DON'T FEAR THE SPREADSHEET

DON'T FEAR THE SPREADSHEET

by
Tyler Nash
Kevin Jones, Tom Urtis, Bill Jelen

Holy Macro! Books
PO Box 82
Uniontown, OH 44685

Don't Fear the Spreadsheet

Printed in USA by Hess Printing

First Printing: May 2012

Author: Tyler Nash, Bill Jelen, Tom Urtis, Kevin Jones

CopyEditor: Ash Glentry

Proofreader: Smit Rout

Layout: Nellie J. Liwam

Cover Design: Shannon Mattiza, 6Ft4 Productions

Published by: Holy Macro! Books, PO Box 82, Uniontown OH 44685

Distributed by: Independent Publishers Group, Chicago, IL

ISBN 978-1-61547-003-7   005.54

Library of Congress Control Number: 2012939999

TABLE OF CONTENTS

ABOUT THE AUTHORS

Bill Jelen is the host of MrExcel.com. You can find his daily Learn Excel podcasts on the bjele123 channel at YouTube. He has written 30+ books but says his Learn Excel 2007-2010 From MrExcel should be your next book purchase after you finish this book. When he isn't writing about Excel, you will find him in a kayak on the Indian River near Merritt Island Florida or at his home near Akron, Ohio.

Tyler Nash is currently pursuing her Master's Degree in English and Philosophy. She is the Copy Editor for Holy Macro! Books. Outside of a love for learning, Tyler also enjoys playing the Didgeridoo and road trips.

Tom Urtis is owner of Atlas Programming Management (www.atlaspm.com), a Microsoft Office business solutions company specializing in Excel project development and training. Tom also created the Excel Aptitude Test (called XAT, xat.atlaspm.com) to measure Excel skills and know-how. When Tom's not at the computer, he enjoys the outdoor life that California offers, and the diverse cultures of the San Francisco Bay Area where he lives.

Kevin Jones has been building applications in too many languages for too many years starting with IBM mainframe Basic Assembly Language. He is known for his ability to use Visual Basic to get Excel to do the most unusual and unexpected things. As "zorvek" he has answered close to 10,000 questions about Excel and Visual Basic on various online forums. NASA wouldn't take him so he spends his free evenings with his daughter Emily at the theater watching 3D superhero films.

DEDICATION

Tom: To my brother, Michael Urtis.

Bill: To Nate Oliver.

Kevin: To Nate, a good man and a friend. You are missed.

Tyler: To Jane Dermody.

ACKNOWLEDGMENTS

Bill wishes to thank Tyler Nash for pitching the idea for this book. He is grateful to Tom Urtis and Kevin Jones for jumping in to keep the book on schedule and into your hands. Various people have contributed stories or anecdotes for the book: Larisa Sadarangani, Mark Doughty, Jane Shiels, Mark Spencer, Patricia Jones, Bryan K, Kevin Marcote and David Rosenthal. Thanks to Scott Pierson for his creative promotions for this book.

Tom wishes to thank Bill Jelen for inviting him as a coauthor. Big thanks to Tyler Nash for conceptualizing the idea for this book, reminding us of the daunting starting point we all felt when opening our first Excel workbook. Thanks to Steve and Nancy Martin for contributions, and to Scott Pierson for the book's early public shout-outs. Special thanks to people using Excel at every level including you, the reader. Your shared questions and solutions have been the Excel community's best teacher.

Tyler wishes to thank Scott Pierson and Bill Jelen for welcoming her to the wild world of Excel. She also thanks Professor of Sociology, Steven Stoll, for driving her to move outside of her Excel comfort zone. Further, she extends her appreciation to all who supported her along the way: Sara Peterson, Nash, Peggy and Jackie Nash, Maureen Harding, Maura Farrell, Sarah Weckerly, Mary Ellen Jelen and Dr. Robert Colson.

Kevin wishes to thank Bill for giving him the opportunity to collaborate on this book and to Tom for taking pictures of the fun.

FOREWORD

Never in my life could I imagine that I would need to use Microsoft Excel for any reason. However, life had different ideas about that and I found myself in the presence of the world's greatest Excel guru and his cohorts. Yes, Bill Jelen, MrExcel himself and his Excel team of any fluctuating number of people suddenly became a fairly consistent part of my life. Interestingly, so did the need for Excel. It's difficult to constantly be surrounded by people using terms like: "Concatenate, Pivot Table, VLOOKUP, Spreadsheet, Cell" and other various Excel terms and not begin to wonder what all this Excel business is about. People get very excited over Excel, which naturally spiked my curiosity. That curiosity is just what gave birth to Don't Fear the Spreadsheet. In May of 2010 I found myself siting in a conference room in Ohio with Bill Jelen and the rest of the MrExcel crew. A few hours into it and several daydreams later it dawned on me that these people had no clue what it was to be 'unfamiliar' with Excel. Needless to say I brought this to their attention as it was becoming increasingly difficult to decode the Excel jargon. "Excuse me," I interrupted. "You are aware that there are people out there who haven't a clue what to do after opening Excel, right?" Crickets…. Followed by a table of people staring at me…. Silent, both astonished and horribly disappointed. After what seemed an eternity of awkward and terrifying silence, Bill Jelen turned to me and said, "I'm not sure what you mean." I repeated my question. It was at that moment that I realized that the group of Excel geniuses that surrounded me had been so far removed from their first days of Excel, that they couldn't fathom such a statement.

> The group of Excel geniuses that surrounded me had been so far removed from their first days of Excel

I expanded on my question and explained to them how terrifying Excel can be, especially for those of us who need to use it for work and don't even know what the fx bar is. I reminded them of what it was like to be an Excel 'newbie.' I watched the lights behind their eyes flicker with confusion, fear for remembering when Excel was foreign to them and the realization that some of us just don't know how to use Excel, let alone program it to talk. Baffled, they began inquiring about this 'clueless' population of people and it became evident that certainly there was something they could do to help people like myself. After going back and forth, Bill asked me to come up with one hundred basic Excel questions that he and his crew of Excel gurus could address. The following week I opened Excel for the third time in my life, played around, made hundreds of mistakes and compiled a list of questions—Don't Fear the Spreadsheet was born. Bill Jelen, Kevin Jones and Tom Urtis came together to tackle my questions and provide the worlds Excel 'newbies' with the most in depth and learner friendly answers. The result: perfection. No longer do we have to spend hours on end searching for answers to Excel's simplest questions, suffering the trials and errors of misinformation or feel foolish asking our fellow employees how to accomplish the simplest of tasks. Today, I can confidently state that I don't fear the spreadsheet.

– Tyler Nash

INTRODUCTION

Microsoft Excel is installed on 750 million desktops worldwide. Assuming some people have Excel both at work and at home, you still have 400 million people 'using' Excel. However, the level of use varies dramatically.

This figure divides the world of people using Excel into groups of 80 million people each:

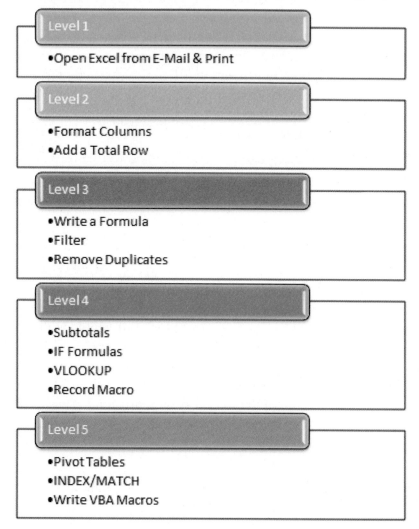

Figure 1 40% of people using Excel have never entered a formula outside of using the AutoSum icon.

That means 80 million people 'use Excel' to open a workbook that they get in their e-mail and print it.

Another 80 million people get some data, do some formatting, add titles, maybe a total row and print.

For these groups of people, Excel can be a confusing and daunting product to use. Excel has many strange behaviors that Excel gurus take for granted. When you ask the department guru why Excel does X, he or she will scoff, wave it off, and say, "That's just the way it happens."

Excel gurus forget when they were in your position, faced with the same challenges that you are facing. Most Excel books out there, even Excel for Dummies, are written for people who are already in Level 3. Those books are trying to take someone from Level 3 to Level 4. Not many Excel books focus on people who are currently in Level 1 or Level 2. This book is designed for you.

Tyler Nash is a complete Excel rookie and had the job of keeping the three Excel gurus grounded. Tyler was able to think like an Excel rookie because she IS an Excel rookie. The questions here are designed to be helpful to the person who is completely new to Excel. That isn't to say that sometimes Bill or Kevin or Tom will try to pull you into Level 4 or even the beginning stages of Level 5 in this book. What might seem like a really easy question requires a bit more than you might think. Or, it might be that the Level 2 approach takes an hour instead of the two minutes required by the Level 3 approach. In these cases, we will show you both ways to solve the problem. It is up to you if you try the intimidating way or the slower way.

As you gain confidence with Excel, I hope you go back and try the other ways to solve the problem. There is a repeated story of people in a Microsoft focus group. They ask how to do X in Excel. The leader of the focus group says that it can easily be solved in six clicks using a "Pivot Table". The person invariably says, "Oh – no… no… I don't want to do that. I don't need a solution that involves a Pivot Table." This is a frustrating position for me as an Excel guru. I can imagine you struggling through the non-Pivot Table method and having it take four hours, but I could teach you the Pivot Table way and the whole thing can be done in two minutes. Chapter 9 is designed to give you a quick introduction to the most powerful tools that Excel has to offer. Don't start there. But that chapter is a jumping off point to move on to another book that will make you a pro at all that Excel has to offer.

There are two longer case studies in the book. One is designed for Level 2 and one for Level 3. These longer case studies show you how to build a small model from start to finish.

Chapter 8 shows every way to accomplish several common tasks in Excel. Often, a manager will want you to do something his way. This will teach you every way to do these common tasks.

Chapter 9 is particularly useful if you are heading off to a job interview this afternoon. Skimming that chapter will give you familiarity with topics that are bound to come up if the job requires knowledge of Excel.

> **Chapter 9 is particularly useful if you are heading off to a job interview this afternoon**

Throughout the book, you will encounter a special section we call "You Did What?" These are true stories of people who went through painful gyrations in Excel when there was a one-minute solution to solve the problem. I did not include these to make fun of the people who went through the long way. Every person using Excel has gone through the long way at some point. These "You Did What?" sections are there to remind you that there might be a faster way. (But, if you actually find yourself doing any of these twelve tasks day after day, please read how to do it faster.)

The screenshots and shortcut keys in the book are from the Windows version of Excel 2010. A few features won't be in Excel for the Mac or in Excel 2007 or earlier on Windows.

Other elements in the book:

The red boxes highlight important quotes along the way.

Tips offer tricks to speed you along your way.

Notes offer asides. Things related to the topic that might help explain why something happens.

Cautions warn you when you should be careful. Not following the instructions exactly will lead to bad things.

The book will use Ctrl+A with a capital A, even though you would actually type Ctrl and the lower case a. Since Ctrl+1 and Ctrl+l look the same, I will remind you that it is Ctrl+1 (the number one). You will not see Ctrl+L used anymore in Excel. When the Ctrl or Alt key might seem ambiguous (such as Ctrl+; or Alt+=), the book will clarify that you should press Alt and the equals sign.

CHAPTER 1 - EXCEL BASICS

Why Do We Need Excel?

What is it for? What does it do? When should I use it?

To understand what Excel is good at, it might help to go back to 1978. At that time, if you had to keep track of any numbers, you had a toolkit with the following items:

- A pad of green ledger paper
- A mechanical pencil
- A Pink Pearl eraser
- An Xacto knife
- An electronic adding machine

Say that you were keeping track of time for a project so you could submit your invoice at the end of the week. You would use the mechanical pencil to log hours on the green ledger paper. You would use the adding machine to keep a column of running total hours and a running total of the money you had earned.

The eraser was used any time that you discovered a mistake in the earlier numbers. You would erase that number and enter the correct number. However, changing that one early number meant that you had to change all of the calculations that came after that number. This would mean that you would be erasing a lot, and doing the calculations all over again.

> You were erasing a lot, and re-doing the same calculations

Sometimes, if you were working on a project that changed frequently such as an annual budget, you would erase a number over and over and over. Eventually, you would erase a hole in the paper! You would then use the Xacto knife to cut a fresh bit of paper from the last page in the tablet and glue it over the hole in your spreadsheet so you could keep using the spreadsheet.

Back in 1978, Dan Bricklin was a college student. For his business classes, he noticed that he was doing the same paper spreadsheets over and over. A case study might have five scenarios, each with a different interest rate. All of the calculations that came after the interest rate entry were identical, but he still had to do them by hand, over and over and over. One of Dan's ideas was to create a calculator with a trackball in the bottom. The ball would let you scroll back through your calculations to the interest rate entry, change the number, and then roll forward to see all of the calculations performed again using the new interest rate. Working with his friend Bob Frankston, they invented a Visible Calculator on the Apple IIe computer. In the fall of 1979, Dan and Bob started selling VisiCalc and sales of VisiCalc and the personal computer skyrocketed. Over the years, many companies sold spreadsheets. VisiCalc, Lotus 1-2-3, Multiplan, Quattro Pro, and Excel became popular. Today, Excel is the leading spreadsheet program, in use on 750 million Windows computers (and 5 million Macs).

- Excel is good at doing calculations, particularly when the numbers used in the calculation might change frequently. Change one number early in the spreadsheet and you get to see all of the calculations reflect the new number.
- Excel is good for creating charts and graphs from numbers.
- Excel is good for holding a lot of rows of data. You can sort that data to find the largest sales, the smallest sales, the earliest sales. You can filter the data to find only sales of red cars to people over the age of 65. You can also use a feature called a Pivot Table to summarize thousands of rows of data down to one page to spot trends in the data.
- And, because it is easy to change the widths of the columns and the height of the rows, it is easy to use Excel any time that you need to do something like a table in Microsoft Word. The big

difference… Excel can hold a bigger table than you can create in Word. Even if you need 20 columns, Excel can do it. Even if you need 16,384 columns and 1.1 million rows, Excel can do it.

If you have never used Excel, take an hour and walk through the case studies in the book (the first one is on page 29). You will gain confidence and learn what Excel can do for you.

What 'Practical' Uses Does Excel Have?

And how do I do ANY of it? Ex: calendar, managing personal finances, address book, and the like?

Excel can be used to do anything. The possibilities are limitless. If you have Excel 2007, you can browse a whole bunch of finished workbooks that you can use.

Open Excel. Go to File. From the left navigation of the File menu, choose New. Excel will show you a whole bunch of files available. In the image below, you can see Agendas, Budgets, Invoices, Labels, Schedules and Time Sheets.

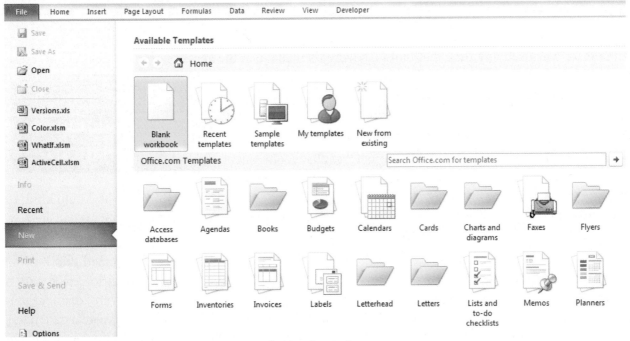

Figure 2 The templates on this opening screen are the tip of an iceberg.

There are free templates available. Use the Search Office Online box. Type: Personal Finance. You have these free choices available:

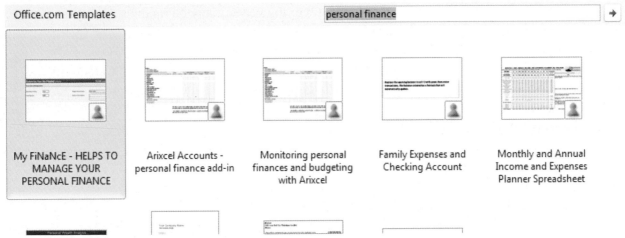

Figure 3 Personal finance? How about check registers, monthly budgets, tax planning, all for free.

Try typing anything in the box. I've found NCAA Brackets. I tried Menu and found a variety of grocery planners, dinner party planners, and more.

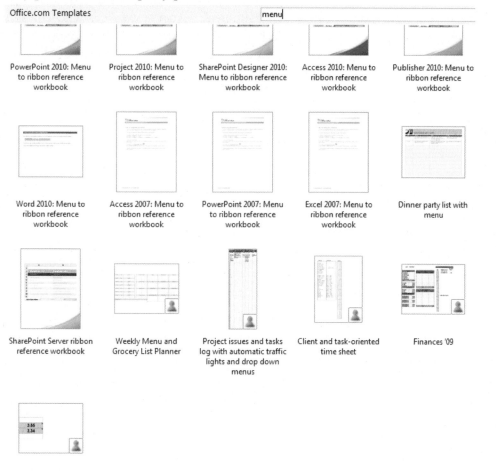

Figure 4 Menu planners, grocery lists, dinner parties.

What Is the Intersection of a Row and Column Referred to As?

I need to learn the lingo. What do you call the box at the intersection of row 10 and column C?

That box is called a "Cell". There are 17 billion cells on a worksheet. By convention, the name of a cell is the column name followed by the row number.

The cell at the intersection of column C and row 10 is called C10.

	A	B	C	D	E
1					
2					
3					
4					
5					
6					
7					
8					
9					
10			C10		

Figure 5 Column name followed by row number.

Note that if you select a cell, the name of the cell appears in the Name Box to the left of the Formula Bar.

If you have a lot of columns, your data might extend past column Z. Excel starts over with column names of AA, AB, and so on. If you actually have a worksheet with more than 701 columns of data, you will get to the point where Excel goes past ZZ and starts over again with AAA. The three character column letters continue all the way out to XFD – a total of 16,384 columns.

Note: Why 16,384? It is 2^14. Similarly, the last row – 1,048,576 is 2^20.

The last cell in the worksheet is called XFD1048576. It is really unlikely that you would ever reach this cell. You could write the name of every living person on earth and only fill up 40% of Sheet 1.

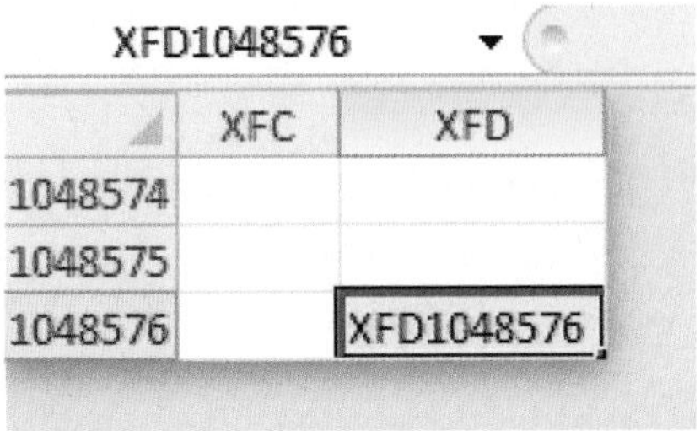

Figure 6 To reach XFD1048576, press Ctrl+Right Arrow then Ctrl+Down Arrow.

Caution: Don't try this trick with all-time world population. According to noted demographer Jean Bourgeois-Pichat, there have been 81 billion people alive on earth since 600,000 BC to 1988. To enter the names of all of those people in Excel, you would have to use Sheet 1 through Sheet 5.

When you have a contiguous collection of cells, those are known as a Range. The name of a range is the name of the cell in the top left corner, a colon, and the name of the cell in the lower right corner. The figure below is B2:D6.

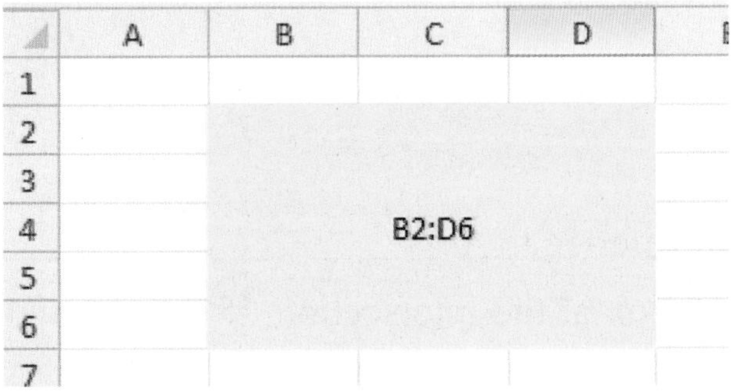

Figure 7 This range runs from B2 to D6.

Note: If you try to refer to B6:D2 in a formula, Excel will automatically rewrite the reference as B2:D6.

What's a Workbook?

Workbook, worksheet, no… workbook. Wait, what's a workbook?

A workbook is a collection of worksheets saved in a single file. Each worksheet is identified by a tab across the bottom of the Excel window. While workbooks often have boring names like Sheet1, Sheet2, Sheet3, you can change the names to be more meaningful.

Figure 8 This workbook has two worksheets.

How Many Worksheets Come in a Workbook?

Three. But you can change this. Typically, a new workbook opens with Sheet1, Sheet2, Sheet3.

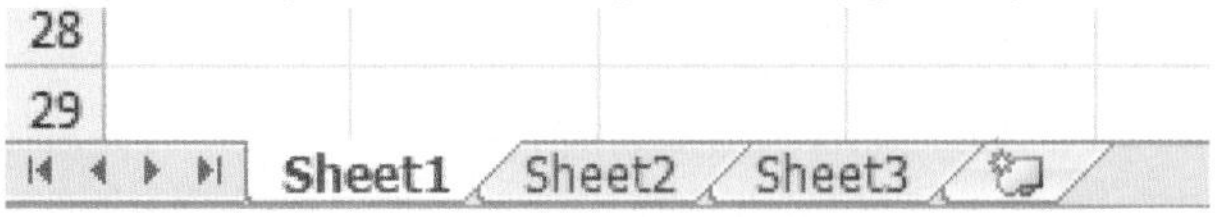

| 28 |
| 29 |

| ◄◄ ◄ ► ►◄ | **Sheet1** / Sheet2 / Sheet3 / ✱ |

Figure 9 By Default, you will get three worksheets in a workbook.

If you are creating a simple one-page worksheet, you don't really need the blank Sheet2 and Sheet3 hanging around back there. Right-click the sheet tab and choose Delete.

Why do they start with three worksheets?

Back in Excel 93, a workbook only contained one worksheet. When Microsoft introduced the ability to include multiple worksheets in a workbook, they decided to make this obvious by including 16 worksheets in every new workbook. I guess they figured that no one would think to use Insert, Worksheet to add new worksheets. This created a lot of silly workbooks with 15 blank worksheets. After that version, Excel changed the setting so that you start with three blank worksheets. They are still doing this because they think that you cannot figure out that the "*" worksheet is how you insert a new worksheet. After reading this book, you will know how to insert worksheets, so there is really no reason to have Excel put three worksheets in every new workbook. To change the setting, go to File, Options. The first panel of the Options dialog is called General in Excel 2010 and Popular in Excel 2007. Use the setting shown here to change the number of new sheets back to 1.

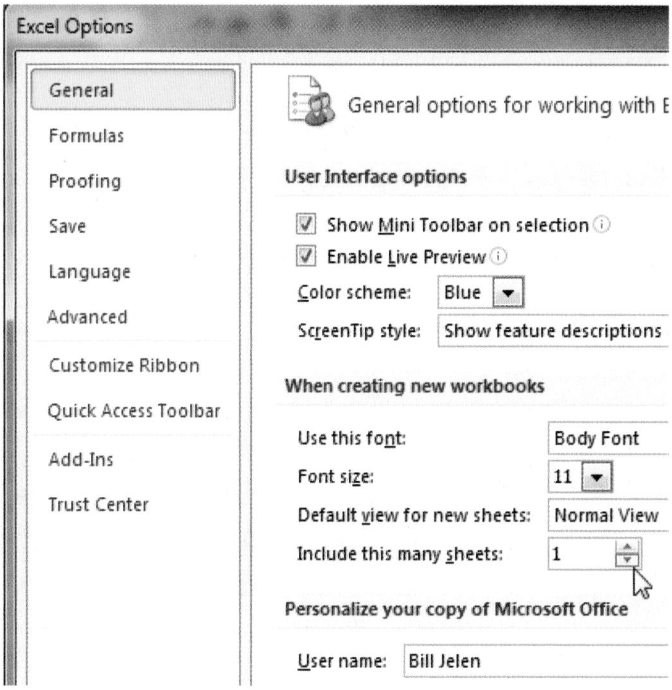

Figure 10 Choose that each new workbook should have one worksheet.

How Do I Insert New Worksheets into a Workbook?

Excel, with all its crafty short cuts must provide a way to quickly insert a new worksheet...Right?

The last worksheet tab in a workbook is a blank worksheet icon with an orange asterisk. This is the New Worksheet icon. Click this sheet tab to add a new blank worksheet as the last worksheet in the workbook.

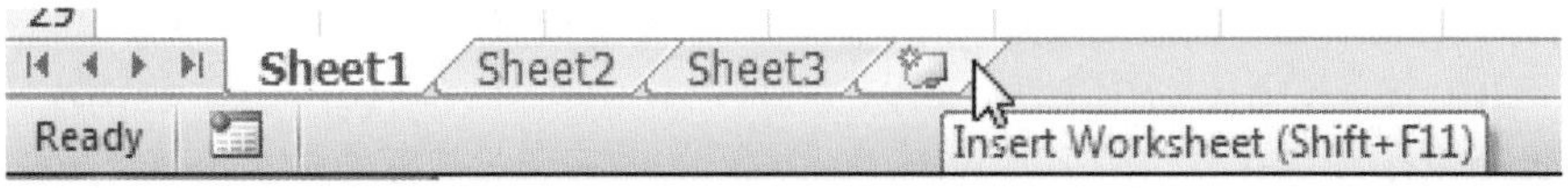

| 25 |

| ◄◄ ◄ ► ►◄ | **Sheet1** / Sheet2 / Sheet3 / ✱ |
| Ready | | | Insert Worksheet (Shift+F11) |

*Figure 11 Click the * sheet tab to add a new sheet to the end.*

What if you don't to move this new worksheet between two other existing worksheets? Click on the worksheet tab and drag it to a new location. A tiny blank triangle will indicate where you are about to drop the new worksheet.

Do you always have to insert the new worksheet at the end and then move it to the new location?

No! There is another way to insert a worksheet exactly where you want it. Say that you want to insert a Feb worksheet between Jan and Mar in this figure. Select the Mar worksheet. From the Home tab, select Insert, Insert Sheet. Excel will insert a new worksheet to the left of the active sheet.

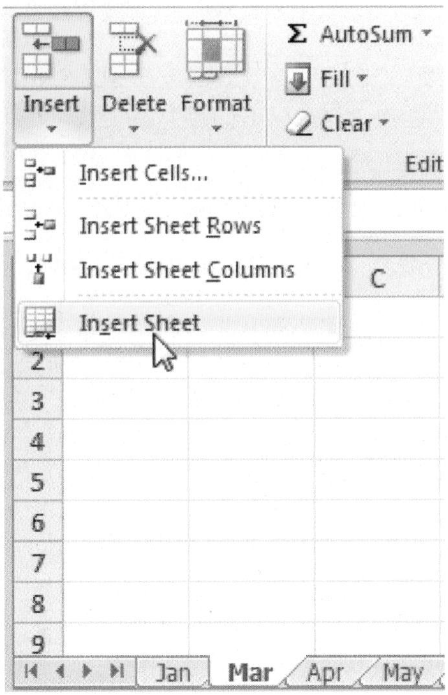

Figure 12 *To insert a new worksheet before the current worksheet, use Alt+I+W or this command.*

👀 You Did What?

What's with the Masking Tape?

Passing by a coworker's cubicle at the office, I noticed a piece of masking tape stuck onto her computer monitor's screen, near the lower left corner. The word "March" had been neatly hand-printed on the piece of tape. It's odd to see anything stuck onto a monitor screen, but I figured she ran out of post-it notes and maybe was reminding herself of a marching-related exercise routine for after work.

The following month I saw "April" written onto a fresh piece of masking tape, stuck onto the monitor screen in the same location as the March piece of tape had been. I asked her: "What's up with the masking tape and month names stuck onto your screen?"

She opened a budget workbook for the company and showed me how the tape covered over the Sheet3 worksheet tab. She told me that part of her job is to type the income and expense numbers into that worksheet for the prior month. Each month she needs to remind herself which month is being entered, and since there is no month named "Sheet3", this was the best way to do it.

Masking tape mystery solved: my coworker did not realize that Excel's worksheet tab names can be changed. There are two easy and fast ways to accomplish this task. In the first pair of figures, notice that the first step would be to either double-click the worksheet tab whose name you want to change, or right-click that worksheet tab and left-click to select Rename from the popup menu.

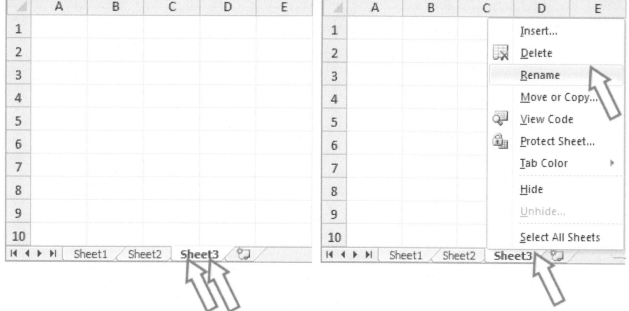

Figure 13 To change a worksheet tab name, start by either double-clicking the tab, or right-click the tab and select Rename.

You will see that the existing worksheet name becomes highlighted, as shown in the left-most figure below. Now all you need to do is simply type the new name for that worksheet tab, such as the month name of April, and press the Enter key. In the figure, the worksheet tab that used to be named Sheet3 is now named April.

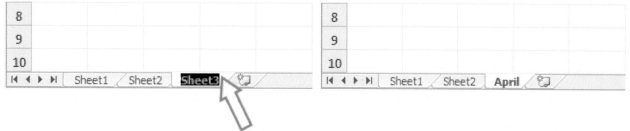

Figure 14 With the existing tab name selected, type in your new name for that worksheet and press the Enter key.

Tip: A few FYI's about naming worksheet tabs. The names can be up to 31 characters in length. The proposed new worksheet name cannot be the same as another worksheet name in that workbook (that is, duplicate worksheet names in the same workbook are not allowed). Finally, a worksheet tab name cannot be blank, and it cannot contain the characters *, :, [,], ?, /, or \.

Oddity: A worksheet name can contain some symbols that cannot be typed on a standard keyboard. This can create some odd-looking worksheet names like in this figure:

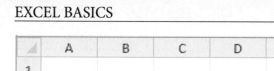

Figure 15 Using a macro, you can create sheet names that can't be typed.

If you want to freak out a co-worker, open the sample files that came with this book. Copy one of these strange sheet names from RenameWorksheet.xlsm to your own book.

How Can I QUICKLY Erase an Entire Sheet?

How can I erase an entire sheet, formatting and all?

First select all cells by clicking the icon above and left of cell A1.

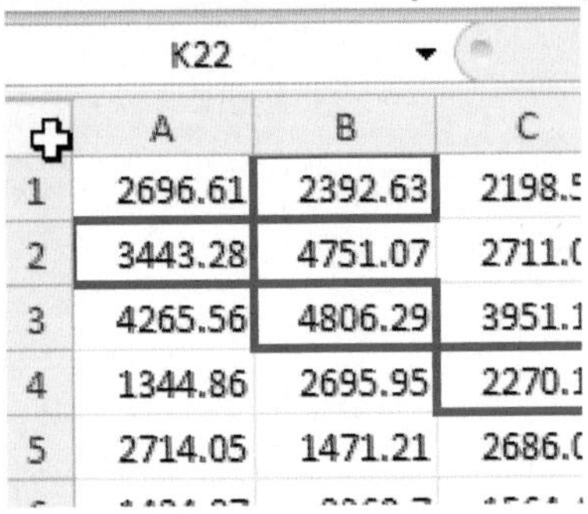

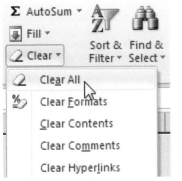

Figure 16 Use this icon to Select All.

On the right side of the Home tab, the Clear dropdown is usually represented by an Eraser icon. Open this dropdown and choose Clear All. Using Clear All will clear cell contents and all formatting. If you want to delete cell contents but leave the existing cell formatting, you can simply press the Delete key.

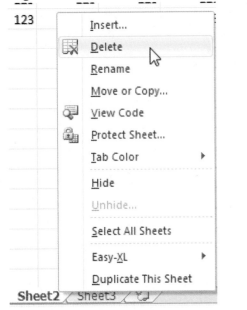

Figure 17 Use the Clear All icon to erase cell contents and formatting.

How Can I QUICKLY Delete an Entire Sheet from the Workbook?

How do I go about deleting an entire sheet from my workbook?

Right-click the sheet tab and choose Delete from the menu that appears.

Figure 18 Right-click the sheet tab that you want to delete.

If the worksheet has always been blank, Excel will delete it without any further interaction. If the worksheet has data, or if the worksheet once held data and that data has been deleted, Excel will show a message warning that the sheet contains data and the deletion can't be undone. You can choose to continue deleting or click Cancel to go take another look at the worksheet.

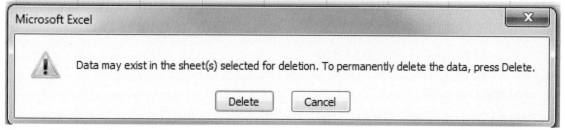

Figure 19 Excel warns you before deleting a worksheet.

Scan through the column numbers to see if one column is missing. This could indicate a hidden column. The hidden column might still have data. Similarly, there might be a hidden row. To unhide all columns and rows, select all cells in the worksheet. Then, select Home, Format, Hide & Unhide. If either Unhide Rows or Unhide Columns is not greyed-out, select those commands.

It is possible that important data is still on a worksheet that appears blank. Perhaps the data is there and someone changed the font color to white. Or, someone used a custom number formatting code of ";;;" to hide the data. After pressing Ctrl+End, press Ctrl+Shift+Home. Excel will select from the bottom right corner back to cell A1. Look in the Quick Sum area to see if any statistics appear. If you haven't done so already, right-click the Quick Sum area and choose all six statistics: Average, Count, Numerical Count, Min, Max, and Sum. The Count statistic will count cells that contain text.

Caution: The Undo command is not available to bring back a worksheet after it has been deleted. If you accidentally deleted the worksheet, you need to go back to the last saved or AutoSaved version of the worksheet.

How Would I Go about Deleting Several Cells at the Same Time?

I have to delete several cells. Right now, I select one cell, then use the Home, Clear, Clear All, over and over and over. Is there a faster way?

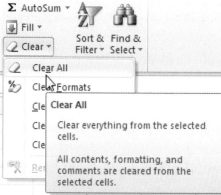

Figure 20 Opening this command over and over is tedious.

There are a lot of tips to make this process easier.

First, selecting a cell or range of cells and pressing the Delete key on the keyboard will clear the cell. Pressing Delete is easier than opening the Clear flyout menu over and over.

Second, there are a few different ways to select all of the cells to delete.

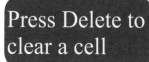

If the cells are in a rectangle, you can use the mouse to click in the top left cell and drag down to the bottom cell. This will select an entire range.

When the cells are not contiguous, you can follow one of these two methods:

- Select the first cell. Hold down the Ctrl key while clicking on all the other cells. As long as you hold down Ctrl, Excel will add the newly selected cells to the selection.
- If using Ctrl seems unnatural, you can press and release Shift+F8. The status bar will indicate that you can Add to Selection. As you click additional cells or ranges, they will be added to the selection.

Figure 21 Shift+F8 toggles you into Add Selection mode.

After you've selected multiple cells using Shift+F8, press the Delete key. Then, use Shift+F8 to toggle back to normal selection mode.

Can I Reset Some Cells in a Worksheet While Keeping Others?

I built this loan payment calculator. I would like to be able to reset the input cells without clearing all of the cells.

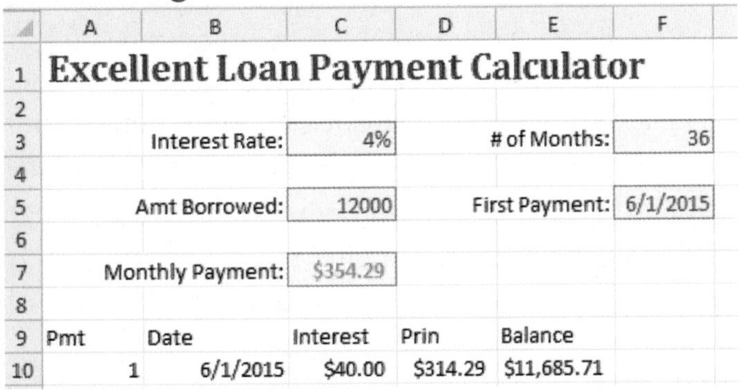

Figure 22 Clear only the input cells but keep everything else intact.

This one sounds really simple, but it will require some work to make it happen.

First thought – do you want to clear all of the numeric cells that are non-numeric in a certain range? It is likely that the input cells are non-formula cells that contain a number or date. If that is true, you can use the Go To Special dialog as described below in Method 1.

Second thought – would you mind changing the fill color of all cells to be cleared to be similar? If this is the case, you can use the Find All Format as described in Method 2.

Third thought – if neither of the above would work, you could use the named range method as described in Method 3.

Method 1: Go To Special.

1. Select the range A3:G6. This range encompasses all of your input cells but also includes other cells.
2. Press F5 or Ctrl+G to display the Go To dialog.
3. In the lower left corner of the Go To Dialog, click Special to display the Go To Special dialog.
4. In the Go To Special dialog, choose Constants. Uncheck the boxes for Text, Logicals, and Errors, leaving only Numbers checked. Click OK. Only cells C3, C5, F3, and F5 will be selected.
5. Press the Delete key.

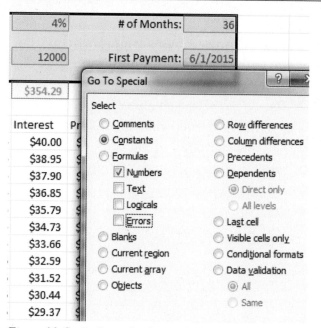

Figure 23 Go To Special selects all of the numeric constants within the selected range.

Tip: In Excel 2007 or newer, you can use Home, Find & Select, Go To Special instead of steps 2 & 3 above.

Method 2: Find All Format. This method requires that you have filled all of the input cells with the same fill color and that no other cells have this fill color. To clear the cells with that color, follow these steps:

1. Select one cell in the worksheet.
2. Ctrl+F to display the Find dialog box.
3. Leave the Find What box empty.
4. Click the Format... button.
5. In the Find Format dialog, go to the Fill tab. Choose the color of your input cells. Click OK.
6. Back in the Find and Replace dialog, click Find All. A list of all matching cells will appear in the bottom of the dialog.
7. Click Ctrl+A to select all of the cells.
8. Use the red X to close Find and Replace dialog.
9. Press the Delete key.

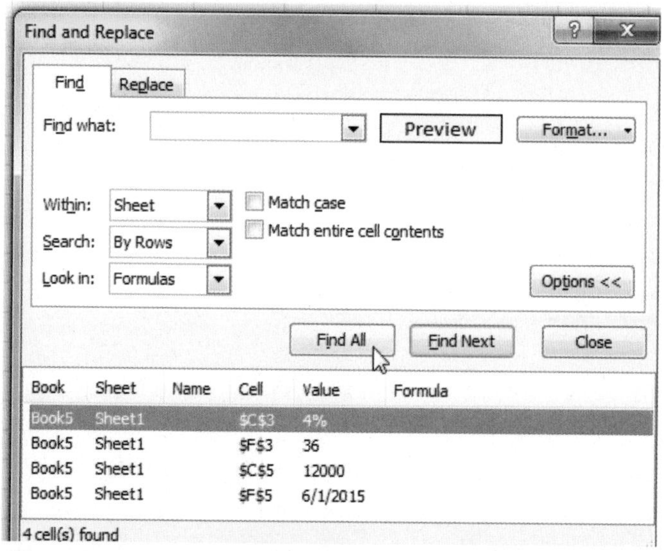

Figure 24 Find All in conjunction with the Format feature.

Method 3: Use a Named Range.

This method requires a little advanced planning. You will have to select all of the input cells one time. Select those cells and click in the Name Box that is located to the left of the Formula Bar. Type a one-word name such as InputCells and press Enter. Because you have multiple cells selected, the name will immediately disappear from the Name Box, but that is OK.

Later, you can easily re-select all of the input cells by opening the dropdown at the right edge of the Name Box and selecting the Input Cells from the list. This will select all of the cells. You can then press Delete.

Figure 25 Using a single name for all of the non-contiguous input cells makes it easy to re-select them all later.

What Does 'Freeze Panes' Do?

What are panes and why do I want to make them cold?

Freeze Panes should be called "Keep the Headings Visible".

Say that you have a worksheet with hundreds of rows. You have a title in row 1, headings in row 3, then data starting in row 4. When you are at the top of the worksheet, you can see the headings, so it is clear what the numbers in each column represent.

	A	B	C	D	E
1	**XYX Company Sales Report**				
2					
3	Region	Date	Customer	Revenue	Profit
4	East	1/1/2014	Ford	22810	12590
5	Central	1/2/2014	Verizon	2257	1273
6	East	1/4/2014	Merck	18552	10680
7	East	1/4/2014	Texaco	9152	5064
8	East	1/7/2014	State Farm	21730	11890
9	East	1/7/2014	General Motors	8456	5068
10	Central	1/9/2014	General Motors	16416	9640
11	Central	1/10/2014	Wal-Mart	21438	12240

Figure 26 At the top of a worksheet, you can see the headings.

As you scroll down further through the data, the headings scroll off the worksheet. Is column E supposed to be profit or cost?

	A	B	C	D	E
34	East	2/16/2014	Boeing	16936	8760
35	East	2/17/2014	Exxon	11430	6348
36	West	2/18/2014	Wal-Mart	20250	11780
37	Central	2/19/2014	Wal-Mart	10385	6150
38	Central	2/20/2014	Wal-Mart	23810	13590
39	Central	2/20/2014	Exxon	11124	6042

Figure 27 Scroll down and you lose the headings.

The solution is to carefully scroll so that the important headings are in the first visible row of the window. In the figure below, rows 1 and 2 have been scrolled off the sheet and row 3 is the first visible row.

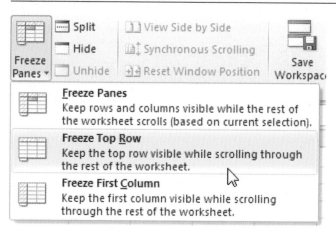

Figure 28 It might take some tweaking of the scrollbars to get row 3 at the top of the window.

Select the View tab in the Ribbon. Open the Freeze Panes menu. Choose Freeze Top Row. As you scroll down through the worksheet, you will always be able to see row 3.

	A	B	C	D	E
3	Region	Date	Customer	Revenue	Profit
550	Central	12/10/2015	General Motors	4492	2524
551	East	12/11/2015	General Electric	4696	2728
552	East	12/13/2015	Verizon	10295	5375
553	West	12/15/2015	CitiGroup	25010	14790
554	East	12/15/2015	Ford	10380	5270
555	East	12/16/2015	IBM	6744	3678

Figure 29 Row 3 stays visible at the top of the worksheet as you scroll through the data.

What if I later need to go back to row 1?

Open the Freeze Panes dropdown and choose Unfreeze Panes.

What if my headings encompass two rows and I always need to see rows 3 and 4?

Carefully scroll so that Row 3 is the first row you can see. Put the cell pointer in A5. Open the Freeze Panes dropdown and choose Freeze Panes (Based on Current Selection). This will lock all of the rows above the cell pointer and to the left of the cell pointer. Since you selected cell A1, no columns are frozen.

> Before selecting Freeze Panes, select the first cell that will NOT be frozen!

> Freeze panes does not print headings at the top of each printed page, use Print Titles instead

Remember these tips:

1. The cell pointer should be in the first unfrozen cell before you freeze panes.
2. Use the scrollbars and arrow keys to make sure only the rows that you want visible can be seen above the freeze point.
3. Unless you want to freeze column A at the left of your screen, you should be in column A when you freeze panes.

Tip: If you accidentally freeze the panes at the wrong place, re-open the Freeze Panes command. The top item will be Unfreeze Panes instead of Freeze Panes.

Caution: Freezing panes only affects the display. It will not force the headings to print at the top of each page. To do this, see the end of Old School Print Titles At the Top of Each Page on page 25.

What Is the Native File Format for Excel?

What's up with XLS, XLSX, XLSB, XLSM? Which one should I use?

You should use XLSX.

XLS files were the only native file format up through Excel 2003. This file format cannot accommodate more than 65,536 rows. This format is known as a binary file format.

XLSB is the Excel 2007 equivalent of XLS. It is also a binary file format, but it can accommodate 1,048,576 rows.

XLSX is a new Excel 2007 file format where all of the data is saved in several XML files, then those files are zipped into a single XLSX file format. The result is smaller files. XLSX is a file format that does not allow macros. If you are reading this book, it is likely that you are not yet creating Excel macros in your workbook, so XLSX is fine.

XLSM is the same as XLSX, but macros are allowed. Since I routinely use macros, this is my favorite file type. But, there are downsides to this choice. For example, GMail refuses to offer a preview of XLSM files.

Excel also supports writing to two dozen other non-native file formats. Over the years, various competitors to Excel have pushed their own file formats. Excel still supports writing to mostly-defunct file types like SYLK, DIF. Microsoft is constantly adding to the list. Excel will now open and write files of the ODS file type. In the past, Excel would open files from Lotus 1-2-3 or Quattro Pro. If a company is seen as a credible alternative to Excel, Microsoft is likely to offer a way to open those files so people can come back to Excel.

There is one frustrating limitation to this policy. Excel for the Mac cannot open files created by Apple Numbers. The Excel for Mac team is separate from the Excel for Windows team. It seems that the Excel for Mac team is focused on adding features to Excel for Mac to keep it compatible with Excel for Windows. They don't seem to have any interest in supporting the competitive files from Numbers. To get your data from Numbers to Excel, you will have to go back to Numbers and save in an Excel format.

Typing Just Enough Characters to Fill a Cell, Then Moving to Next Cell

Jane S. sends in a report from the field. She was at a co-worker's computer. The co-worker had some long text to type in Excel. Rather than typing the entire text in cell A1 and letting the text automatically spill over to B1, C1 and so on, the co-worker had typed just enough characters to fill column A. She then moved over to column B and typed just enough characters for column B. She continued in this fashion until she had typed the whole title.

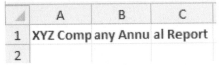

Figure 30 Something doesn't look quite right here.

So you can see what the co-worker was doing, the next figure shows the row height increased and each cell set to Top, Middle, or Bottom align.

	A	B	C
1	XYZ Comp	any Annu	al Report

Figure 31 The co-worker was typing about eight letters in each cell.

Why this is bad: You want to keep that entire title in one cell. Provided you don't put anything in B1 and C1, the text characters that won't fit in cell A1 will automatically spill over and appear in B1 and C1.

XYZ Company Annual Report

	A	B	C	D	E
1	**XYZ Company Annual Report**				
2					

Figure 32 Type the entire title in A1.

I Can't Select the Right Cell

I have a long title that starts in A1 and stretches out to column H. The date in the title appeared around column F. Every time I wanted to change the date, I click in cell F1. There is nothing in the Formula Bar to edit!

F1   ▼   *fx*

	A	B	C	D	E	F	G	H
1	**OurCo Company Report As of May 15, 2015**							
2								

Figure 33 Clicking in F1 won't let you edit the date.

If you click in F1 and nothing shows up in the Formula Bar, use Ctrl+Left Arrow to go back to the cell that contains the text. You can now click in the Formula Bar to edit the part of the title that you need to edit.

A1   ▼   *fx*   OurCo Company Report As of May 15, 2015

	A	B	C	D	E	F	G	H
1	**OurCo Company Report As of May 15, 2015**							
2								

Figure 34 Ctrl+Left Arrow goes back to the text that you are seeing in cell F1.

My Laptop Screen Is Too Small. I Can't Manage to Click on the Right Cell

I have this little 13" screen. I try to click on cell C9, but I end up on D10.

There is a zoom slider in the lower right corner of Excel. Try kicking the zoom up to 200%. You will see less cells, but you should be able to select cells easily.

How Can I Add More Rows or Columns to My Spreadsheet?

What to do when you need more rows or columns than Excel is giving you.

A common question that gets asked among people new to Excel is how to add more rows or columns to your worksheet. The short answer is, unfortunately, you can't.

In earlier versions of Excel such as version 2003, there were 256 columns and 65,536 rows. For many years there was a clamor for Microsoft to add more rows and columns to the Excel spreadsheet grid.

Microsoft finally expanded those limits starting with version 2007, when the Ribbon was introduced to the Office suite of products. Now, current versions of Excel, including and after version 2007, have 16,384 columns (A:XFD) and over 1 million rows (1,048,576 rows to be exact).

And that's where we all stand. If you need more rows or columns beyond what's offered with your version of Excel, sorry to say, but it's not possible. Unless you use PowerPivot in Excel 2010.

What Allows Me to Access Popular Commands from Any Ribbon Tab?

I find that I mostly use commands on the Home tab, but there are a few commands from the Data tab and Page Layout tab that I use frequently. How can I access those commands without switching to those tabs?

Microsoft created the Quick Access Toolbar (QAT) as a place to store your favorite commands. Since the QAT is visible from every tab of the Ribbon, you can access commands on the QAT without switching to another Ribbon tab.

The QAT starts out as a strip above the Ribbon with icons for Save, Undo and Redo. A dropdown at the end of the QAT offers a dozen popular commands that you might want to add to the QAT. Of particular interest in this list are Quick Print and Open Recent File.

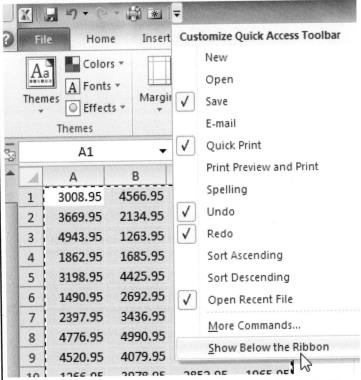

Figure 35 The dropdown offers popular icons to add to the QAT.

If you find a favorite command on another Ribbon tab, right-click the icon and choose Add to Quick Access Toolbar.

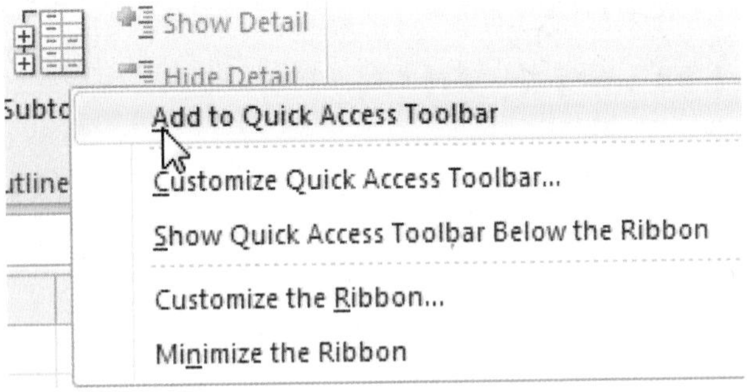

Figure 36 Add any Ribbon command to the QAT by right-clicking the command.

There are also many more commands that you cannot find in the Ribbon that you can add to the QAT. Follow these steps:

1. Right-click the QAT and choose Customize Quick Access Toolbar.
2. In the left dropdown, choose All Commands.
3. You can now scroll through 2000+ commands arranged alphabetically in the left list. When you find a desired command, choose that command and click the Add>> button in the center of the page.
4. Click OK to close the Excel Options dialog.

Customize the Quick Access Toolbar.

Choose commands from: ⓘ

| All Commands ▼ |

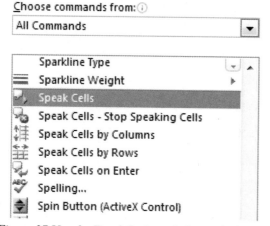

Sparkline Type
Sparkline Weight ▶
Speak Cells
Speak Cells - Stop Speaking Cells
Speak Cells by Columns
Speak Cells by Rows
Speak Cells on Enter
Spelling...
Spin Button (ActiveX Control)

Figure 37 Use the Excel Options dialog to find 2000+ commands that you can add to the QAT.

Tip: You might want to move the QAT below the Ribbon. There is room for more icons when the QAT is below the Ribbon. It is also closer to the worksheet grid.

How Do I Use the Arrows Keys to Navigate More Efficiently?

I have this HUGE spreadsheet with 300 rows of data. Is there a faster way to navigate to the top or bottom?

Yes – there are a few simple keystrokes you can use.

When you're anywhere in your data and you press Ctrl+Down Arrow, you will jump to the last row with data.

	A	B	C	D	E	F	G
1	123	123	123	123			123
2	123	123	123	123			123
3	123	123	123	123			123
4	123	123	123	123			123
5	123	123		123			123
6	123	123	123	123			123
7	123	123	123	123			123
8	123	123	123	123			123
9	123	123	123	123			123
10							
11							
12							

Ctrl ↓

Figure 38 Ctrl+Down Arrow jumps to the last cell in this column.

Ctrl+Right Arrow jumps to the last column with data. Notice that it stops before the blank cell in E9, assuming that the data in G must be a grocery list or something unrelated to the main data set.

	A	B	C	D	E	F	G
1	123	123	123	123			123
2	123	123	123	123			123
3	123	123	123	123			123
4	123	123	123	123			123
5	123	123		123			123
6	123	123	123	123			123
7	123	123	123	123			123
8	123	123	123	123			123
9	123	123	123	123			123
10							
11							
12							

Ctrl →

Figure 39 Ctrl+Right Arrow jumps right to the edge of the data.

If you are already sitting at the edge of the data and press Ctrl+Right Arrow again, Excel will jump the gap of blank cells and go to the first cell in the next data range.

◢	A	B	C	D	E	F	G
1	123	123	123	123			123
2	123	123	123	123			123
3	123	123	123	123			123
4	123	123	123	123			123
5	123	123		123			123
6	123	123	123	123			123
7	123	123	123	123			123
8	123	123	123	123			123
9	123	123	123	123	→		123
10							
11			Ctrl →				
12							
13							

Figure 40 Ctrl+Right Arrow when you are at the edge jumps the blank cells.

Of course, the Ctrl+Up Arrow works to go back to the top or the to left.

◢	A	B	C	D	E	F	G
1	123	123	123	123			123
2	123	123	123	123			123
3	123	123	123	123			123
4	123	123	123	123			123
5	123	123		123			123
6	123	123	123	123			123
7	123	123	123	123			123
8	123	123	123	123			123
9	123	123	123	123			123
10							
11			Ctrl ↑				
12							

Figure 42 Use Ctrl+Up Arrow to go back to the top of the data.

Caution: The navigation can be fooled by a blank cell. If you are in C1 and press Ctrl+Down Arrow, the cell pointer will stop at C4 because of the blank in C5.

What if there isn't more data? Then you go to the edge of the grid. Pressing Ctrl+Down Arrow from D9 would go to D1048576. Pressing Ctrl+Right Arrow from G9 would go to XFD9.

◢	A	B	C	D	E	F	G
1	123	123	123	123			123
2	123	123	123	123			123
3	123	123	123	123			123
4	123	123	123	123			123
5	123	123		123			123
6	123	123	123	123	Ctrl ↓		123
7	123	123	123	123			123
8	123	123	123	123			123
9	123	123	123	123			123
10							
11				↓			
12		to D1048576!					

Figure 41 Ctrl+Right Arrow at the edge of the data could take you to edge of grid if non-blank cells are not found.

There isn't a good solution for this. If you know that column C is sparsely populated and column B is completely filled in, do the Ctrl+Down Arrow from B1 instead of C1.

◢	A	B	C	D	E	F	G
1	123	123	123	123			123
2	123	123	123	123			123
3	123	123	123	123			123
4	123	123	123	123			123
5	123	123		123			123
6	123	123	123	123			123
7	123	123	123	123			123
8	123	123	123	123			123
9	123	123	123	123			123
10							
11		Ctrl ↓ :-(					
12							

Figure 43 Blank cells will cause the cell pointer to stop early.

Tip: If you hold down Ctrl+Shift+Arrow, Excel will select all of the cells from the current cell to the edge of the data.

There are some other navigation tricks that do not use the arrow keys:

- Pressing Home will go back to column A of the current row no matter if there are blank cells or not.

- Pressing Ctrl+Home will go back to cell A1 from anywhere.
- Pressing Ctrl+End will go to the last used cell.

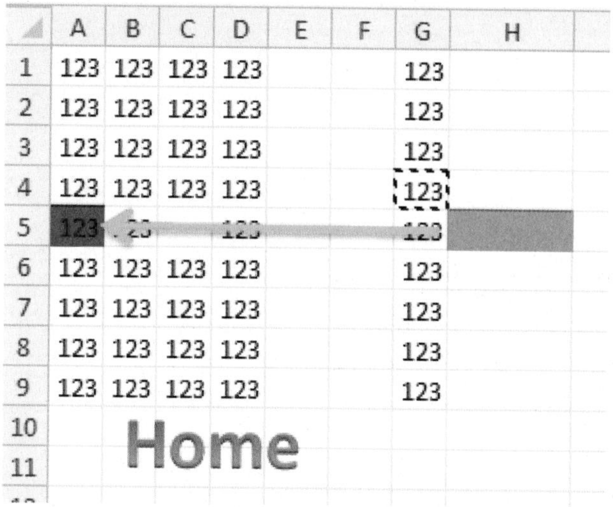

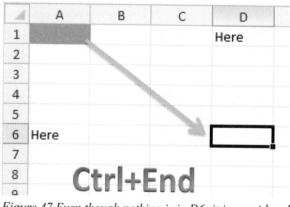

Figure 44 Jump to column A of this row with Home.

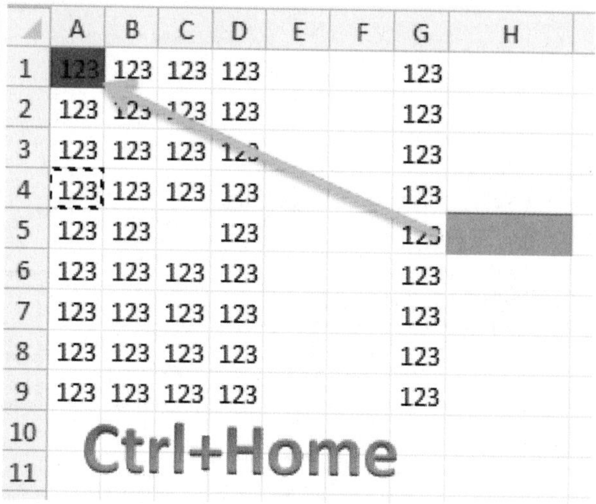

Figure 45 Jump to A1 with Ctrl+Home.

Caution: The concept of the last used cell can be confusing. In Figure 45, I used a green fill in cell H5. This would make Excel think that the last used cell is H9. In Figure 47, only three cells are used. Excel finds the cell that is in the right-most column (Column D). It finds the cell in the lowest row (6). The last used cell will be D6. Further, if you accidentally type in Z99, then clear the cell, Z99 will remain the last used cell until you save the workbook.

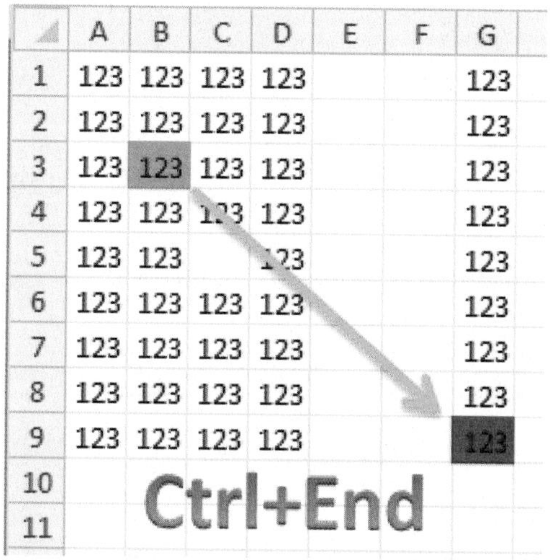

Figure 46 Jump to the last used cell with Ctrl+End.

Figure 47 Even though nothing is in D6, it is considered the last used cell.

How Can I See a List of Worksheet Names, and Quickly Go to a Sheet If I Can't See Its Sheet Tab?

Is there a way to display a list of all of my worksheets?

When your workbook has a lot of worksheets and you can't see all the tabs, here's a way to show a list of the worksheet names. As the following figure shows, you can right-click what are called the sheet navigation buttons, located at the immediate left of the left-most sheet tab. If there are many sheets, click the More Sheets item to see them all.

When the pop-up list of worksheets appears, you can jump to a sheet by clicking its name on the list.

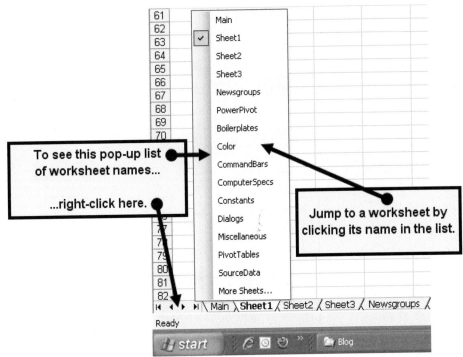

Figure 48 The pop-up list of your workbook's sheets appears when you right-click the sheet navigation buttons.

How Can I Quickly Move between Several Excel Files That I Have Open?

I have five workbooks open and need to switch quickly between them.

Use Ctrl+Tab to switch between open workbooks.

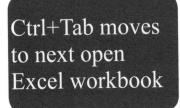

Ctrl+Tab moves to next open Excel workbook

Say that you open five workbooks called 1, 2, 3, 4, 5. If 5 is the active workbook, pressing Ctrl+Tab will switch to 4.

If 5 is the active workbook and you want to switch to 3, hold down the Ctrl key while you press the Tab key twice.

If you currently are at 3 and you want to go to workbook 4, use Ctrl+Shift+Tab to go backwards through the list.

When Selecting a Range, the Corner That I Started in Is Not Also Highlighted.

I click and drag to select a range. The starting cell is not highlighted. Is this information still included in the selection?

▲	A	B	C	D	E
1					
2		138	186	271	114
3		142	187	269	108
4		307	253	245	199
5		103	299	139	195
6		294	115	293	106
7		163	390	387	291
8		230	220	112	267
9					

Figure 49 Is A2 part of the selection?

Yes – the thick border defines the selection. The lighter cell is how you know which is the Active Cell.

If you do any formatting, it will apply to the whole selection. But, if you start typing anything, it will only be entered in the active cell.

Note: If you want to enter the same value in the whole selected range, type the value and press Ctrl+Enter.

Tip: In case you have a large data set, you can move the active cell to another corner by pressing Ctrl+Period. This is a great way to move from the top to the bottom of the data set without losing the selection.

To change the active cell without losing the whole selection, press the Tab key repeatedly.

How Do I Select a Large Area of Cells without Having to Click and Drag?

I opened a file with thousands of rows. It is a pain to click and drag to select this data.

Select one cell in the data and press Ctrl+* (hold down Ctrl and press the asterisk). Excel will extend the selection in all directions until it encounters the edge of the spreadsheet or the edge of the data.

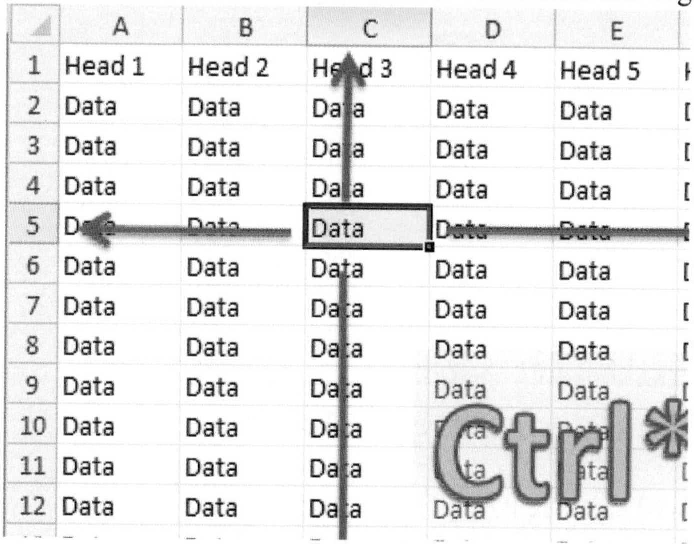

Figure 50 Select C5 and press Ctrl+. Excel will select A1:F14.*

Ctrl+* selects something known as the "Current Region". When determining the current region, Excel can ignore some blank cells, provided there is still a diagonal path to the edge of the data. While this usually works pretty well, it sometimes works against you. In the following figure, there is a diagonal path from C5 to B6 to A5, so Excel figures that you wanted to select back to column A. However, there is also a diagonal path to the grocery list that you jotted in column H, so two extra columns are considered part of the current region. Had you moved the heading from G3 to H3, Excel would not have included G or H in the current region.

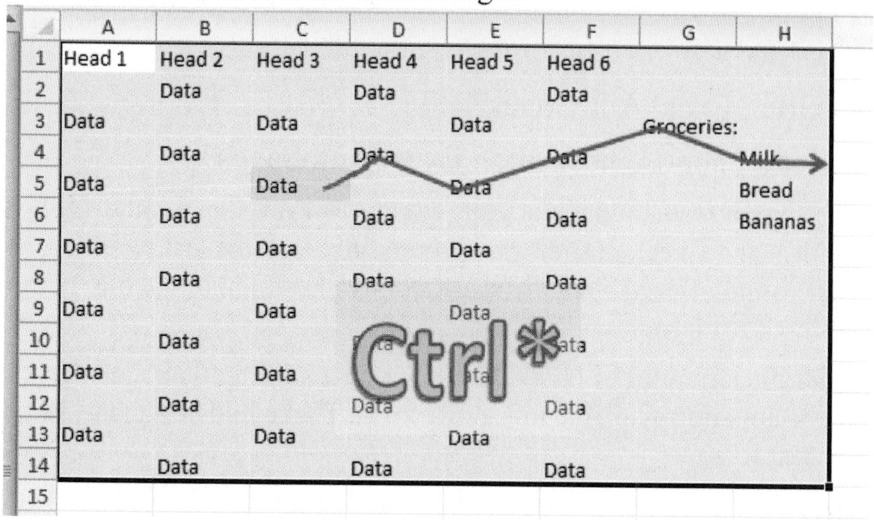

Figure 51 Keep one blank column between a data set and any other notes.

The other common requirement is to select from the current cell down to the end of the current column or row. If you select a cell and use Ctrl+Shift+Down Arrow, Excel will select down to the cell before the first blank cell. Similarly, Ctrl+Shift+Right Arrow will select to the right edge of the data.

⊿	A	B	C	D	E
1	Head 1	Head 2	Head 3	Head 4	Head 5
2	Data	Data	Data	Data	Data
3	Data	Data	Data	Data	Data
4	Data	Data	Data	Data	Data
5	Data	Data	Data	Data	Data
6	Data	Data	Data	Data	Data
7	Data	Data	Data	Data	Data
8	Data	Data	Data	Data	Data
9	Data	Data	Data	Data	Data
10	Data	Data	Data	Data	Data
11	Data	Data	Data	Data	Data
12	Data	Data	Data	Data	Data
13	Data	Data	Data	Data	Data
14	Data	Data	Data	Data	Data
15					

Figure 52 Ctrl+Shift+Down Arrow will select to the end of the column.

Caution: While Ctrl+* can skip over the occasional blank cell, Ctrl+Shift+Arrow will not jump over a blank cell.

Can I Cut and Paste Cells from One Worksheet into Another?

Can I cut data from one worksheet and paste it into another worksheet?

Yes – this generally is not a problem. However, say that you want to cut H1:H10 from Sheet 1. If these cells contain formulas that point to A1:A10 and you paste to Sheet 2 and there are not 7 columns to the left of where you paste the data, the formula will be pointing outside the grid, which will cause a #REF! error.

1. Select the cells that you want to cut.
2. Use Ctrl+X or the cut icon.
3. Use Ctrl+PgDn to quickly move to worksheets to the right of the current worksheet. Or, to switch to another workbook, use Ctrl+Tab until you are in the new workbook.
4. Use Ctrl+V to paste.

Caution: You want to be careful not to invoke most commands after the cut. Many commands will clear the cut range from the clipboard and you will have to start over.

Is It Possible to Change How Often Excel AutoSaves?

I'm paranoid to lose my work, can I choose how often Excel AutoSaves?

By default, Excel will save AutoRecover information about your workbook every ten minutes. If you were using a workbook for 52 minutes and Excel crashed, you would only lose the last two minutes of your work. After Excel restarts, it would offer to open the last AutoSaved version of the file. In this scenario, this isn't bad… you only lost 2% of your work.

However, what if Excel crashes after nine minutes of use? Then, since you have not had a workbook open for ten minutes, there will not be anything available to AutoRecover. That could be a painful way to learn about the shortcomings of AutoRecover.

To change the AutoRecover setting, go to File, Options, Save. You can set Excel to AutoRecover every one to 120 minutes. Change this setting to five minutes or three minutes or whatever you are comfortable with.

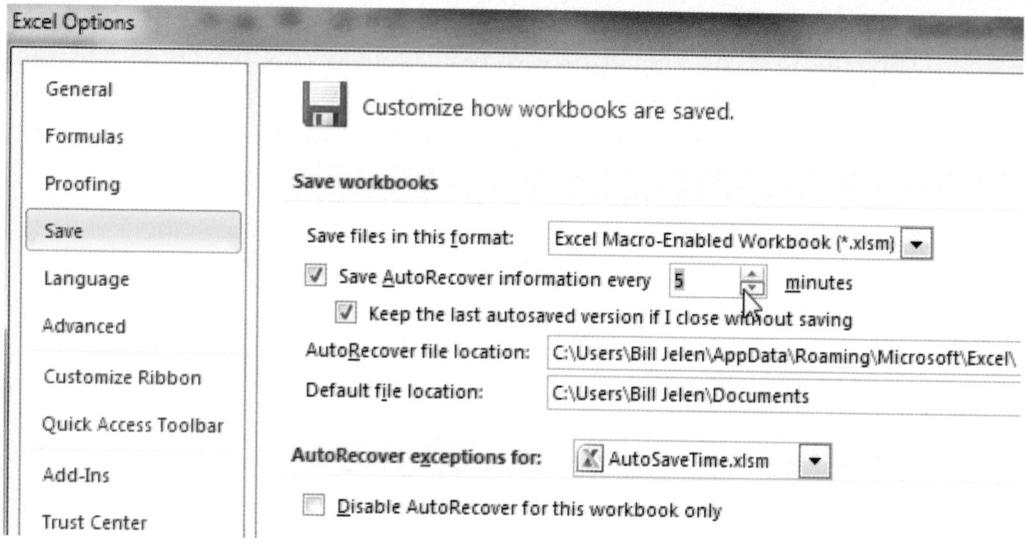

Figure 53 Use Excel Options to choose a shorter AutoSave time.

There is a downside to a short AutoRecover time. If you have a 20-row worksheet saved to a local hard drive, it can save in a second or two. But, if you have 10,000 rows of data and save it to a network drive, the AutoSave might take 20 or 30 seconds. You cannot type any data while Excel is saving the AutoRecover information. If Excel were to pause for 30 seconds every minute, you would become very frustrated. While the AutoSave time is a global setting, you can specify that the currently active workbook should be excluded from the AutoSave regimen. Use the checkbox at the bottom of the figure above. If you do this, you will have to manually remember to save every so often.

How Do I Add Headers and Footers to My Worksheet When I Print It?

I have a worksheet that I want to print and distribute. It contains sensitive information. How can I add a title, page numbers, confidentiality information and the date and time it was printed?

Excel has the ability to add a header and footer to any worksheet that is included on every page printed. Both the header and the footer have three sections: a left justified section, a center section and a right justified section. In addition to custom text such as "My Special Report" you can instruct Excel to include the date and time printed, the page number, total number of pages, file name and some other workbook attributes.

To add or edit headers and footers on the currently selected sheet, navigate to the View tab and click Page Layout in the Workbook Views group.

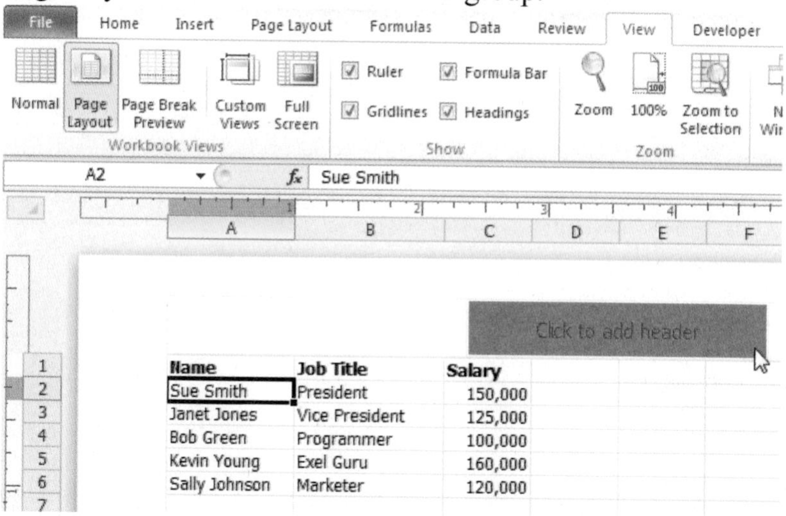

Figure 54 Page Layout view offers easy access to headers and footers.

Excel now displays an area for the header and the footer, each split into three sections: left, center, and right. Click in a section and enter the text you want displayed. When you are editing a header or footer Excel adds to the Ribbon a new tab named Header & Footer Tools Design. To insert a predefined value such as the page number or date printed click one of the buttons in the Header and Footer Elements group of that tab.

Figure 55 Inserting header and footer elements using the "Design" tab.

If you want to use a different header or footer for the first page versus the rest of the pages check on the Different First Page checkbox in the Options group of the Design tab. To display different headers on odd and even pages check on the Different Odd & Even Pages checkbox. When using either of these two features, you have to navigate to a page on which that header and footer will print in order to add or edit it. For example, if you choose to print a different header on the first page, you have to navigate to the second page to add or edit the header that appears on all but the first page.

Note: Excel provides a number of useful predefined headers and footers. You can view and use them by clicking either Header or Footer in the Header & Footer group on the Design tab.

Caution: Excel does not provide a way to adjust the left and right margins used to format the header – only the top and bottom (using the Margins tab of the Page Setup dialog box.) The left and right margins are set at 0.75 inches and cannot be changed. If you want to align the headers, footers and content, set the left and right margins for the content at 0.75 inches.

Tip: Excel offers three views; Normal, Page Layout, and Page Break Preview. The Page Layout view is the only one of the three that displays headers and footers. When you switch back to Normal view, the headers will not be displayed. They are still there and will appear in Print Preview and on the print out.

You will notice that when you work with headers and footers using the Page Layout view, when you return to Normal view Excel displays the page breaks on the sheet. If you don't want the page breaks displayed, navigate to the File tab (or click the Office Button in Excel 2007) and select Options then select Advanced in the left column and uncheck the Show Page Breaks checkbox in the section Display Options for This Worksheet section as seen below:

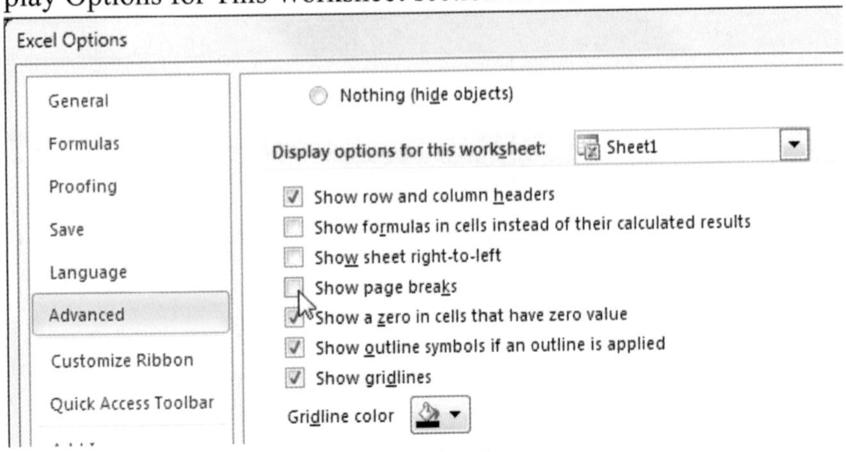

Figure 56 Turning off the display of page breaks.

👀 You Did What?

Old School Print Titles at Top of Each Page

David R. wrote about his manager. The manager had a huge report in Excel that went on for thousands of rows. When the manager tried to print the report, the headings only appeared on page one and never anywhere else. This is annoying. The manager had used Freeze Panes so he could always see the headings, but they did not print out on each page.

	A	B	C	D
1	**My Awesome Report**			
2				
3	Log ID	Jan	Feb	Mar
4	123001	3185	4708	1017
5	123002	3821	4256	2752
6	123003	3236	1845	1893

Figure 57 You need to print pages and pages of data like this.

The co-worker thought it would be easier for the report recipients to see the headings at the top of each page. It is cool that after you do a Print Preview, Excel shows you where each automatic page break is going to happen. In the following figure, right after row 34, you can see the dotted page break line:

So – the co-worker inserted three new blank lines before row 35. He copied and pasted the titles and headings from rows 1:3 to these blank lines.

	A	B
1	**My Awesome**	
2		
3	Log ID	Jan
31	123028	2382
32	123029	1354
33	123030	3259
34	123031	2746
35	123032	3128
36	123033	4578

Figure 58 The dotted line shows that the next page will start with row 35.

34	123031	2746	2593	1004
35	**My Awesome Report**			
36				
37	Log ID	Jan	Feb	Mar
38	123032	3128	2772	1730
39	123033	4578	2482	3830
40	123034	3038	3554	3777

Figure 59 Insert three blank rows for the headings and paste the headings at the top of page two.

By the way, I hope the co-worker adjusted the margins before he started this process. Otherwise, it would be a major problem because a change to the margins would change where the automatic page breaks occur. Or, he could select each title and use Insert, Breaks, Insert Page Breaks to add a manual page break.

After a day's worth of work, the manager had added title and heading rows to all 399 pages of the report.

13530	136122	4985	2311	3515	2462	1871	2748	4685	4345
13531	136123	4340	3722	1398	4647	2029	1671	2016	3663
13532	136124	2275	2967	1245	1661	2094	3889	1397	4442
13533	**My Awesome Report**								
13534									
13535	**Log ID**	**Jan**	**Feb**	**Mar**	**Apr**	**May**	**Jun**	**Jul**	**Aug**
13536	136127	1867	1995	2167	3790	4059	2522	2792	1182
13537	136128	4957	3977	3309	3842	3133	1670	4051	1812
13538	136129	3708	4351	1837	1045	4752	1948	1627	3958
13539	136130	2842	3439	4094	1789	2407	4751	1416	2211
13540	136131	2396	4766	3009	4137	2023	3979	3132	1182
13541	136132	3612	4351	3354	3393	1637	1940	1328	1593
13542	136133	1165	1317	2914	4209	3532	4908	4047	3717
13543	136134	2083	3137	2729	3946	3353	2533	3418	3209
13544	136135	4477	2984	4343	1307	3989	3734	2283	3728
13545	136136	1575	1902	2944	1244	3904	1980	4070	2516
13546	136137	3716	2186	2850	2770	3583	2099	3495	3779
13547	136138	2762	5000	3828	4452	1663	1673	4609	1699
13548	136139	2790	2701	2633	3051	3575	1192	3000	3893
13549	136140	2747	3159	3229	3735	3820	4941	4356	3136
13550	136141	1120	2112	1604	4984	1422	4770	3553	2148
13551	136142	2211	4460	4625	2978	3600	2028	3598	4549
13552	136143	2402	1171	2015	2548	4328	4559	2345	2105
13553	136144	4010	4113	2281	3003	4866	4009	2882	4893

Figure 60 Insert, Copy, Paste, PgDn over and over and over.

Note: It undoubtedly took David's co-worker all day to do this. I did it here in a minute using a three line macro.

Why didn't you show me this *yesterday*?

David showed the co-worker the technique shown below. The co-worker had a look on his face, along the lines of "Why Didn't You Show This To Me Yesterday?"

Why this is bad: The faster way to go is to specify that rows 1:3 should repeat at the top of each printed page. You would follow these steps:

1. On the Page Layout tab of the Ribbon, select the Print Titles icon. This opens up the Excel 2003 legacy dialog for Page Setup. You will be on the fourth tab – labeled Sheet.
2. Click in the box for Rows To Repeat At Top.
3. Type 1:3 in order to repeat rows 1-3 at the top of each printed page. You can also specify those rows using the mouse and the RefEdit button on the right side of the box. However, it is just as easy to type 1:3.

Figure 61 Use Rows to Repeat at Top in order to force rows 1:3 to print at the top of each page.

How Do I Center My Work in Excel?

I need to center my report in the middle of a page. How many columns should I insert to the left of column A to get it to center?

There is a much better way to do this. You will rarely discover this setting, so grab a sticky note and mark this page.

Set up your report starting in column A and row 1. Select the entire range of the report (perhaps A1:H15). Go to the Page Layout tab in the Ribbon. Choose Print Area, Set Print Area.

Look in the bottom right corner of the Page Setup group. There is a symbol there called the Dialog Launcher. It looks like the top left corner of a rectangle, with a diagonal arrow pointing towards the bottom right. Click this icon in the Page Setup group to open the old Page Setup dialog box.

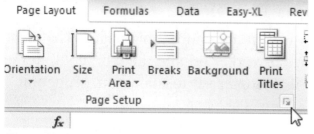

Figure 62 Use the Page Setup dialog launcher.

In the Page Setup dialog, there are four tabs across the top. Choose the Margins tab. In the bottom of this tab, there are two checkboxes under Center on Page. To center your report between the left and right margins, choose Horizontally. To center your report between the top and right margins, choose Vertically. Click OK.

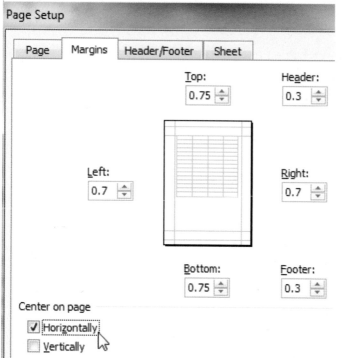

Figure 63 Center the report horizontally in the middle of the page.

When you print this worksheet, the report will print out in the center of the page. This also works if you create a PDF of the report.

👀 You Did What?

Print to Blueprint Printer Then Reduce on Copier Three Times

Jane's co-worker had a huge document that was printing on multiple pages. The manager wanted everything to fit to one page. The co-worker printed the workbook to the company Blueprint printer. She then used a photocopier set to maximum reduction – twice – to get the information to fit to a page.

I give this person an "R" for Resourcefulness. There is an easier way. Go to the Page Layout tab in Excel. There is a group called Scale To Fit.

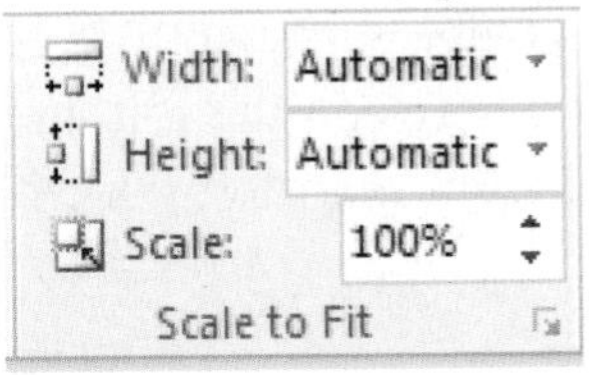

Figure 64 With Width and Height set to Automatic, the worksheet prints at 100% of normal size.

Open the Width and Height dropdowns and choose 1 Page from each.

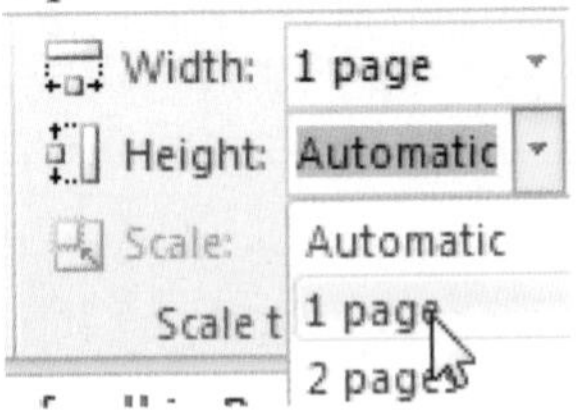

Figure 65 Excel will automatically scale the size of the printed text until it fits on one page.

CHAPTER 2 - FORMATTING

Is There a Way to Make a Sheet with Only a Few Cells and Columns?

For example, sign-up sheets, to-do lists and so on.

Sure! Here are the steps to build a simple sign-up schedule for a conference room.

Note: this is a longer case study that walks completely through a small project from beginning to end. There are a lot of concepts introduced here, but this project should not be intimidating. There are no formulas in this project, only formatting. If you can master the steps to do this project, you will officially be in "Phase 2" of your Excel journey.

Case Study 1
Build your confidence with Excel by following this case study step by step

Start with a completely blank worksheet.

	A	B	C	D
1				
2				
3				
4				

Figure 66 Start with an empty worksheet.

Put a long title in cell A1. You do not have to worry about merging cells or using wrap text since there will be nothing to the right of this title in row 1. If there are no values to the right of the cell, it is fine for the cell text to extend past the right edge of the cell.

	A	B	C	D	E
1	2nd Floor Conference Room Sign-Up Sheet				
2					
3					
4					

Figure 67 Add a title.

Now is a good time to Save the file with a good name. AutoSave will save a copy of your workbook every ten minutes, but manually saving now will help you to remember to save the document when you close Excel later. Use File, Save As and choose a folder. Type a good name such as Conference-RoomSignup and click OK.

When you press Enter after typing the title, Excel normally moves to cell A2. You want to format the title so select cell A1 again.

	A	B	C	D	E
1	2nd Floor Conference Room Sign-Up Sheet				
2					

Figure 68 Move back to cell A1.

Starting in Excel 2007, Microsoft bundled several cool Cell Styles with Excel. Look towards the right side of the Home tab and open the Cell Styles dropdown to reveal the built-in styles. No one says that you have to use any of these. But, it is a quick way to format the title. Choose the Title style.

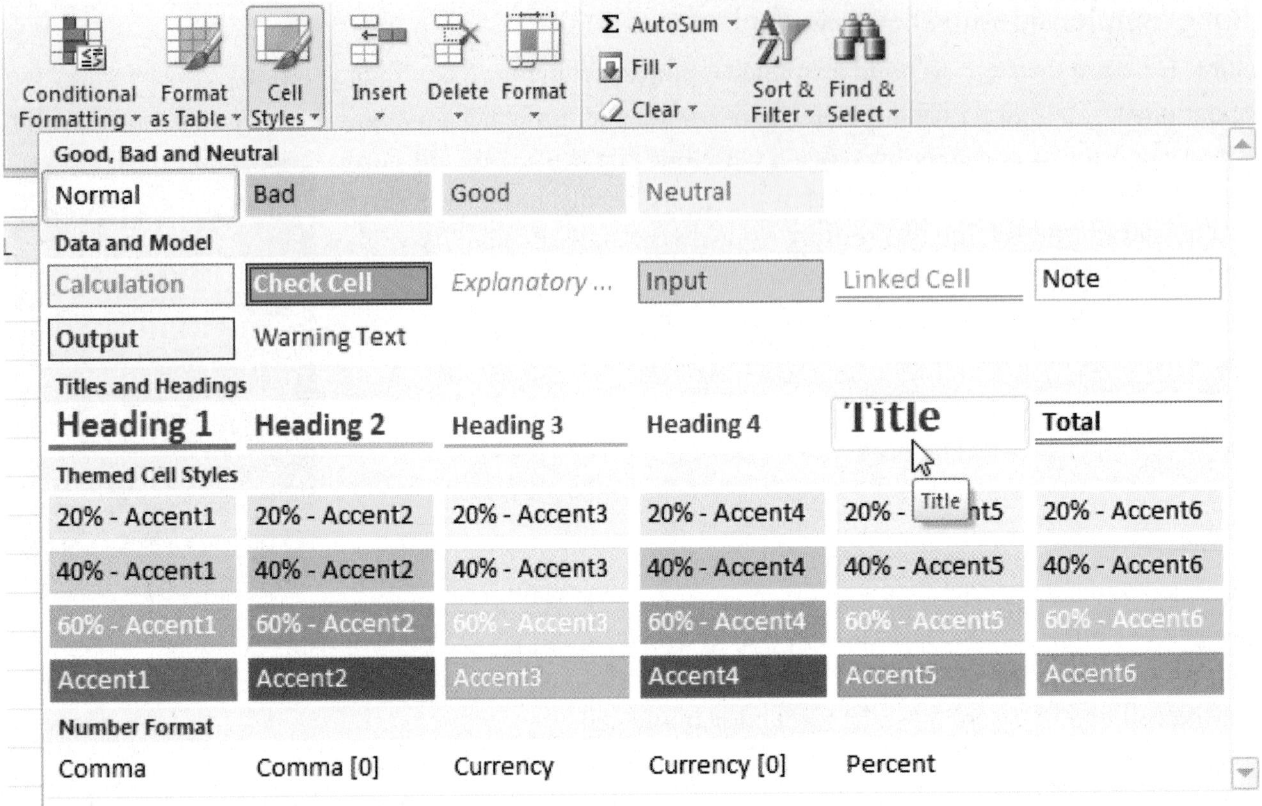

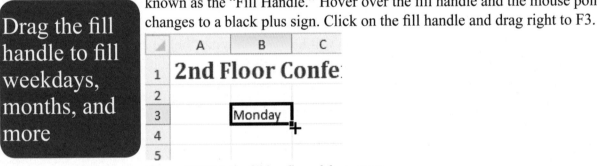

Figure 69 Use a Title style for cell A1.

Select cell B3. Type Monday. To prevent Excel from moving to B4, press Ctrl+Enter.

The active cell has a thick border. The bottom right corner of that border is a square dot. That dot is known as the "Fill Handle." Hover over the fill handle and the mouse pointer changes to a black plus sign. Click on the fill handle and drag right to F3.

> Drag the fill handle to fill weekdays, months, and more

Figure 70 Click the fill handle and drag across.

Amazingly, Excel will fill the days of the week for you! This trick also works with month names, dates and more.

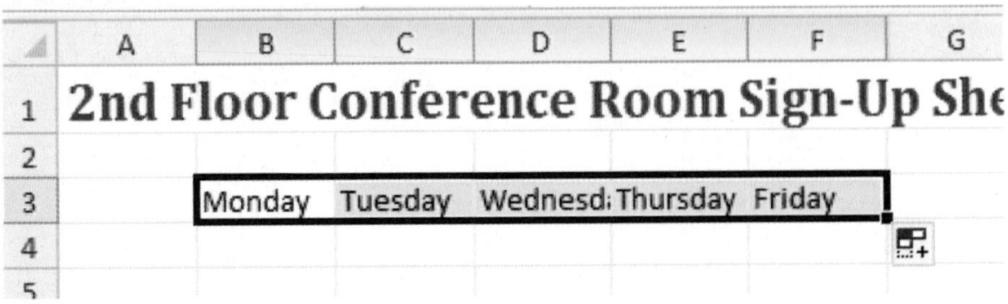

Figure 71 Dragging the fill handle is easier than typing Wednesday.

While the weekday names are still selected, open the Cell Styles dropdown and choose Heading 4. There are several heading styles, but the first three have a too-large underline, so I always go for Heading 4.

While the weekday names are still selected, open the Format dropdown and choose AutoFit Column Width.

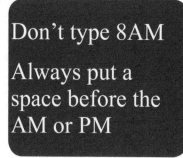

Don't type 8AM

Always put a space before the AM or PM

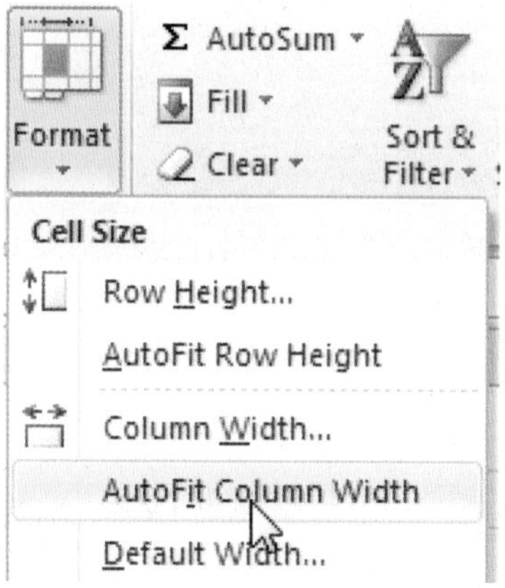

Figure 72 Excel will make the columns wide enough for the text in the selection.

Go to cell A4. Type the number 8, a space, and AM. This is a quirk, but that space before the AM in times is absolutely critical. Don't miss the space!

Press Enter and Excel changes what you typed to 8:00 AM. Is this annoying? Well, it is part of the "Excel letting you use certain shortcuts when entering date and time" problem. It didn't work to your advantage today, but it is possible to fix it.

Figure 73 Another gotcha in Excel is not typing a space before AM or PM.

Figure 74 Excel changes 8 AM to 8:00 AM.

Select cell A4. Drag the fill handle down until the tool tip shows that you are at 5:00 PM. Let go of the mouse button and Excel has put in all the hours for you.

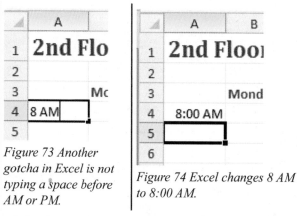

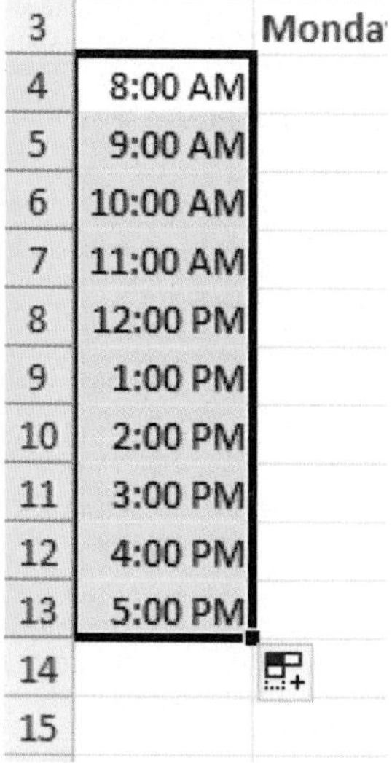

Figure 75 Keep this up, and your co-workers will start calling you "Dr. Fill".

While all of the times are still selected, open the Format Cells dialog. If you are a keyboard person, use Ctrl+1 (the number one). If you prefer to use the mouse, look for the tiny arrow pointing southeast from the bottom right of the Number group on the Home tab. Microsoft calls this little symbol a "Dialog Launcher." You will see them throughout the Ribbon. This particular dialog launcher is the correct one to fix the format of your times.

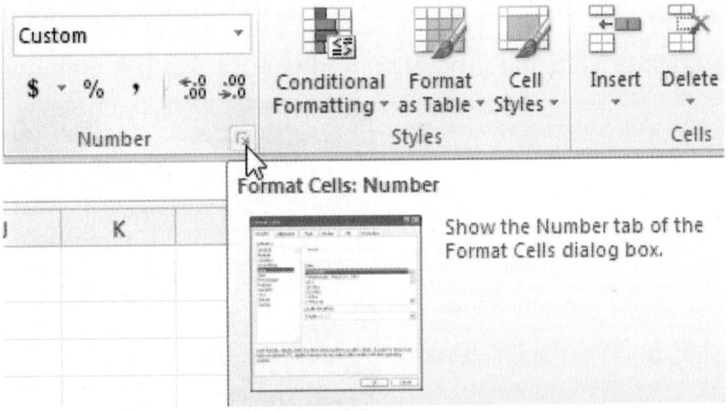

Figure 76 Ctrl+1 (the number one) or this little icon will get you to the Format Cells dialog.

Provided you clicked the correct dialog launcher, you will already be on the Number tab of the Format Cells dialog. If not, click the first tab across the top of the dialog.

There is a Category dropdown along the left side of the Number tab. There are categories for Date, Time and so on. Click on the Time category to look at the built-in number formats for time.

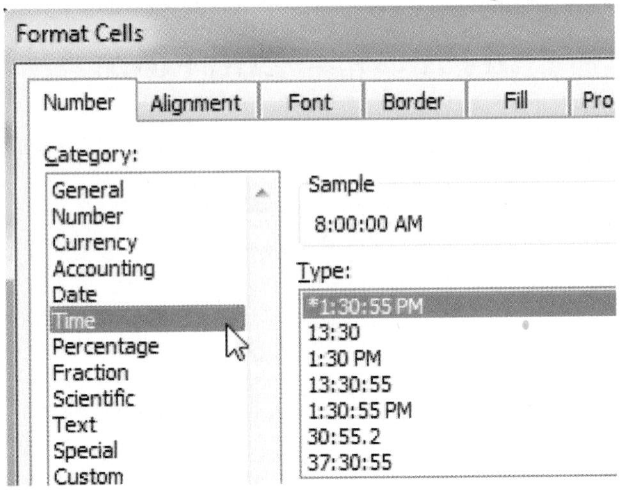

Figure 77 Start with the Time category to see if they have anything close.

In the Type: box above, you can see several time formats that are available. None of those formats look like "8 AM". That's OK, because you can create your own format easily. Move to the Custom category.

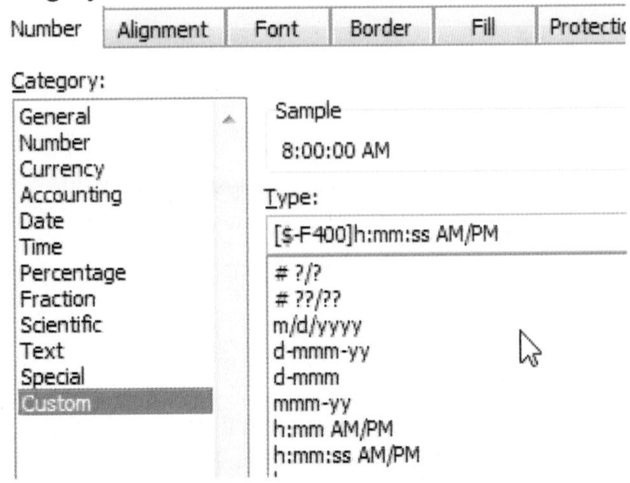

Figure 78 Choose the Custom category and you can build your own format.

When you select the Custom category, Excel shows you the code for the current number format. In Figure 78, you can see it is [$-F400]h:mm:ss AM/PM.

First rule: delete anything in the square brackets at the beginning. Those numbers are a locale code that varies from country to country. They define a default format. Always delete the square brackets before trying to figure out what is going on.

> Custom number formats let you show dates or time in thousands of variations

That leaves you with a code of h:mm:ss AM/PM.

Is that hard to figure out? H=hours. M=Minutes. S=Seconds. There are colons between each.

Excel Help goes through pages and pages of minutiae about custom number formats, but you can easily figure this one out. You don't want minutes or seconds, so edit the code in the type box to be: h AM/PM. The dialog even shows how the active cell will appear with this code: 8 AM. Perfect! Click OK to close the dialog.

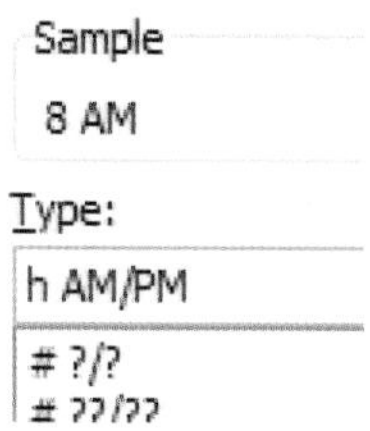

Sample

8 AM

Type:

h AM/PM

?/?

??/??

Figure 79 Custom number formats are not difficult most of the time.

While you have the times selected, go to Home, Cell Styles, and choose the style called Heading 4.

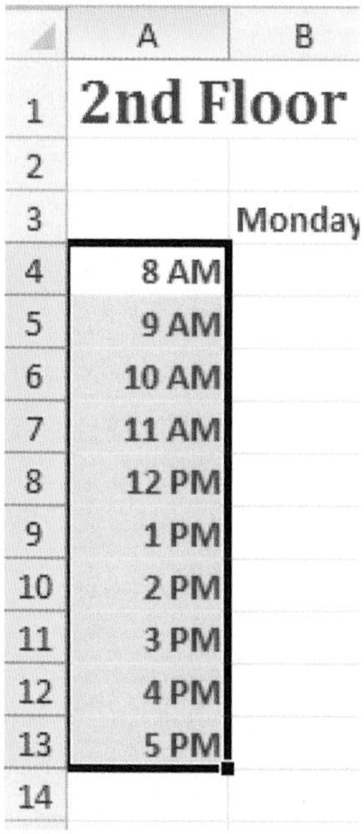

	A	B
1	**2nd Floor**	
2		
3		Monday
4	8 AM	
5	9 AM	
6	10 AM	
7	11 AM	
8	12 PM	
9	1 PM	
10	2 PM	
11	3 PM	
12	4 PM	
13	5 PM	
14		

Figure 80 The times along the left side look good.

If this is a printed sign-up form that you hang on the door of the conference room, you will need boxes that people can write in. Select B4:F13. Remember, you can select this range with this fluid motion: Click in B4, hold the mouse button down and move to F13. Release the mouse button.

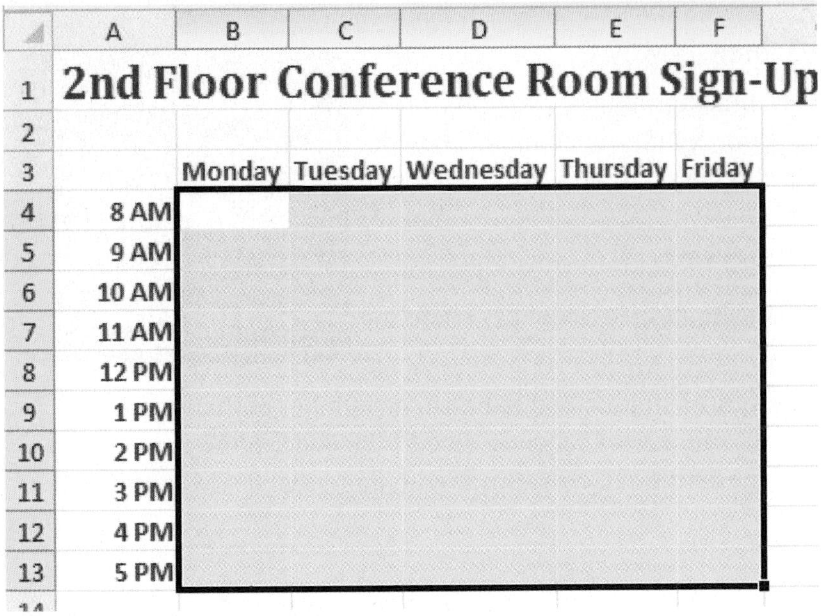

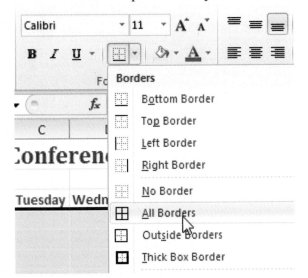

Figure 81 Select the area for the boxes.

There are a million choices for borders in the Format Cells dialog, but in many cases, the Borders dropdown has exactly what you need. Look for the Borders dropdown to the right of the Bold/Italic/Underline icons. Open this dropdown and choose All Borders.

Figure 82 Apply borders.

You now have boxes. Two things strike me when I look at Figure 83. The boxes are not tall enough for anyone to write in them. And, the Wednesday column is wider than the other columns. This happened when you did AutoFormat column width. It make column D wide enough to hold the characters in "Wednesday", but it looks asymmetrical with each column having a different width.

A row height of 35 gives people enough room to write in the printed form

	A	B	C	D	E	F
1	**2nd Floor Conference Room Sign-U**					
2						
3		Monday	Tuesday	Wednesday	Thursday	Friday
4	8 AM					
5	9 AM					
6	10 AM					
7	11 AM					
8	12 PM					
9	1 PM					
10	2 PM					
11	3 PM					
12	4 PM					
13	5 PM					
14						

Figure 83 Each column is a different width.

To make the boxes taller, you want to adjust the row height. You should still have B4:F13 selected. Go to Home, Format, Row Height.

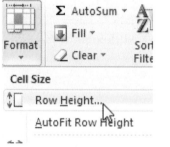

Figure 84 Make the boxes taller by adjusting the row height.

The Row Height will tell you that the rows are currently a height of 15. (Your actual number will vary depending on the fonts that you used over in column A.)

Row Height	?	X
Row height:	15	
OK	Cancel	

Figure 85 Currently, the rows have a height of 15.

Note: You might ask "15 what?" What is the unit on row height? It is points. There are 96 points in an inch.

This next step requires a guess. If I want someone to write in a cell, I usually double the row height. But since someone might need to write "Budget Meeting with Auditors" in the box, go a little bit bigger. Try a height of 35. Click OK to see how it looks.

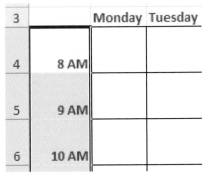

Figure 86 Guess at a good row height.

You now have taller boxes for each row.

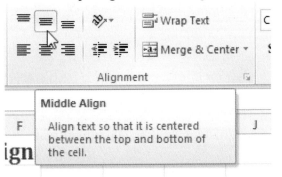

Figure 87 These look tall enough for someone to write in.

In the figure above, notice that the times are appearing at the bottom of each row. It happens that all text is always at the bottom of the cell, but you only notice it when the row is taller. There are three icons for Top Align, Middle Align, and Bottom Align in the Home tab. Choose Middle or Top Align.

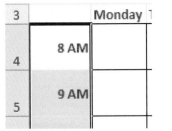

Figure 88 Excel added Top, Middle, Bottom icons starting in Excel 2007.

Here are the times with Middle Align:

Figure 89 Top or Middle vertical alignment would work here.

When fixing the row height, you used the Row Height dialog to see the current row height. That worked because all of the rows have the same height. When the rows or columns have a different height, you need a different method for determining the current row height or column width.

One of my favorite tricks is to click on the line separating two column letters. In Figure 90, clicking between D and E shows a tool tip that column D currently has a width of 10.86. You will want columns B:F to be at least 10.86 wide, maybe wider.

Figure 90 Click here to pretend you are going to resize the column. Excel displays a tooltip showing the current width.

Note: You might ask "10.86 what?" What is the unit on column width? It sounds ridiculous, but it is the number of digits of Courier New 9 point that can fit in a cell. Hardly anyone uses Courier font any more, yet that is still how Excel measures column width.

Select cells B3:F3. Go to Home, Format, Column Width.

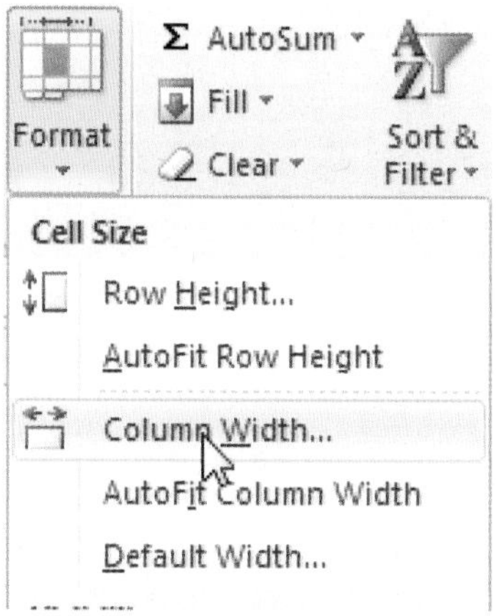

Figure 91 Choose Column Width from the Format dropdown.

Type a large column width. If Wednesday is currently 10.86 wide, go with about 15 to create columns that are bigger than Wednesday.

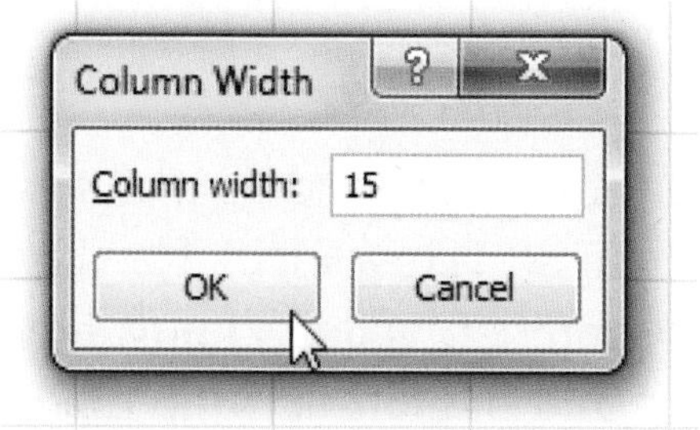

Figure 92 Use a column width of 15.

To center the headings, click the Center Align button while the headings are selected.

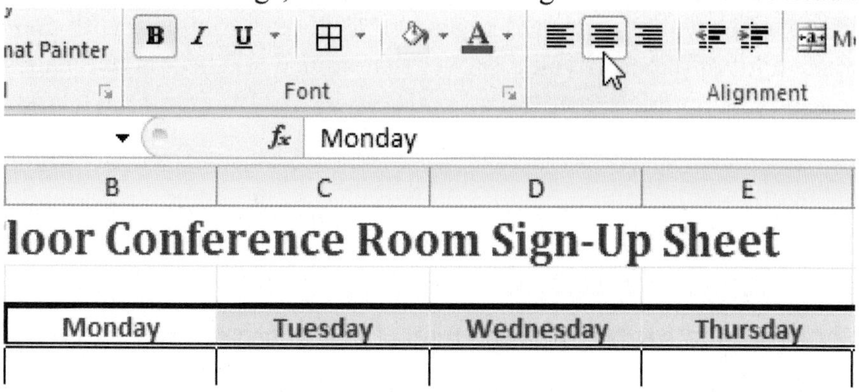

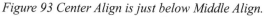

Figure 93 Center Align is just below Middle Align.

Select A1:F13. On the Page Layout tab, choose Print Area, Set Print Area. Setting the print area makes sure that only this range gets printed. This is not necessary if your form is the only text on the worksheet as in this case. But, since I tend to jot grocery lists to the right of any worksheet that I happen to have open, setting the print range keeps me from accidentally letting everyone know that I need to buy soap and oatmeal.

Figure 94 It is a good habit to explicitly set the print range.

Click Ctrl+P then click Print to print a copy of your sign-up sheet. Tape it to the conference door and let people start reserving the conference room. (For the next case study, see page 125).

That Dotted Line Isn't There for Centering!

I was working on a spreadsheet, entering a lot of data. I did something and all of a sudden, a dotted line runs down the middle of the screen. I thought, "How nice! They are showing me the midpoint of the report so I can keep things centered!" I don't know how I turned it on, but OK, whatever. Then I printed the report and the left half the report printed on pages 1-3 and the right half of the report printed on pages 4-6.

That dotted line is the arcane way of letting you know that there will be a page break. Before printing, go to View, Page Layout. You will get to see what the printed pages will look like, complete with margins. This is a great way not to waste a lot of paper. If you discover that your worksheet is two pages wide instead of one, you can try these three simple remedies:

- Page Layout, Margins, Narrow
- Page Layout, Orientation, Landscape
- Page Layout, Width: 1 Page

How Do I Put the Path and File Name in the Footer?

Ten weeks ago, I created the conference room sign-up sheet. I made ten copies and used one each week. Someone used the last one without making a copy. The only one left is hanging on the conference room door and people have written on it. I cannot remember what I called the file when I saved it.

There is a built-in footer setting that would put the complete path and filename of the document in the footer area of the document. While you've already seen how to edit headers on page 23, here is a different way to add a header or footer.

1. Go to the Page Layout tab of the Ribbon.
2. Click the dialog launcher (the arrow pointing southeast) in the lower right corner of the Page Setup group. This displays the old Excel 2003 Page Setup dialog.
3. There are four tabs across the top of the Page Setup dialog. Choose the third tab: Header/Footer.
4. Open the Footer dropdown. Scroll down until you see the footer that includes the path and file name. Choose that footer. Click OK.

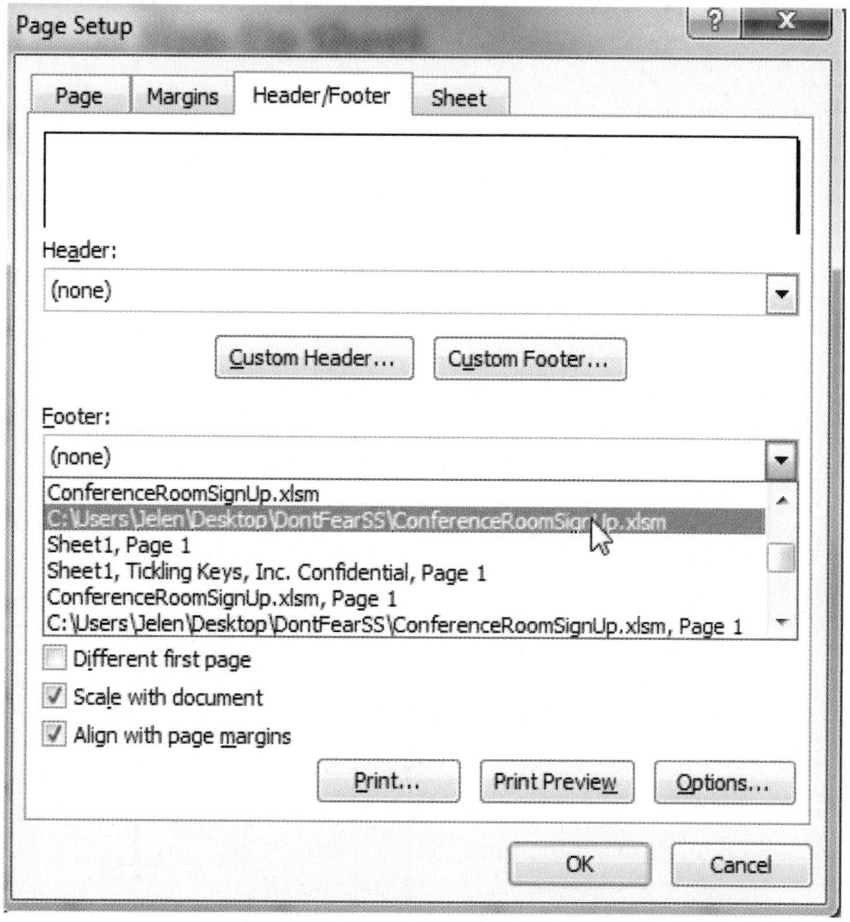

Figure 95 Choose a footer to help you remember where you saved this form.

You Did What?

Word Wrap Woes

Jane reports that her co-worker kept a monthly cheat-sheet for how to type the headings for certain reports. The cheat-sheet said that Column B would have the word Budget, then 13 spaces, then Amount. Column D would have Something, then 40 spaces, then Else.

The co-worker is trying too hard to create a cell with wrap text.

If you've never used wrap text, here is how it works.

Say that you want a multi-line heading above a column. You might start with a long line of text as shown in this figure:

◢	A	B	C	D	E	F	G
1	This is a really long heading that I want to wrap above this column (Unaudited)						
2	$ 150,023,456.79						
3	$ 150,023,456.79						
4	$ 150,023,456.79						
5	$ 150 023 456 79						

Figure 96 Start with all the text in one long line.

On the Home tab, choose the icon for Wrap Text.

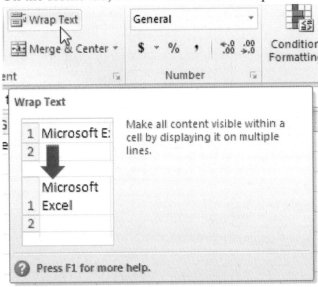

Figure 97 Wrap Text was buried on the Alignment tab of the Format Cells dialog box until Excel 2007.

When you turn on Wrap Text, the words will be wrapped to fill the available width in the column. This forces the cell to be taller, but that is better than using many rows for your heading.

To make the cell look better, use center alignment.

Excel breaks the heading at off places. You might want the lines to break as shown in Figure 99.

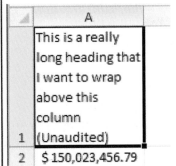

Figure 98 Excel fills the available width of the column.

◢	A
	This is a really
	long heading
	that I want to
	wrap
	above this
	column
1	(Unaudited)
2	$ 150,023,456.79
3	$ 150 023 456 79

Figure 99 You want to move the word "that" from line two to line three.

One way to do this, as discovered by Jane's co-worker is to type a bunch of spaces before the word that will begin the next line. In this figure, you can see that it required a few spaces before the word "that", but a bunch of spaces before the word "above". This is all achieved through trial and error.

heading	that I want to wrap	above this column	(Unaudited)

Figure 100 Add a bunch of spaces to force certain words to go to the next line.

Once Jane's co-worker figured out the right spacing, it was smart of her to create the cheat sheet to save the hassle the next time.

Why this bad: There is already a very fast way to control where the lines wrap. As you are typing the long title, press Alt+Enter to insert a line break. Don't even put a space after the last word in line one. Type line one, Alt+Enter, line two. In the figure below, the heading in A1 was created by typing the sequence shown in red.

Use Alt+Enter to move to a new line in the cell

A1	fx	This is a long label
		that I want to wrap
		Above this column

	A	B	C	D	E	F
1	This is a long label that I want to wrap Above this column					
2	$ 150,023,456.79					
3	$ 150,023,456.79					
4	$ 150,023,456.79					

This is a long label<Alt+Enter> that I want to wrap<Alt+Enter> Above this column<Enter>

Figure 101 Use Alt+Enter to go to a new line in a cell.

How Can I Merge Multiple Cells into a Single Cell?

I have a table containing multiple columns, each with its own header. Some of the columns are related to each other and I would like to show their relationship by adding a header above the existing column headers that spans the related columns.

I understand why you asked this question. Right there on the Home tab, Excel offers a big, inviting dropdown called Merge & Center, with four choices.

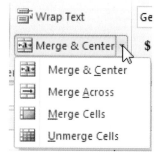

Wrap Text	Ge
Merge & Center ▾	$

- Merge & Center
- Merge Across
- Merge Cells
- Unmerge Cells

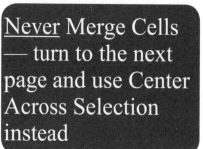

Never Merge Cells — turn to the next page and use Center Across Selection instead

Figure 102 As Microsoft gave these a premium location on the home tab, you might think they are useable.

Using any of those four choices will cause you untold misery. Your ability to copy and paste, sort, even select cells will be hampered. The better alternative is hidden deep in the Format Cells dialog.

Since merged cells can be problematic when copying and pasting, a better solution is to use a feature that centers a text value across multiple cells without actually merging the cells. To apply this format to more than one cell, select the cells across which you want the text to span, press the Dialog Box Launcher in the Alignment group on the Home tab to open the Format Cells dialog with the Alignment tab displayed. Select Center Across Selection for the horizontal text alignment. In the figure below, you would select A1:B1 and Center Across Selection. Then choose C1:E1 and press F4 to repeat the Center Across Selection command.

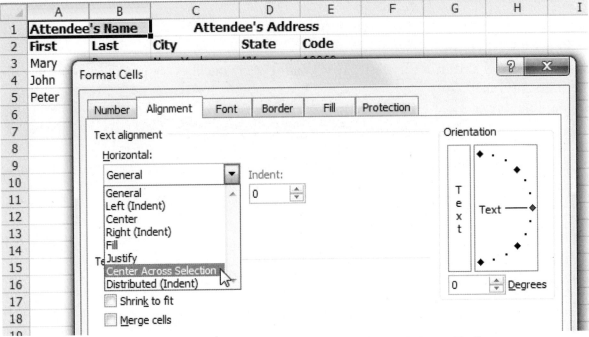

Figure 103 Center Across Selection isn't even available as an icon on the Quick Access Toolbar.

Tip: Pressing F4 repeats the last command. It happens to work great after applying Center Across Selection.

How Can I Copy Cell Formatting?

I have a series of identically shaped regions. I've formatted the first report and want to copy the formatting to the other reports.

	A	B	C	D	E	F	G	H	I
1		East	Central	West	Total			East	Central
2	A	63	171	75	309		A	63	171
3	B	159	222	78	459		B	159	222
4	C	135	30	144	309		C	135	30
5	D	48	132	165	345		D	48	132
6	E	171	207	168	546		E	171	207
7	Total	576	762	630	1968		Total	576	762
8									
9									

Figure 104 Copy the formatting from A1:E7 over to G1:K7.

There is a Paste Special option that makes this almost easy, with one exception.

Select A1:E7 and copy.

Select G1:K7. If you are in Excel 2007 or earlier, use Alt+E+S to display Paste Special. Select Formats and click OK. If you are in Excel 2010 or newer, you can right-click, choose Paste Special... and then hover over the Paste Formats dialog as shown in Figure 105.

	G	H	I	J	K	L
		East	Central	West	Total	
A		174	60	15	249	
B		144	138	78	360	
C		174	192	180	546	
D		150	132	111	393	
E		189	189			
Total		831	711	3		

Figure 105 Paste Formatting copies the formatting but not the values.

The exception? Using Paste Formatting does not bring the column widths over. One solution is to use Alt+E+S to redisplay the Paste Special dialog and choose Column Widths, OK.

	G	H	I	J	K	L	M
		East	Central	West	Total		
A		174	60	15	249		
B		144	138	78	360		
C		174	192	180	546		
D		150	132	111	393		
E		189	189	15	393		
Total							

Paste Special

Paste
- All
- Formulas
- Values
- Formats
- Comments
- Validation

- All using Source theme
- All except borders
- ● Column widths
- Formulas and number formats
- Values and number formats
- All merging conditional formats

Figure 106 Do Paste Special again and choose Column Widths.

After doing two pastes; one for formatting and one for widths, you have copied the formatting from the first report to the second report.

	A	B	C	D	E	F	G	H	I	J	K
1		East	Central	West	Total			East	Central	West	Total
2	A	63	171	75	309		A	174	60	15	249
3	B	159	222	78	459		B	144	138	78	360
4	C	135	30	144	309		C	174	192	180	546
5	D	48	132	165	345		D	150	132	111	393
6	E	171	207	168	546		E	189	189	15	393
7	Total	576	762	630	1968		Total	831	711	399	1941
8											

Figure 107 Two Paste Special operations will bring the formatting and column widths over.

There is a faster way to copy both the formatting and column widths, but only if there is nothing above or below your report. Just follow these steps:

1. Select the entire columns A:E
2. Ctrl+C to Copy
3. Select the entire columns G:K
4. Use Paste Special, Formats, OK. This will copy the formatting and column widths.

	A	B	C	D	E
1		East	Central	West	Total
2	A	63	171	75	309
3	B	159	222	78	459
4	C	135	30	144	309
5	D	48	132	165	345
6	E	171	207	168	546
7	Total	576	762	630	1968
8					

Figure 108 Copy the entire columns and paste formats to entire columns to copy column widths as well.

Note: There is a completely different solution to copying formats called the Format Painter. The Format Painter icon is found in the Clipboard group on the left side of the Home tab. Select columns A:E, click the Format Painter, then immediately choose columns G:K. Excel will copy the formats and column widths. Read more about the Format Painter on page 94.

How Can I Remove Cell Formatting?

I want to keep all the numbers and formulas in a range, but get rid of the borders or any other cell formatting.

	A	B	C	D
1	Item	Qty	Price	Total
2	A	450	27.95	12578
3	B	300	64.95	19485
4	C	350	63.95	22383
5	D	250	76.95	19238
6	E	100	39.95	3995
7	F	200	80.95	16190
8	G	450	80.95	36428
9	H	350	47.95	16783
10	I	300	73.95	22185
11	J	200	46.95	9390

Figure 109 Remove the cacophony of formatting.

The most common problem with formatting is errant borders. If your problem is borders, select the range of cells, then open the Border dropdown from the Font group on the Home tab. Choose No Borders.

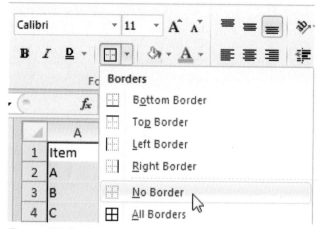

Figure 110 To clear only the borders, select No Borders from this dropdown.

To get rid of all formatting, select the range. Open the Clear dropdown and choose Clear Formatting.

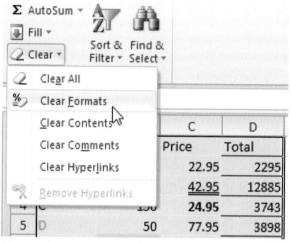

Figure 111 To clear all special fonts, formatting, and borders, use Clear Formatting.

Caution: Using Clear Formatting also removes any custom number formatting.

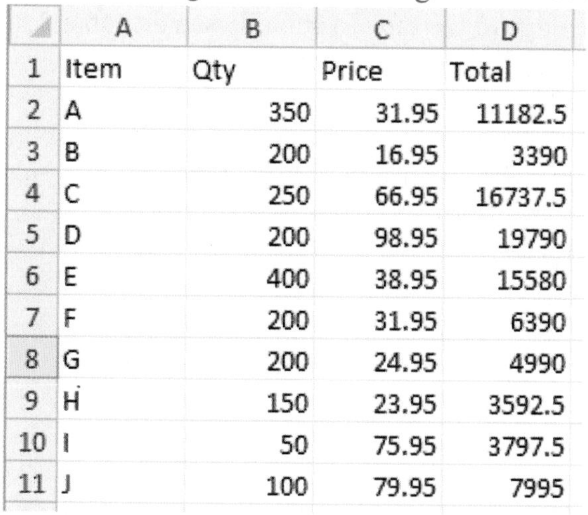

	A	B	C	D
1	Item	Qty	Price	Total
2	A	350	31.95	11182.5
3	B	200	16.95	3390
4	C	250	66.95	16737.5
5	D	200	98.95	19790
6	E	400	38.95	15580
7	F	200	31.95	6390
8	G	200	24.95	4990
9	H	150	23.95	3592.5
10	I	50	75.95	3797.5
11	J	100	79.95	7995

Figure 112 Clearing formatting resets everything to a General number formatting.

Is It Possible to Change the Color of a Worksheet Tab?

It would be helpful to have my worksheet tabs color-coded; certainly, there must be a way to do that.

It is possible to color the worksheet tabs, although there is one confusing part.

As shown below, each worksheet tab has a different color. But you can barely see the active worksheet tab. The active worksheet tab turns white to let you know that it is the active tab. And…in order to change the color of the worksheet tab, it has to be the active tab. So, after you apply color to a tab, you will barely see the color of the tab, until you switch to another tab.

Figure 113 A variety of different tab colors.

To change the tab color, right-click the tab and hover over the Tab Color… item. A flyout menu will appear with variations of the current theme, some standard colors and a More Colors choice.

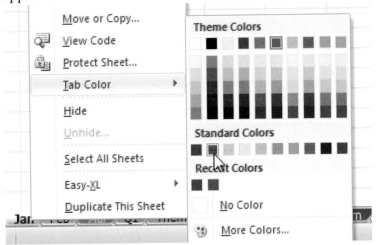

Figure 114 Choose from theme colors or standard colors on this tab.

Caution: Be careful when choosing from the first six rows – the Theme Colors. If you choose a nice red and later switch to a new theme, the tab colors may switch.

If you choose More Colors, you will have the option to either choose from 170 standard colors, or to use the Custom tab where you can enter Red, Green, Blue values for a color.

Caution: After changing the tab color, that tab will naturally be the active tab. For the active tab, the color will be 90% white, with just a tiny bit of color at the edge of the tab. To actually see the tab color, switch to another tab.

Can I Customize Color?

This little dropdown offers about 70 colors. Is that all I can use?

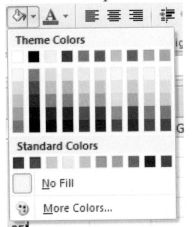

Figure 115 Both the paint bucket and font color dropdown offer these colors.

There are millions more colors than those. If you choose More Colors at the bottom of the color dropdown, you get to the color wheel with 145 colors. The colors on the color wheel are always the same.

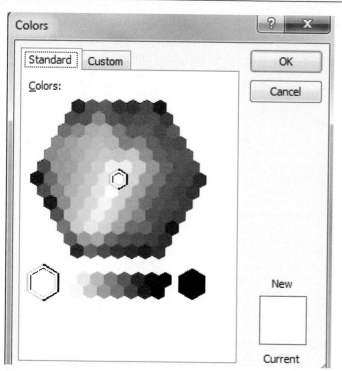

Figure 116 Some of your favorite colors from Excel 2003 are found here.

There are two tabs across the top. Click the Custom tab and you can enter any RGB color. Your company's web designer can tell you the RGB codes for the colors used by your company in their logo and web page. RGB stands for Red Green Blue. You can enter a value from 0 to 255 for each of the three colors to make any of 16 million colors.

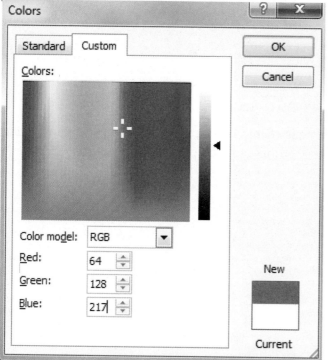

Figure 117 You can make 16 million different colors here.

Caution: Because your web designer is a geek, they will likely give you the color code as six characters like CCD044. When they give you this, they are using hexadecimal codes for each color. Ask them if they can give you the decimal values instead. Or – go to your favorite search engine and search for "convert hex color codes to RGB". There are several free converters.

You should understand something cool about the colors at the top of the original color menu in this topic. Those are all "theme colors". When you choose the orange from the top right of the menu, Excel does not record "orange". Instead it records "Theme Color 6 at the normal brightness".

Say that you use all theme colors for designing your worksheet.

	A	B	C	D	E	F
1	**Office Theme**					
2						
3	86	83	84	85	100	50
4	91	93	100	89	100	50
5	95	88	100	88	100	50
6	96	98	84	83	100	50
7	87	100	97	95	100	50
8	83	88	82	87	100	50

Figure 118 This worksheet uses all six theme colors.

If you go to the Page Layout tab and either open the Colors dropdown or the Theme dropdown, you can quickly change the colors to another set of six complementary colors.

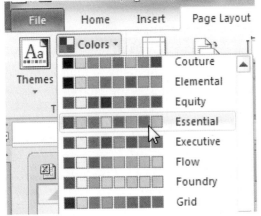

Figure 119 Excel 2010 offers forty color themes plus more at Office Online.

If you use the Colors dropdown, you change only the theme colors. If you choose the same theme name from the Themes dropdown, you will get those colors plus some different fonts and effects.

	A	B	C	D	E	F	G
1	**Essential Theme**						
2							
3	86	83	84	85	100	50	
4	91	93	100	89	100	50	
5	95	88	100	88	100	50	
6	96	98	84	83	100	50	
7	87	100	97	95	100	50	
8	83	88	82	87	100	50	

Figure 120 Notice that the Title font in A1 changed because you changed the theme.

Tip: If you are building documents in Word, PowerPoint and Excel that will go into the same report, use the same theme in all three products to make sure that the documents have a similar look and feel.

You Did What?

All My Numbers Are Corrupt!

Larisa received an urgent call from a co-worker. "You have to come over here. I just corrupted the worksheet – all of the numbers are missing!"

Larisa headed over to her co-worker's computer. Instantly, Larisa recognized the problem.

E		F
Tot $		Sales Rep
#######		Dan

Figure 121 Column E has become corrupt!

Here's what's happened: If you open the Undo dropdown, you can see that the last action was Format Cells. In fact, Larisa's co-worker had just formatted column E as currency. Normally, Excel would auto-fit the column, but someone had previously adjusted the width of column E, so Excel will not automatically expand the column.

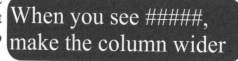

When you see #####, make the column wider

Excel has different rules for dealing with text and numbers that are wider than the current cell.

In the figure below, cell A1 contains long text and there is nothing to the right of the cell. In this case, the letters in cell A1 are allowed to spill over and cover up cell B1, C1, and so on. Note that those letters are not in B1, they are still considered part of cell A1. If you later would enter something in column B, such as in cell B2, then Excel will only show the first few letters from column A as shown in cell A2 below:

	A	B	C	D	E	F
1	This is some long text that spills outside of column A					
2	This is son	123				
3	This is some long text that spills outside of column A					
4	This is some long text that spill		123			

Figure 122 When a cell contains text, it is allowed to spill into the next blank column.

However, the rules are different when a cell contains a number or a date. If there is no room to display the entire number, Excel will fill the cell with #####. This is your indication that you need to consider making the column wider. Cell A3 below contains a number (which you can see in the Formula Bar). Since the adjacent cell is not empty, there would not be room to show all the digits, so Microsoft decided to not show you any of the digits. Note that even in row 4, where cell B4 is empty and Microsoft could have allowed the extra digits to spill over to cover part of cell B4, they still show the ####.

A3		▼		f_x	234567890123	
	A	B	C	D	E	
1	This is some long text that spills outside of column A					
2	This is son	123				
3	########	Some text in B3				
4	########					
5						

Figure 123 Numbers and dates are not allowed to spill over to an adjacent column.

To fix it, you could do any of these:

- Make column A wider.
- Make the font in column A smaller.
- Choose a narrower font such as Arial Narrow.
- Choose another number format such as Scientific Notation (too geeky of a choice for this book).
- Use the hidden Shrink to Fit option for the cells.

To make the column wider, move the mouse between the column letters at the top of the worksheet. When you hover on the line between the A and B column label, you will see a bar with arrows pointing left and right. Click and drag to the right until the #### signs disappear. Or, double-click the line to make the column wide enough for the longest value in the column.

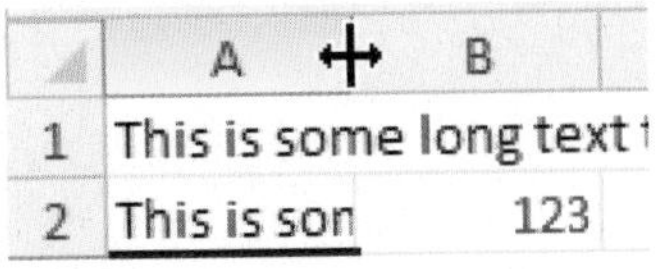

Figure 124 Click and drag right to make Column A wider.

Making the font smaller sounds easy, but it may not be that easy. On the Home tab, there is a font size dropdown. Next to that dropdown is a Large A icon and a Small A icon. To make the font size smaller, click the Small A icon several times. Eventually, you will get to the point where the font is only 8 point and then Excel will beep as you try to make the font smaller. In the figure below, 8 point is small enough to show the date in cell A5, but not small enough to show the numbers in A3:A4.

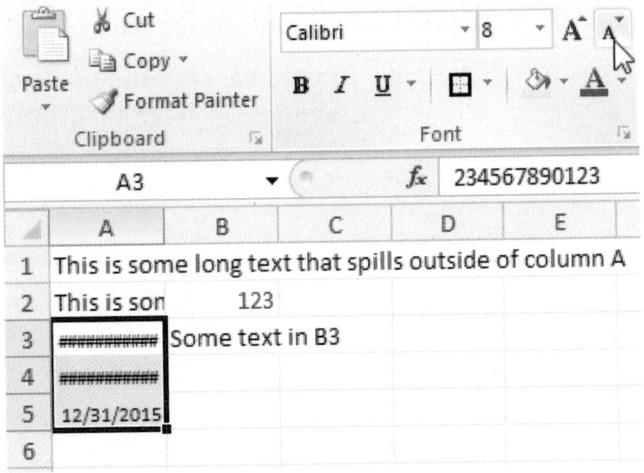

Figure 125 Use the Decrease Font Size icon until you get to 8 point.

One option is to switch to a narrower font, such as Arial Narrow. This font is designed to fit more information in a small space. As the next figure shows, you can show the numbers using 9 point Arial Narrow, when they would not have fit using 8 point Calibri.

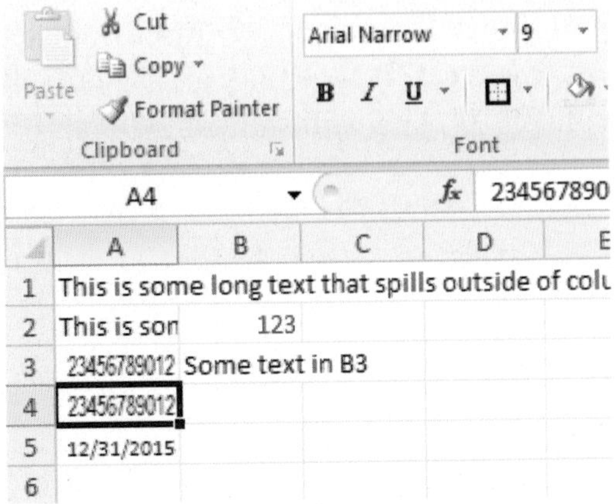

Figure 126 Arial Narrow will allow more characters to fit in a column.

Tip: Some fonts are known for being extremely wide. Even a number like 1234 will change to #####
if you try and use a font like Wide Latin.

There is, however, a way to use a font smaller than 8 point. Most people would choose a font size by
opening the font dropdown and choosing from the list. Instead, you
can type a new value in the top of the dropdown. Close the dropdown
and instead of clicking on the arrow, click next to the 8. You can now
backspace and type a 7. Press Enter to see the new font size in the
worksheet. As shown in the figure below, it is now small enough to
show the numbers instead of ####.

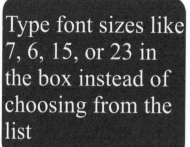

Type font sizes like 7, 6, 15, or 23 in the box instead of choosing from the list

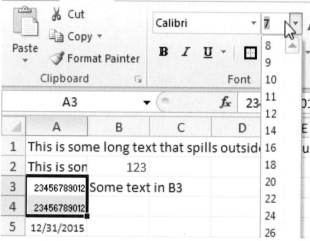

Figure 127 Click here and type a smaller number.

My favorite method for solving this problem is Shrink to Fit. To turn on shrink to fit, follow these
steps:

1. Select a range that contains numbers.
2. Type Ctrl+1 (the number one) to display the Format Cells dialog.
3. In the Format Cells dialog, click the Alignment tab across the top.
4. About half way, down on the left side is a checkbox for Shrink to Fit. Turn this on.
5. Click OK to close the dialog box.

Excel will automatically choose a smaller font size rather than using ####.

![Format Cells dialog showing Alignment tab with Shrink to fit checked]

Figure 128 Shrink to Fit is hidden in the Format Cells dialog box.

Note: Some managers hate to see the smaller font size. Try to explain that you would rather have a
smaller font size that shows the number rather than printing ##### where no one can see the number.

Can I Delete Data from a Spreadsheet without Changing the Formatting?

I need to delete some data from my spreadsheet, but I don't want to delete all of the formatting. Can I do that?

Yes – select the range of data and press the Delete key on the keyboard. Pressing Delete will clear the words and text in the cells, but keep the fill color, font color, font size, borders and cell comments.

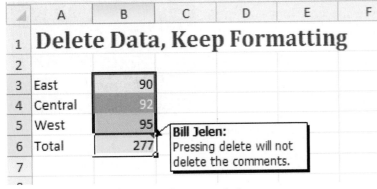

Figure 129 Select the formatted range with data.

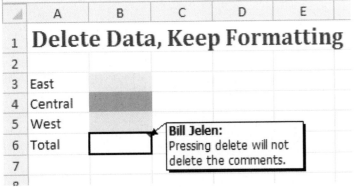

Figure 130 Press the Delete key on the keyboard to clear the contents and keep formatting.

Tip: Deleting the cell contents will not delete any cell comments. If you regularly use comments (from Excel's Reviewing tab), you can clear the comments using a command on the Ribbon. Look at the right-most group on the Home tab. There is a dropdown next to the eraser icon. Open this dropdown and choose Clear Comments to clear comments from a cell.

How Do I Set up Cells to Show Dollars and Cents?

I want a column to always show two decimal places and to show a dollar sign.

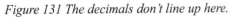

	A	B
1	Product	Price
2	A	13.5
3	B	5.95
4	C	7.5
5	D	12.95
6	E	15.5
7	F	12
8	G	10.5
9	H	6.95

Figure 131 The decimals don't line up here.

Excel offers two competing number formats with a dollar sign. One format is known as Accounting and one is known as Currency. Personally, I prefer Currency over Accounting.

There is a big $ icon in the Number group of the Home tab. Clicking this icon applies the Accounting format.

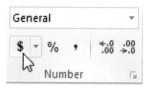

Figure 132 This icon chooses the Accounting format.

In Accounting Format, the dollar signs are along the left edge of the column. The numbers are right-aligned, but there is an annoying gap at the right edge of the column.

◢	A	B
1	Product	Price
2	A	$ 13.50
3	B	$ 5.95
4	C	$ 7.50
5	D	$ 12.95

Figure 133 There is a gap at each edge of the column.

To skip the Accounting format and choose Currency, open the large dropdown above the $ icon. Choose Currency from this dropdown.

Figure 134 Open the dropdown to choose Currency instead of Accounting.

With Currency format, there is no gap to the right of the number. The currency symbols are flush against the number.

◢	A	B
1	Product	Price
2	A	$13.50
3	B	$5.95
4	C	$7.50
5	D	$12.95
6	E	$15.50
7	F	$12.00

Figure 135 This is Currency format.

The other difference between Accounting and Currency is how they handle negative numbers. Currency uses a minus sign to indicate negative numbers. Accounting uses parentheses instead.

◢	A	B	C
1	Product	Currency	Accounting
2	A	$13.50	$ 13.50
3	B	-$3.00	$ (3.00)
4	C	$7.50	$ 7.50
5	D	$12.95	$ 12.95

Figure 136 Negative numbers are shown in parentheses in Accounting format.

I Type 0345 in a Cell and Excel Changes It to 345

We have part numbers that start with leading zeroes. I need the leading zeroes to appear. Excel keeps removing them.

If you will never need to do math with the part numbers, the easy solution is to type an apostrophe then type 0345 ('0345). Excel will not show the apostrophe, but it will keep the leading zero.

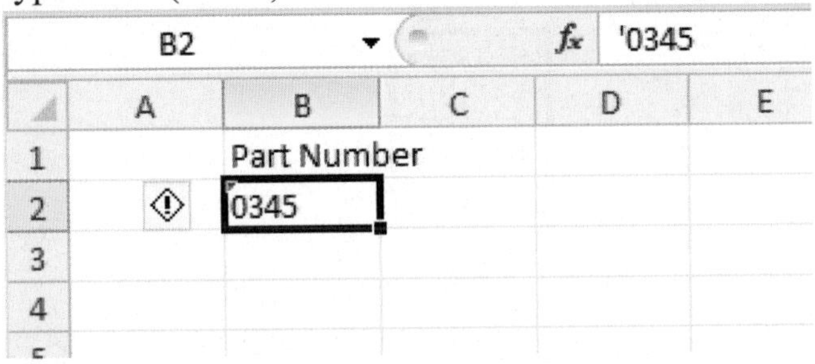

Figure 137 Use an apostrophe to declare a cell as text.

If you have to enter 100 part numbers, it would be faster to format the range as text before you begin. Select the range where you will be entering the part numbers. Open the dropdown in the Number group of the Home tab. Near the bottom, choose Text. Now, any number that you type in that range will keep the leading zeroes.

Caution: It is impossible to enter a formula in a cell that has been formatted as text. Instead of seeing the answer to the formula, Excel will display the formula.

What if you already have data in Excel that needs leading zeroes?

You can select the range and set up a custom number format.

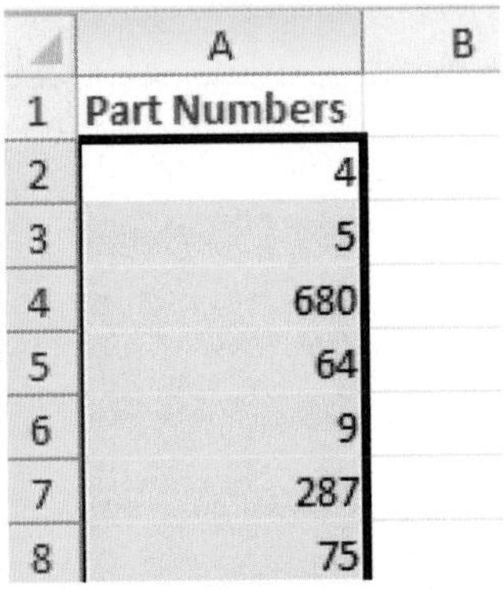

Figure 138 These part numbers should be four digits, with leading zeroes.

Follow these steps:
1. Select the range of part numbers.
2. Press Ctrl+1 (the number one) to display the Format Cells dialog.
3. Across the top of the dialog, choose the Number tab.
4. In the Category list, choose Custom.
5. In the Type box, enter four zeroes. The number of zeroes should correspond to the desired length of the part number.
6. Click OK.

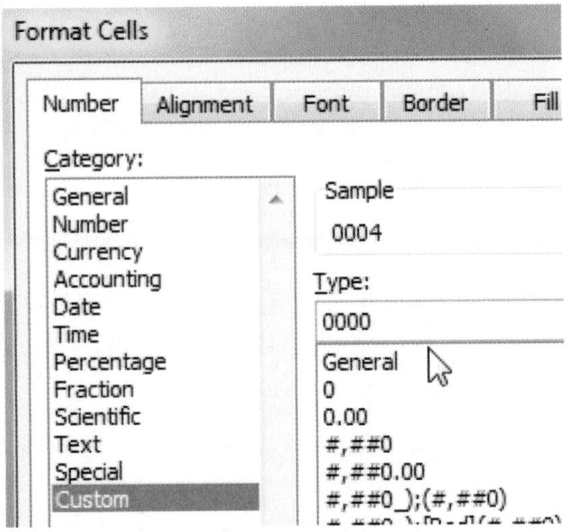

Figure 139 Set up a custom number format of 0000.

Result: Excel will display leading zeroes when the part number contains less than four digits. If a part number has more than four digits, Excel will display all of the digits.

	A	E
1	Part Numbers	
2	0004	
3	0005	
4	0680	
5	0064	

Figure 140 Although cell A4 contains 680, Excel displays 0680.

One advantage of the custom number format: you can still do math operations with these cells since they are stored as numbers.

When I Enter 36.80, Excel Leaves off the Zero

How do I make Excel stop rounding my decimals?

Usually, Excel will show all of the numbers before the decimal point and any significant numbers after the decimal. For a value like 1.23, all three of the digits are considered significant, so you will see 1.23 instead of 1 or 1.2300. Following the same logic, $36.80 is considered to have only one significant digit after the decimal. Excel wants to show you $36.8 instead of $36.80 or $36.8000.

The trick is to change from General format to either Number or Currency format. In these formats, you can explicitly ask for Excel to always show two places after the decimal (or any number of digits) after the decimal).

One of the fast ways to convert to Number format is to use the Increase Decimal or Decrease Decimal icons. How these work might seem confusing. In the figure below, the numbers have varying numbers of decimal places. Although 44 cells are selected, the 246.7729 in A1 is the active cell. You can tell this because the cell has a lighter highlight. You could also look in the Name Box to the left of the Formula Bar to see that it says A1. Note that all of these cells are formatted in the General style.

The Decrease Decimal icon is the one showing Excel going from one decimal place to two decimal places. Many people get Decrease and Increase Decimal icons confused. If you can't remember, hover until you see the tooltip.

	A1			f_x	246.7729	
	A	B	C	D	E
1	246.7729	96063.95	8.230226	42269.25	
2	5940.592	2225.206	7.871452	399.6977	
3	88.41277	55.08037	199747.4	4.39155	
4	906.3558	903.2529	6.447169	20210.21	
5	36326.18	559.2171	72060.15	0.218163	
6	5818.151	9973.74	7065.187	594.0093	
7	6101.1	0.655556	7.074422	39901.41	
8	6083.697	71243.7	405050.1	8048.032	
9	165.7689	361.915	54594.01	54503.07	
10	103.9143	29765.64	700.5455	1428.955	
11	7.32399	96880.37	51.95235	5702.388	

Figure 141 The active cell is displaying four decimal places.

General				
$ ▾ % ,	.0 .00	Conditional Formatting ▾	Format as Table ▾	Cell Styles ▾
Number			Styles	

Decrease Decimal

Show less precise values by showing fewer decimal places.

J	K

Figure 142 Using either of the Decimal icons will convert from General to Number.

When you click the Decrease Decimal button, Excel sees that the active cell is showing four decimal places. It will change all of the cells in the selection to have a Number format with three decimal places.

In the figure below, note that clicking Decrease Decimal forced column C to be wider. The value in C3 is now showing extra decimal places that were not there originally.

	A	B	C	D
1	246.773	96063.950	8.230	42269.250
2	5940.592	2225.206	7.871	399.698
3	88.413	55.080	199747.400	4.392
4	906.356	903.253	6.447	20210.210
5	36326.180	559.217	72060.150	0.218
6	5818.151	9973.740	7065.187	594.009
7	6101.100	0.656	7.074	39901.410
8	6083.697	71243.700	405050.100	8048.032
9	165.769	361.915	54594.010	54503.070
10	103.914	29765.640	700.546	1428.955
11	7.324	96880.370	51.952	5702.388

Figure 143 All cells are showing three decimal places.

Click the Decrease Decimal icon one more time and all of the cells in the range will now show two decimal places. Note that Excel did not make the columns narrower here. Excel will only widen columns to fit the extra decimals. Also note that the 2225.206 stored in B2 is rounded for display purposes only to 2225.21. Excel still stores 2225.206 in the cell and would use 2225.206 in any formulas that point to this cell.

> You are only changing the way Excel displays the decimals in the cell; they are still storing the complete number and using that number in any calculations

B2			fx	2225.206	
	A	B	C	D	
1	1246.77	96063.95	8.23	42269.25	
2	5940.59	2225.21	7.87	399.70	
3	88.41	55.08	199747.40	4.39	
4	906.36	903.25	6.45	20210.21	
5	36326.18	559.22	72060.15	0.22	
6	5818.15	9973.74	7065.19	594.01	
7	6101.10	0.66	7.07	39901.41	
8	6083.70	71243.70	405050.10	8048.03	
9	165.77	361.92	54594.01	54503.07	
10	103.91	29765.64	700.55	1428.96	
11	7.32	96880.37	51.95	5702.39	

Figure 144 Excel rounds in order to display the number, but the real number is still stored in the cell.

In this format, there are no commas used as the thousands separator and no currency symbols. You might notice the $ icon and the , icon in the same area as the Increase Decimal icons. I personally don't like either of those icons because they change the format to Accounting format instead of Number or Currency format. The next figure shows the effect of the $ icon if it had been applied to the original General format. All of the numbers are set to show two decimal places. The currency symbol is always on the left edge of the cell. Also, the final digit is not quite at the right edge of the cell, since this format shows negative numbers in parentheses.

	A	B	C	D
1	$ 1,246.77	$96,063.95	$ 8.23	$42,269.25
2	$ 5,940.59	$ 2,225.21	$ 7.87	$ 399.70
3	$ 88.41	$ 55.08	$199,747.40	$ 4.39
4	$ 906.36	$ 903.25	$ 6.45	$20,210.21
5	$36,326.18	$ 559.22	$ 72,060.15	$ 0.22
6	$ 5,818.15	$ 9,973.74	$ 7,065.19	$ 594.01
7	$ 6,101.10	$ 0.66	$ 7.07	$39,901.41
8	$ 6,083.70	$71,243.70	$405,050.10	$ 8,048.03

Figure 145 The results of the Currency icon look bad.

Using the , icon does the same thing, except there is no currency symbol.

All of these icons are shortcut methods for choosing settings in the Format Cells dialog box. If you are trying to get to a currency format, it is easier to go straight to the Format Cells dialog.
1. Select a range of numbers.
2. Press Ctrl+1 (the number one) to display the Format Cells dialog.
3. Select the Number tab across the top.
4. Select Currency from the side.
5. Choose the number of decimals, the currency symbol, and how to display negative numbers.

Note: The Currency format always displays a thousands separator.

To apply a thousands separator without a dollar sign:
1. Select a range of numbers.
2. Press Ctrl+1 (the number one) to display the Format Cells dialog.
3. Select the Number tab across the top.
4. Select Number from the side.
5. Choose the number of decimals, the Use 1000 Separator checkbox, and how to display negative numbers.

The next figure compares numeric formats. Column A was formatted with the $ icon. Column B was formatted with the , icon. Column C was formatted with the Format Cells dialog, Number format, with 1000 Separator. Column D was formatted with the Format Cells dialog, Currency format. Since I prefer not to have the extra space to the right of my numbers, and since I prefer the currency symbol to be next to the number instead of at the left edge of the cell, it is worth it to me to visit the Format Cells dialog to achieve the results in C and D.

	A	B	C	D
1			Format Cells Dialog	
2	$ Icon	, Icon	Currency	Number
3	$ 1,246.77	1,246.77	$1,246.77	1,246.77
4	$ 5,940.59	5,940.59	$5,940.59	5,940.59
5	$ 88.41	88.41	$88.41	88.41
6	$ 906.36	906.36	$906.36	906.36
7	$36,326.18	36,326.18	$36,326.18	36,326.18
8	$ 5,818.15	5,818.15	$5,818.15	5,818.15
9	$ 6,101.10	6,101.10	$6,101.10	6,101.10
10	$ 6,083.70	6,083.70	$6,083.70	6,083.70

Figure 146 Columns C and D were created using the Format Cells dialog box instead of the icons on the Home tab.

How Can I Show My Numbers as Thousands or Millions?

I am preparing a report for the executives and I have been asked to show all the revenue and expense numbers in thousands so that they are easier to read – they don't care about $1 here and $10 there.

We're going to use custom number formatting to accomplish this. Start by selecting the numbers that you want to show as thousands. Press Ctrl+1 (the number one) to display the Format Cells dialog. Select Custom in the Category list. In the Type Text entry box enter:

```
#,##0,
```

Click OK to apply the format you just created to the selected cells.

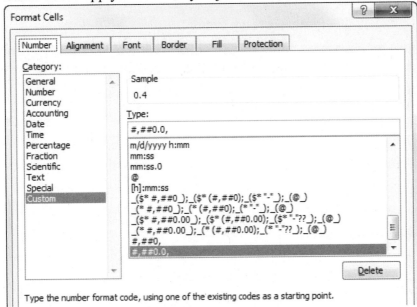

Figure 147 The Format Cells dialog.

If you want to display millions instead of thousands, use the custom number format:

```
#,##0,,
```

Note: how does the formatting work? Notice that there are commas at the end of the format text. Each comma at the end instructs Excel to drop three least significant digits – one comma removes three digits, two commas removes six digits.

Original Value	Custom Format	Displayed Value
123,456,789	#,##0	123,456,789
123,456,789	#,##0,	123,457
123,456,789	#,##0,,	123

Note: In the second example above, Excel is smart enough to round the last displayed digit up to 7 instead of leaving it at 6.

Caution: Remember to inform your audience that the amounts are in thousands or millions! A well-placed notation such as "All monetary amounts are in thousands" in the header area of your report serves this purpose well.

But maybe just thousands is not quite enough information. Perhaps you want to keep the hundredths position to present a bit more granularity for values that are not as large as the other values in your presentation. This is accomplished by adding a decimal and a zero before the first trailing comma. For example, the value 1,234, when formatted with the custom format string:

```
#,##0.0
```

is displayed as 1.2

Caution: Do not mix your formatting in the same report! If you choose to format your values as thousands then format all values as thousands. Of course there will be exceptions such as percentages and those values should be easily identified as such. Be consistent or your audience will get confused – and no one likes a confused audience, especially if it's your boss!

Another way to display thousands or millions is to append a "K" or an "M" to the number. This allows different formats to be displayed on the same report while minimizing confusion. To display a K at the end of a number use this format:

```
#,##0," K"
```

Or, to display an M for millions:

```
#,##0," M"
```

#,##0,K is HOT!

How Can I Remove the Lines from Excel?

The gridlines are giving me a headache! How can I get rid of them?

There are many options for getting rid of gridlines!

Method 1: Go to the View tab. In the Show group, uncheck Gridlines to remove all gridlines from the current worksheet. This is a worksheet-level setting. If you remove gridlines from Sheet1, you will still have to remove them from Sheet2.

Method 2: The exact same setting is found on the Page Layout tab, in the Sheet Options group. Uncheck View under Gridlines.

Figure 148 Turn off the gridlines for this worksheet.

If you are tired of the gridline color, you can change the color for one worksheet. Go to File, Options. Choose the Advanced category from the left navigation of the Excel Options dialog. Scroll down about 65% of the way until you see a category called Display Options For This Worksheet. There is a dropdown where you can change the gridline color.

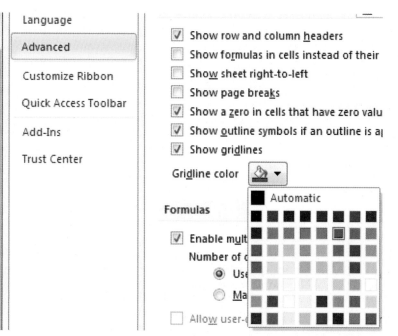

Figure 149 Be careful, some of the gridline color choices are startling.

To remove gridlines from one section of the worksheet, fill that range with either a white fill from the Paint Bucket or white borders from the Format Cells dialog. Using a white fill will remove the gridlines from the range.

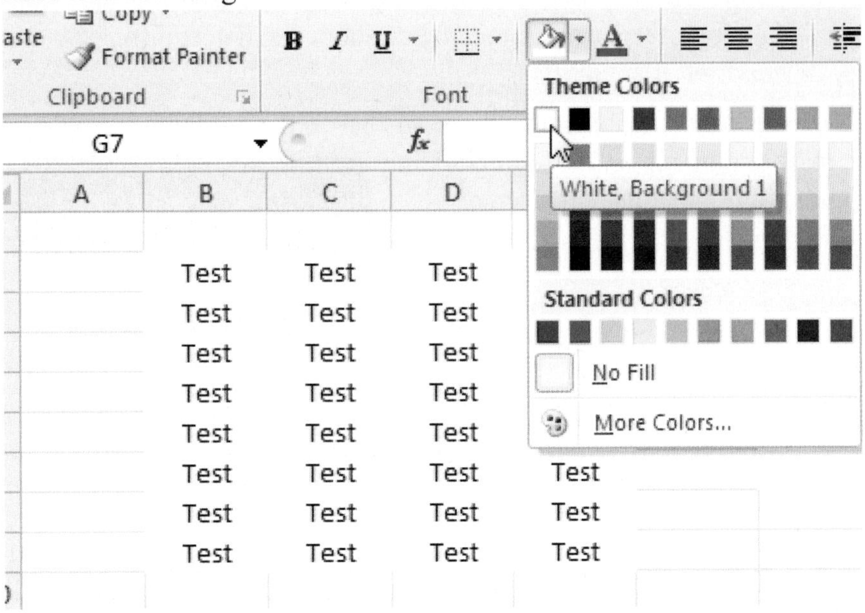

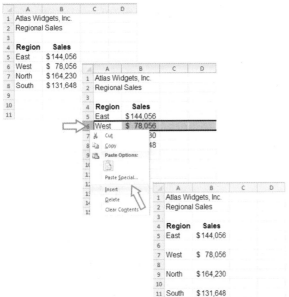

Figure 150 To hide gridlines in one range, use a white fill from the Paint Bucket dropdown.

How can I Insert Rows or Columns within My Existing Data?

I really need a little space between my rows and columns. How can I do that?

Changing the look of your data by inserting rows or columns.

When you want to insert rows or columns inside your existing data, there are a few easy ways to do that. Creating some visual space between rows or columns of data is a common thing to do. Also, you may discover that after developing your worksheet a new column must be inserted between existing columns.

As done in the following figure, you want to put an empty row between the regions of East, West, North, and South. You can right-click directly in the "6" row header for row 6, and from the pop-up menu click Insert. A new row will be inserted there. Simply repeat the process for the other regions' rows to arrive at the final result.

Figure 151 The sequence for inserting a row between existing rows of data.

The same approach will work for inserting a column between existing columns of data. You can right-click onto the column B header and select Insert from the pop-up menu as was done in the figure below:

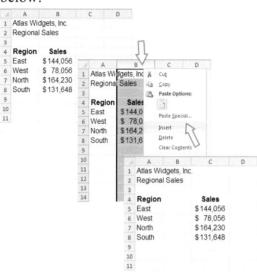

Figure 152 The sequence for inserting a column between existing columns of data.

Can I Make Part of the Text in a Cell Red?

When I use the Font color dropdown, it changes the color of all the text in the cell to red. Can I format part of the cell?

Select the cell. In the Formula Bar, select the characters that will have the special formatting. Clicking in the Formula Bar forces you into Edit mode and you temporarily won't see all of the characters in the grid itself.

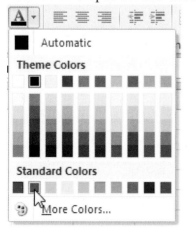

Figure 153 Select characters in the Formula Bar.

Even though you are editing the cell, several formatting tools are available. You can open the Font color dropdown and choose a color.

You can format each word in a cell with a different color by repeating the steps. Common formatting shortcuts like Ctrl+B for bold, Ctrl+I for italic, and Ctrl+U for underline also work while you have only certain characters selected.

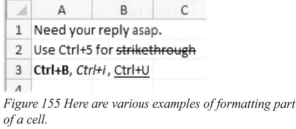

	A	B	C
1	Need your reply asap.		
2	Use Ctrl+5 for ~~strikethrough~~		
3	**Ctrl+B**, *Ctrl+i*, <u>Ctrl+U</u>		

Figure 155 Here are various examples of formatting part of a cell.

Figure 154 Choose a color for those characters.

Can I Double Space Lines in Excel?

It is easy to double-space in Word. How do I do it in Excel?

Double-spacing in Excel, allows you to add height to each row. This will add extra space between each row.

First, select your data. If you have data in A1:E99, you can simply select A1:A99.

On the Home tab, open the Format dropdown and choose Row Height.

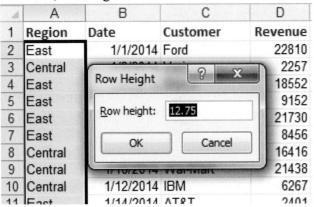

Figure 156 Open the Row Height dropdown.

Provided all of the rows are the same height, Excel will show you the current height of the rows. In this case, the height is 12.75.

	A	B	C	D
1	Region	Date	Customer	Revenue
2	East	1/1/2014	Ford	22810
3	Central			2257
4	East			18552
5	East			9152
6	East			21730
7	East			8456
8	Central			16416
9	Central			21438
10	Central	1/12/2014	IBM	6267
11	East	1/14/2014	AT&T	2401

Row Height

Row height: 12.75

OK   Cancel

Figure 157 Do a little mental math to determine 12.75 x 2 is 25.5.

Type a new row height, such as 25.5 in the Row Height dialog box. Click OK. As shown below, it will appear that the data is double-spaced.

	A	B	C	D	E
1	Region	Date	Customer	Revenue	Profit
2	East	1/1/2014	Ford	22810	12590
3	Central	1/2/2014	Verizon	2257	1273
4	East	1/4/2014	Merck	18552	10680
5	East	1/4/2014	Texaco	9152	5064
6	East	1/7/2014	State Farm	21730	11890
7	East	1/7/2014	General Motors	8456	5068

Figure 158 There is extra space between the text in each row.

Are There Any Other Formatting Tips?

Once you get your numbers looking good, you might need to create an eye-catching cover page. Although Excel's forte is numbers and calculation, it includes several graphic tools.

The figure below shows WordArt, SmartArt, and a picture. All three are found on the Insert tab.

Figure 159 Jazz up a worksheet using these graphic tools.

To use WordArt, select Insert, WordArt, and choose a basic style. Type your words in place of Your Text Here. As long as the WordArt is selected, you will have access to a Drawing Tools Format tab in the Ribbon.

To achieve the bendy type look of classic WordArt, open the Text Effects dropdown in the WordArt Styles group. Open the Transform menu to see 30 different shapes for your WordArt.

SmartArt business diagrams were introduced in Excel 2007 to replace the old Excel 2003 diagrams tool. You can create process charts, cycle charts, pyramid charts, Venn diagrams, org charts and more. With SmartArt, you type Level 1 and Level 2 bullet points in a Text Pane and Excel handles updating the graphic.

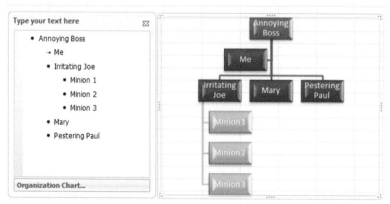

Figure 160 Use tab and shift-tab to change levels in the text pane.

As long as the SmartArt is selected, you have two Ribbon tabs for SmartArt Tools. Use the Change Colors dropdown on the Design tab to add color to the diagram. Use the SmartArt Styles to add a bit of 3-D formatting to the diagram.

You've always been able to use Insert, Picture to add a picture the spreadsheet. With today's digital cameras, almost any picture will come in way too large. Zoom out and resize the picture to get it to fit to a single page instead of taking up three pages.

When the picture is selected, you have access to the Picture Tools Format tab in the Ribbon. Tools such as Artistic Effects, Color, Correction, Remove Background and a gallery of picture styles allow you to achieve various effects quickly in Excel.

In the figure below, the top left image is the result of Color, Recolor. The top right image has one of the Glass effect from the Artistic Effects gallery. The bottom left image uses a built-in style from the Picture Styles gallery. The bottom right image used Background Removal to keep only two trees.

Figure 161 Apply various effects to photos in Excel for an eye-catching cover page.

CHAPTER 3 - FORMULAS I

When Is It OK to Use a Calculator with Excel?

Is there a time when I may need to use a calculator because Excel cannot calculate certain things?

NEVER! If you ever find yourself reaching for a calculator while using Excel, you need to know the following:

Excel can do every calculation that your calculator can do. It can do it faster. The two guys who invented spreadsheets were so tired of using their calculator to do similar calculations over and over, they invented the spreadsheet as a Visible Calculator (which they marked as VisiCalc) and made millions. The whole reason for the invention of the spreadsheet is to keep you from having to reach for your calculator.

You Did What?

My Coworker Used an Adding Machine to Add a Column of 100 Numbers!

I could not believe it. Every time that he had to add a column, he plugged every number into a 10-key, then compared the tape to the spreadsheet, then keyed the answer into the total cell.

This is bad, all the way around. It is a waste of time. All of the other people in your office are going to expect that total cell to be a formula, which would automatically change when they change a number.

Here is how you can tell that someone used a calculator. Select the total cell in Excel. You should see the total in the cell, but you should see a formula in the Formula Bar. If you see the total repeated in the Formula Bar, then you know that this is not a live formula.

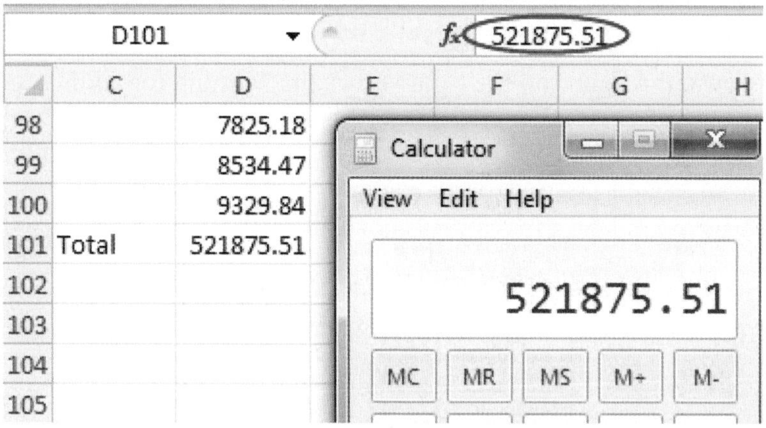

Figure 162 The total is correct, but using a calculator or adding machine is not the right way to find the total.

Sometimes this happens because they don't know Excel can do calculations or don't know how. Sometimes this happens because AutoSum didn't work for them in the past. Perhaps they have numbers stored as text or typed their numbers with a lower case "L" instead of a 1, or the letter "O" instead of a zero. If you follow some basic guidelines, your AutoSum will reliably work.

To replace the total in the figure above, select cell D101. Press Alt+= and then Enter. The total will be the same, but the formula bar will show a formula of =SUM(D1:D101).

How Do I Total All the Rows and Columns in My Table of Numbers?

You have a table of numbers that need to be added up vertically and horizontally. Take a look at how quickly and easily this can be done.

Here are a couple of methods and shortcuts to painlessly total the numbers in rows and columns for a table of data.

Suppose you have an expense budget as shown by example in this first set of figures. Notice that you need to total the numbers going across the rows, and the numbers going down the columns.

	A	B	C	D	E	F	G
1	Quarterly Expenses for Atlas Widgets, Inc.						
2							
3	Item	Qtr 1	Qtr 2	Qtr 3	Qtr 4	Total	
4	Payroll	33,692	36,504	37,788	39,340		
5	Maintenance	2,588	3,740	792	2,272		
6	Landscaping	2,328	2,052	668	3,768		
7	Postage	3,848	3,468	2,476	3,740		
8	Telephone	3,160	2,668	704	1,368		
9	Computers	1,112	3,756	2,712	3,864		
10	Office rent	1,576	536	1,032	3,500		
11	Utilities	3,104	1,084	1,484	3,304		
12	Taxes	2,116	2,632	3,244	1,680		
13	Total						
14							

	A	B	C	D	E	F	G
1	Quarterly Expenses for Atlas Widgets, Inc.						
2							
3	Item	Qtr 1	Qtr 2	Qtr 3	Qtr 4	Total	
4	Payroll	33,692	36,504	37,788	39,340	147,324	
5	Maintenance	2,588	3,740	792	2,272	9,392	
6	Landscaping	2,328	2,052	668	3,768	8,816	
7	Postage	3,848	3,468	2,476	3,740	13,532	
8	Telephone	3,160	2,668	704	1,368	7,900	
9	Computers	1,112	3,756	2,712	3,864	11,444	
10	Office rent	1,576	536	1,032	3,500	6,644	
11	Utilities	3,104	1,084	1,484	3,304	8,976	
12	Taxes	2,116	2,632	3,244	1,680	9,672	
13	Total	53,524	56,440	50,900	62,836	223,700	
14							

Figure 163 Before and after: a table of numbers to be totaled, and all the numbers totaled in rows and columns.

The next set of figures shows one way to add up the numbers using the popular SUM function. In the figure, numbers in the rows are totaled with this formula, entered into cell F4 and copied down to cell F12

`=SUM(B4:E4)`

Tip: You can enter this (or any) formula quickly to an entire range all at once. For example, select range F4:F12 as seen in the figure. Type in the formula as usual, then (and here's the trick), press Ctrl+Enter, not just Enter. The formula will be entered into all the cells you had selected.

Similar to how you entered the totals for rows, the figure on the right shows the formula for adding up numbers in the columns, from cell B13 to cell F13.

`=SUM(B4:B12)`

SUM	▼	X ✓ fx	=SUM(B4:E4)

	A	B	C	D	E	F	G
1	Quarterly Expenses for Atlas Widgets, Inc.						
2							
3	Item	Qtr 1	Qtr 2	Qtr 3	Qtr 4	Total	
4	Payroll	33,692	36,504	37,788	39,340	=SUM(B4:E4)	
5	Maintenance	2,588	3,740	792	2,272		
6	Landscaping	2,328	2,052	668	3,768		
7	Postage	3,848	3,468	2,476	3,740		
8	Telephone	3,160	2,668	704	1,368		
9	Computers	1,112	3,756	2,712	3,864		
10	Office rent	1,576	536	1,032	3,500		
11	Utilities	3,104	1,084	1,484	3,304		
12	Taxes	2,116	2,632	3,244	1,680		
13	Total						
14							

SUM	▼	X ✓ fx	=SUM(B4:B12)

	A	B	C	D	E	F	G
1	Quarterly Expenses for Atlas Widgets, Inc.						
2							
3	Item	Qtr 1	Qtr 2	Qtr 3	Qtr 4	Total	
4	Payroll	33,692	36,504	37,788	39,340		
5	Maintenance	2,588	3,740	792	2,272		
6	Landscaping	2,328	2,052	668	3,768		
7	Postage	3,848	3,468	2,476	3,740		
8	Telephone	3,160	2,668	704	1,368		
9	Computers	1,112	3,756	2,712	3,864		
10	Office rent	1,576	536	1,032	3,500		
11	Utilities	3,104	1,084	1,484	3,304		
12	Taxes	2,116	2,632	3,244	1,680		
13	Total	=SUM(B4:B12)					
14							

Figure 164 Enter a SUM formula to total down the rows, and another SUM formula to total across the columns.

The SUM functions in the previous figure did the job, but there are two faster and easier methods that will instantly add up all the numbers in the rows and columns at the same time.

As the next figure shows, select the range of numbers, but extend your selection to include the empty Total column at the right and the empty Total row at the bottom. To fill the Total cells, you can either double-click the AutoSum icon (located on the Formulas tab of the Ribbon), or from your keyboard you can simultaneously press the Alt and = keys.

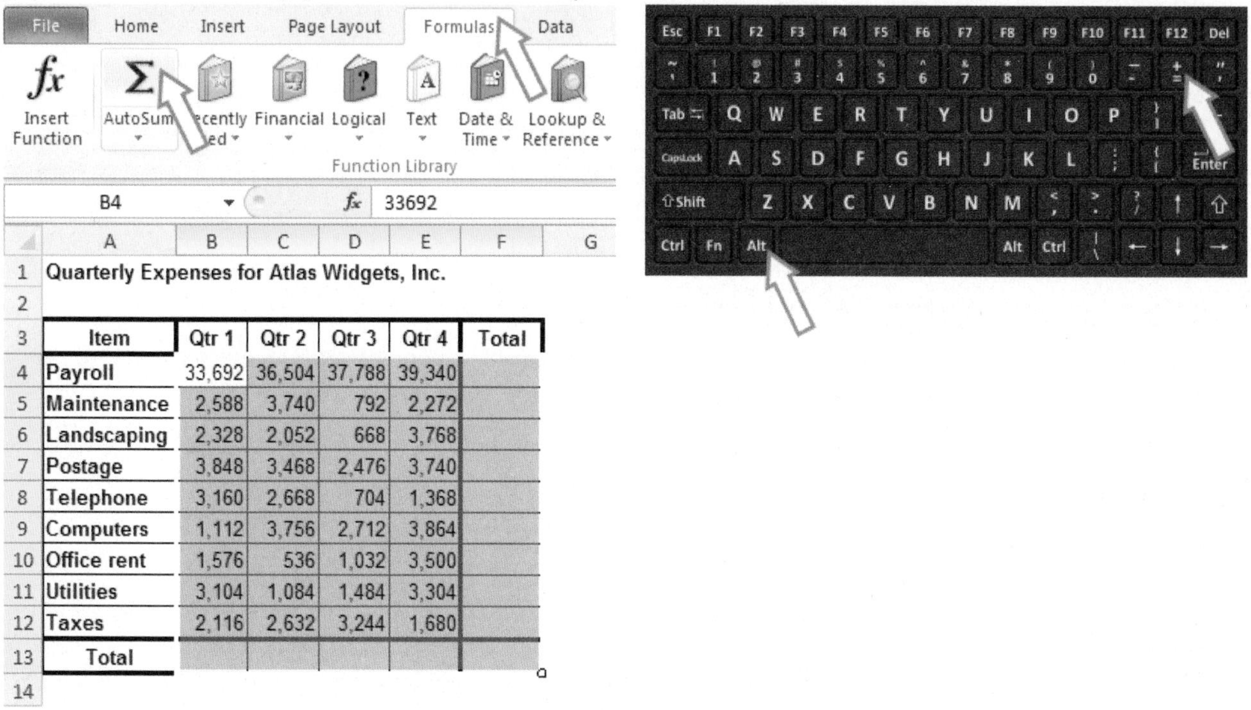

Item	Qtr 1	Qtr 2	Qtr 3	Qtr 4	Total
Payroll	33,692	36,504	37,788	39,340	
Maintenance	2,588	3,740	792	2,272	
Landscaping	2,328	2,052	668	3,768	
Postage	3,848	3,468	2,476	3,740	
Telephone	3,160	2,668	704	1,368	
Computers	1,112	3,756	2,712	3,864	
Office rent	1,576	536	1,032	3,500	
Utilities	3,104	1,084	1,484	3,304	
Taxes	2,116	2,632	3,244	1,680	
Total					

Figure 165 Two shortcuts for quickly summing rows and columns.

I Added up a Column of Numbers with a Formula of =A2+A3+A4+A5+A6+A7+A8+A9+A10.

A nasty co-worker of mine saw my formula, cackled, and walked away. What's her problem?

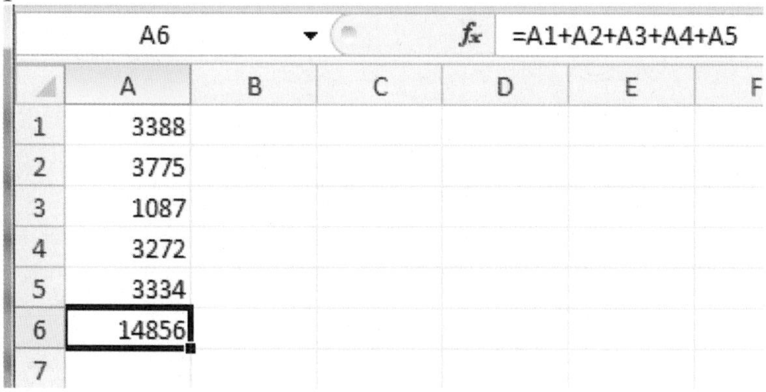

	A
1	3388
2	3775
3	1087
4	3272
5	3334
6	14856

Figure 166 What's wrong with this formula??

Hey – don't feel bad. I remember when I used to do the same thing. Your method *does* produce the correct answer, but imagine if you had 20 numbers or 100 numbers. It would take a much longer time to enter the formula.

◢	A	B	C	D	E	F	G	H	I	J	K	L	M	N
1	=A2+B2+C2+D2+E2+F2+G2+H2+I2+J2+A3+B3+C3+D3+E3+F3+G3+H3+I3+J3+A4+B4+
2	C4+D4+E4+F4+G4+H4+I4+J4+A5+B5+C5+D5+E5+F5+G5+H5+I5+J5+A6+B6+C6+D6+
3	E6+F6+G6+H6+I6+J6+A7+B7+C7+D7+E7+F7+G7+H7+I7+J7+A8+B8+C8+D8+E8+F8+
4	G8+H8+I8+J8+A9+B9+C9+D9+E9+F9+G9+H9+I9+J9+A10+B10+C10+D10+E10+F10+
5	G10+H10+I10+J10+A11+B11+C11+D11+E11+F11+G11+H11+I11+J11	
6	30	30	59	46	14	25	20	27	76	87
7	68	55	42	63	96	39	90	79	91	34
8	55	92	14	81	36	89	11	25	90	88
9	35	22	32	77	77	92	42	65	88	74
10	55	99	46	21	22	18	87	12	51	78
11	80	72	16	64	25	62	93	42	42	96
12	

Figure 167 That method becomes unwieldy when you have more than a few numbers.

Also, there is a limit to the number of characters in a formula. Even if you had the patience to enter =A2+A3+…+A30000, the formula would be too long. There is an easier way.

The solution is to use the =SUM() function. Inside of the function, you can put up to 255 numbers, cells, or ranges of cells. So, you could use:

```
=SUM(1,2,3,4,5)
```

to produce a result of 15. You can also use:

```
=SUM(A2:A10)
```

to add up all of the cells from A2 to A10. This formula is easy to expand without getting too much longer. Say that you need to add from A2 to A20. The formula is:

```
=SUM(A2:A20)
```

Say that you need to add the numbers from A2:A30000. The formula is:

```
=SUM(A2:A30000)
```

This is dramatically shorter than typing the 198,892 characters in =A2+A3+A4+A5+…+A30000.

A1	▼	●	*fx*	=SUM(A2:J11)

◢	A	B	C	D	E	F	G	H	I	J	K	L
1	5696											
2	31	54	79	70	15	88	58	92	76	60
3	98	40	33	44	81	13	51	97	13	81
4	44	68	77	97	11	85	74	86	35	32
5	40	36	72	79	38	45	83	23	93	67
6	30	30	59	46	14	25	20	27	76	87
7	68	55	42	63	96	39	90	79	91	34
8	55	92	14	81	36	89	11	25	90	88
9	35	22	32	77	77	92	42	65	88	74
10	55	99	46	21	22	18	87	12	51	78
11	80	72	16	64	25	62	93	42	42	96
12	

Figure 168 Use the SUM function instead of adding each cell.

How Can I Average a Set of Numbers?

I need to figure out the average starting salary. You've shown me that Excel can sum. Can it find the mean?

Sure – Excel can average. In fact, the process is very similar to using the AutoSum button.

If you look closely at the AutoSum, you will see a dropdown arrow next to Auto-Sum. Open the dropdown and there are choices for SUM, AVERAGE, COUNT, MAX, and MIN.

To average a column of numbers, select the blank cell below the numbers. Open the AutoSum dropdown and choose Average. Excel will propose a formula. Verify the range is correct and press Enter.

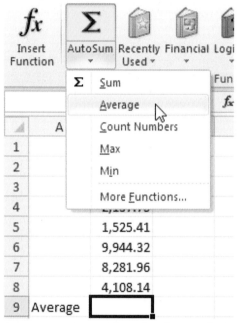

Figure 169 The AutoSum dropdown includes choices for four other functions.

	A	B	C	D	E
		=AVERAGE(B2:B8)			
1		Amounts			
2		8,590.87			
3		7,933.76			
4		2,137.73			
5		1,525.41			
6		9,944.32			
7		8,281.96			
8		4,108.14			
9	Average	6,074.60			
10					

Figure 170 The AutoSum's Average option will write this formula.

By the way, the smaller AutoSum icon on the Home tab offers the same dropdown.

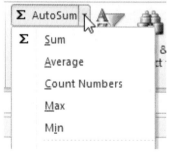

Figure 171 You can use the AutoSum dropdown on the Home tab as well.

Can I Change the Default Setting for My AutoSum?

I would like it to Auto-Average instead of AutoSum. Can I make the AutoSum icon automatically do Average instead of summing?

You cannot change the default behavior of the AutoSum button, but Excel offers four alternative icons that you can add to your Quick Access Toolbar. In a fit of lunacy, however, Microsoft made the four icons all look identical in the Quick Access Toolbar – a green crystal ball. Apparently, you have to be a fortune teller to tell which is which.

Follow these steps:

1. Right-click the Quick Access Toolbar and choose Customize Quick Access Toolbar.

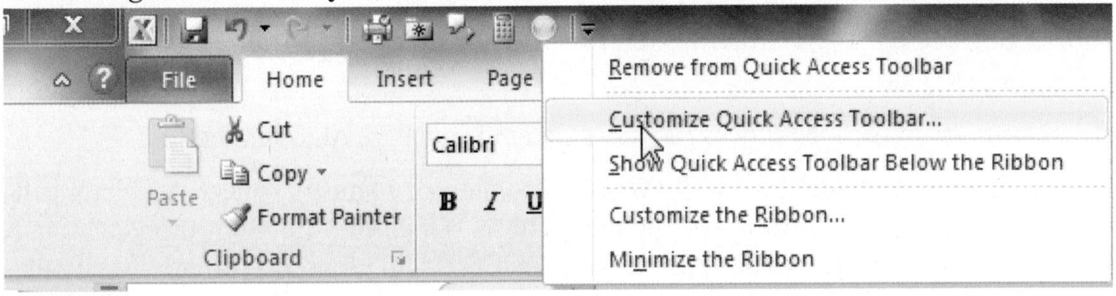

Figure 172 Customize the QAT.

2. Open the left dropdown and choose All Commands.

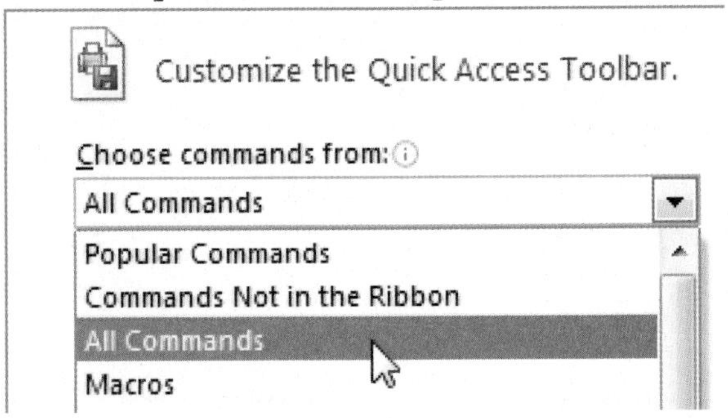

Figure 173 These icons aren't popular. No one knows they are there.

3. Scroll down in the left list to Average. It happens to be right under AutoSum, but that is a coincidence. Hover over the command to see more about the command. Sure enough, this is the Average that is in the AutoSum dropdown on the Home tab.

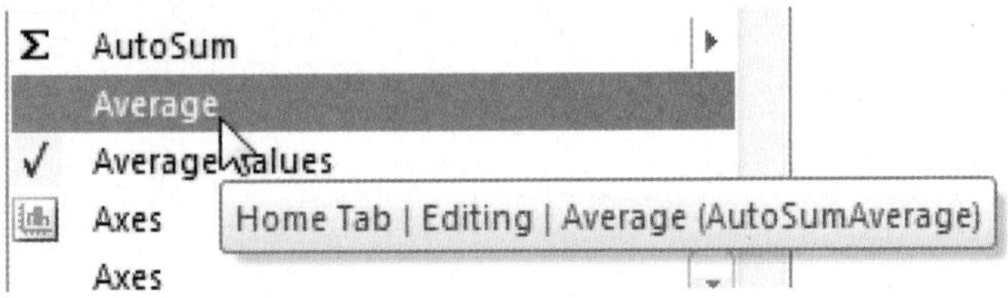

Figure 174 Brilliant – Microsoft made an icon for Auto-Average.

4. Select Average and click the Add>> button in the center of the screen.

5. Repeat for Count, Max, and Min. You will now have four new icons in the right list.

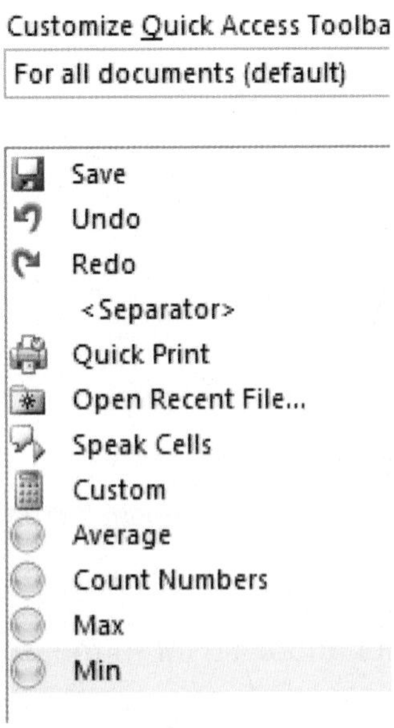

Figure 175 Microsoft uses this annoying green crystal ball as an icon whenever they don't have an existing icon for the command.

You now have four green crystal ball icons in your QAT. Remember they are arranged alphabetically, Average, Count Numbers, Max, Min.

Figure 176 Annoying, Annoying, Annoying, and Annoying. I mean, Average, Count, Max and Min.

These four icons work just like the AutoSum! Set up data as shown here. Select the data plus one extra row and one extra column.

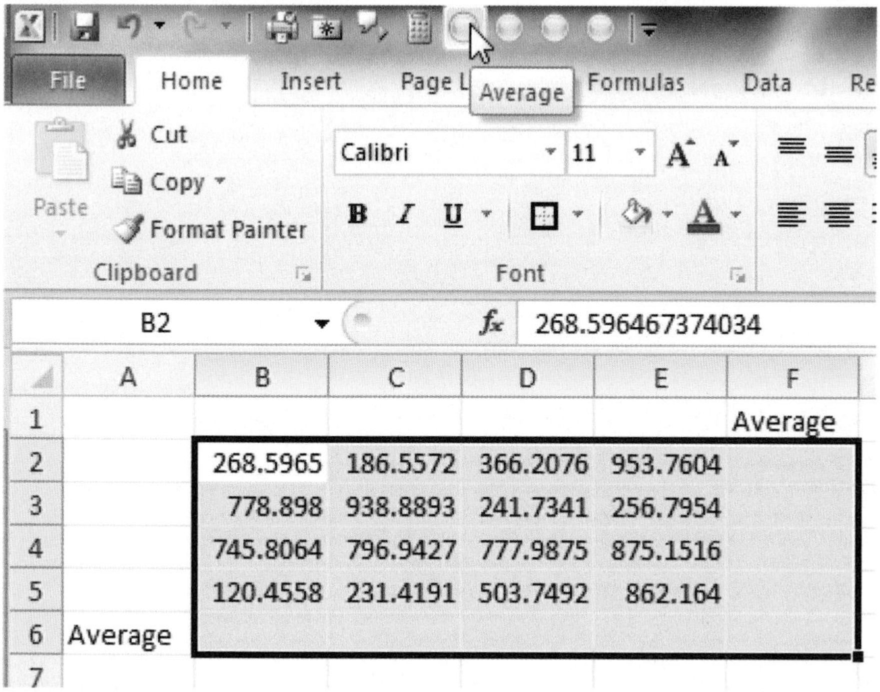

	A	B	C	D	E	F
1						Average
2		268.5965	186.5572	366.2076	953.7604	
3		778.898	938.8893	241.7341	256.7954	
4		745.8064	796.9427	777.9875	875.1516	
5		120.4558	231.4191	503.7492	862.164	
6	Average					
7						

Figure 177 Normally, you could AutoSum like this.

Instead of hitting AutoSum, click the green crystal ball for Average. Presto – you have average formulas all around.

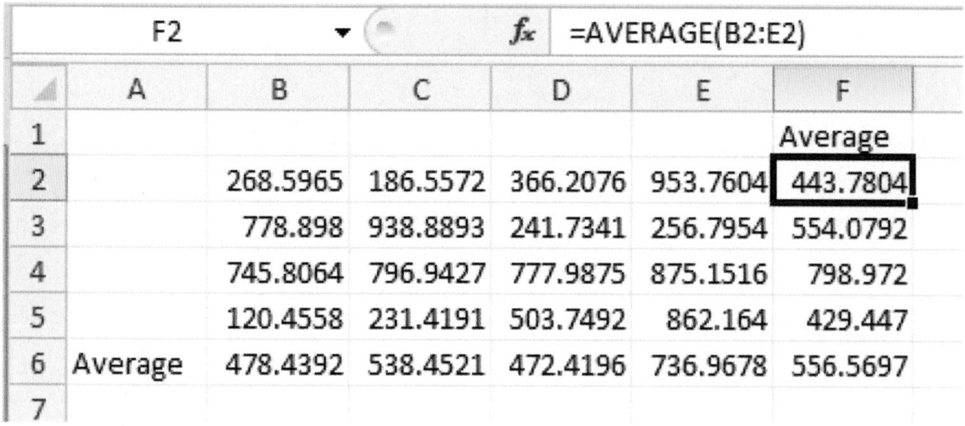

F2   fx   =AVERAGE(B2:E2)

	A	B	C	D	E	F
1						Average
2		268.5965	186.5572	366.2076	953.7604	443.7804
3		778.898	938.8893	241.7341	256.7954	554.0792
4		745.8064	796.9427	777.9875	875.1516	798.972
5		120.4558	231.4191	503.7492	862.164	429.447
6	Average	478.4392	538.4521	472.4196	736.9678	556.5697
7						

Figure 178 Auto-Average!

Do I Have to Put the Sum Formula in the Same Row or Column as the Data?

The AutoSum only totals numbers that are just above or left of my cell. Can I put the total somewhere else?

You can put the SUM formula wherever you want, even on another worksheet if you need to. This topic will show you three different methods, all are very easy – you select the one that works best for you.

Method 1: Type the SUM function:
1. Go to where you want the sum to appear.
2. Type =SUM(
3. Using the mouse, select the range that should be summed.
4. Type the closing parenthesis.
5. Press Enter.

	A	B	C	D	E
1	Amounts				
2	8,590.87		TOTAL		
3	7,933.76		=SUM(		
4	2,137.73		SUM(**number1**, [number2], ...)		
5	1,525.41				
6	9,944.32				
7	8,281.96				
8	4,108.14				

Figure 179 Start typing the formula using the keyboard.

	A	B	C	D	E
1	Amounts				
2	8,590.87		TOTAL		
3	7,933.76		=SUM(A2:A8		
4	2,137.73		SUM(**number1**, [number2], ...)		
5	1,525.41				
6	9,944.32				
7	8,281.96				
8	4,1□8.14				
9		7R x 1C			
10					

Figure 180 Switch to the mouse. Highlight the numbers to add.

C3			▼	f_x	=SUM(A2:A8)

	A	B	C	D	E
1	Amounts				
2	8,590.87		TOTAL		
3	7,933.76		42,522.19		
4	2,137.73				
5	1,525.41				
6	9,944.32				
7	8,281.96				
8	4,108.14				
9					

Figure 181 Type the closing parenthesis and press Enter.

Method 1 requires a bit of typing, but it is not that much typing. If it is too much typing, try Method 2.

Method 2: Use AutoSum, but select a new range:
1. Go to where you want the sum to appear.
2. Click the AutoSum icon on either the Home tab or Formula tab. (Or, type Alt+=). Excel might make a guess of what to sum, but ignore the guess.

3. Using the mouse, select the range that should be summed.
4. Press Enter.

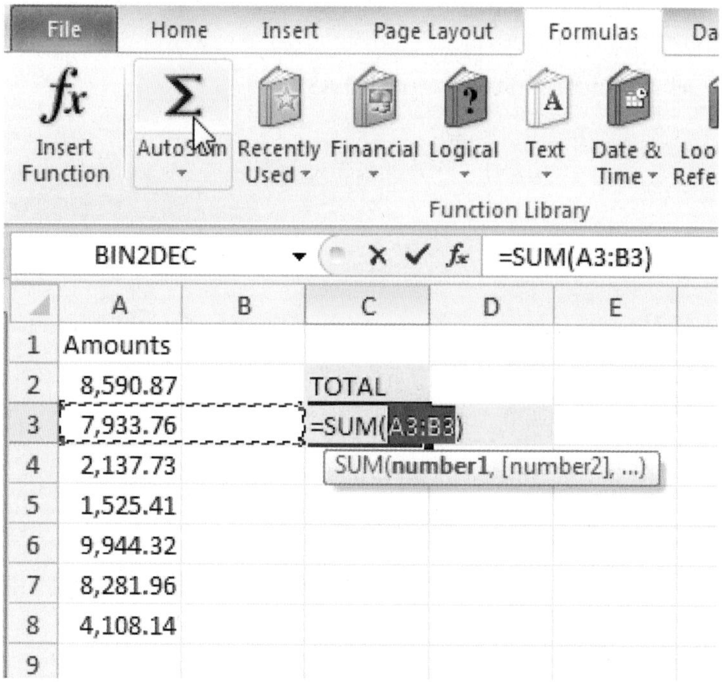

Figure 182 When you click the AutoSum, Excel guesses wrong. Use the mouse to select the correct range instead.

This method does not require you to type anything, not even the closing parenthesis.

Method 3: Let the AutoSum work, then Cut and Paste to the correct location:

1. Even though you want the total in C3, go to where the AutoSum would work correctly. Select A9, as in the figure below, and hit the AutoSum icon followed by Ctrl+Enter to stay in the same cell.
2. Press Ctrl+X to Cut.
3. Select where you want the total to appear.
4. Ctrl+V to Paste. Excel copies the correct formula to the new location. Unfortunately, you lose whatever formatting was in the cell where you pasted.
5. Re-apply the format that was in the cell before pasting.

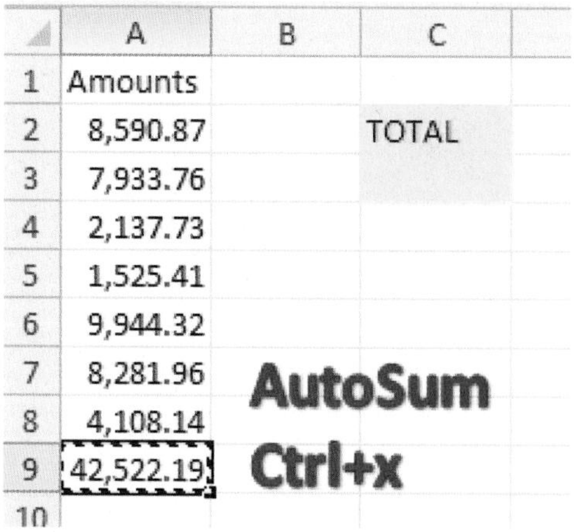

Figure 183 Use AutoSum where it will work, then Cut the formula.

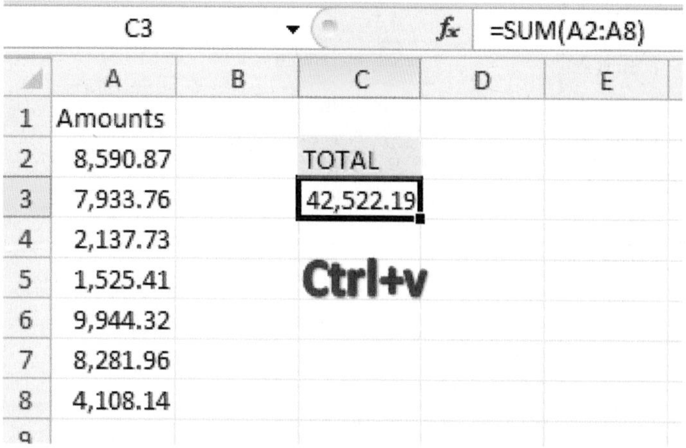

Figure 184 Use Ctrl+V to Paste. The formula will be correct.t

Note: It is critical that you cut instead of copying. When you copy and paste a formula, the references in the formula will move relative to the new location. When you cut and paste, the references stay the same as in the original formula.

What if you want the sum to appear on another worksheet?

It is easiest to use Method 3 above, but then paste to the other worksheet. As shown below, Excel added the proper syntax to point back to the original worksheet.

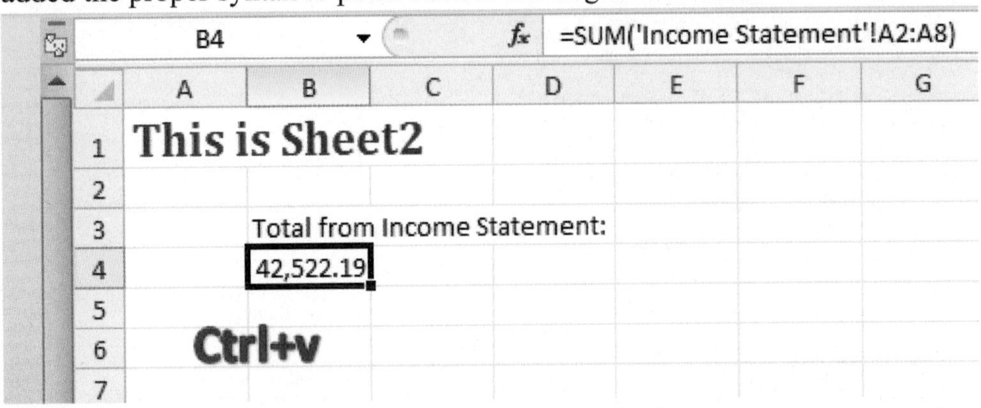

Figure 185 Cut, then paste to another worksheet. Excel will add the syntax to point to another sheet.

Can My Formula Be Open Ended to Accomodate New Numbers?

I am unsure of how many rows my data will take up. Is there a way to keep the formula open ended?

First, I will show you the old fashioned way that you had to use before Excel 2007. There is a new method that works starting in Excel 2007.

Method 1: Include a bunch of extra cells in the original formula.

Right now, you have seven numbers to add. Write the sum function to handle the next 20+ cells. Use:

`=SUM(A2:A24)`.

Provided the extra cells are blank, you will still get the correct answer for the SUM function. Heck, you could use

`=SUM(A2:A20000)`

if you wanted to.

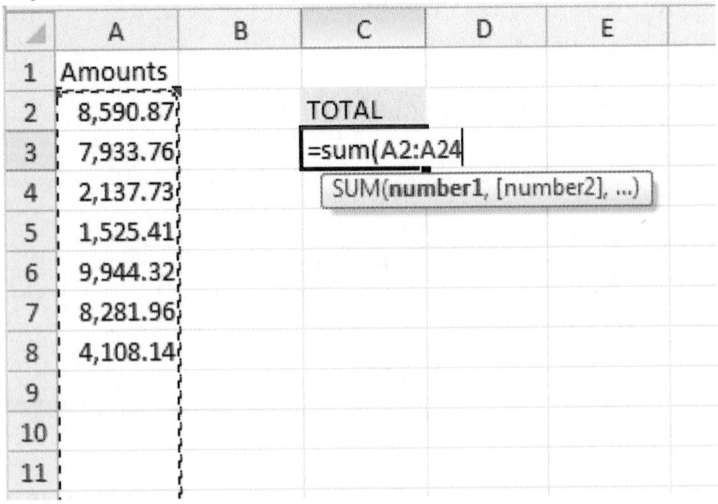

Figure 186 Include a bunch of extra cells in the formula.

As you type new numbers, the formula will automatically pick them up since they are in the A2:A24 range.

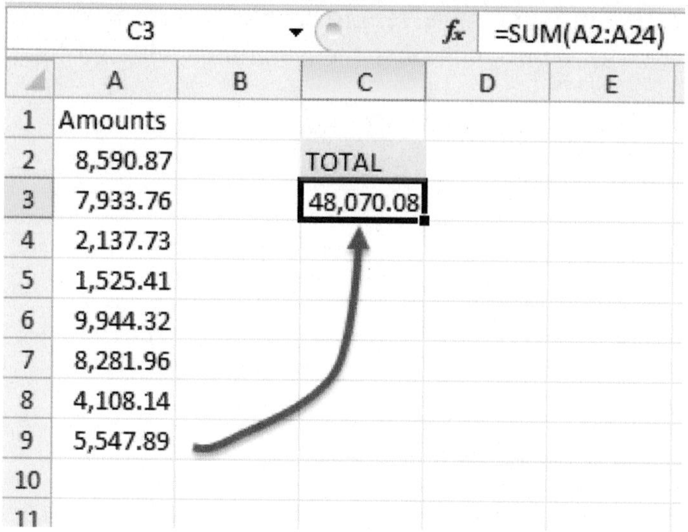

Figure 187 Because the formula is summing down to row 24, new numbers typed in the range automatically add to the total.

The problem with this method is that you might eventually reach cell A25, and you could forget that the sum range only goes down to A24. Unless you are really paying attention, you might type a few numbers before you realize that the total is not going up.

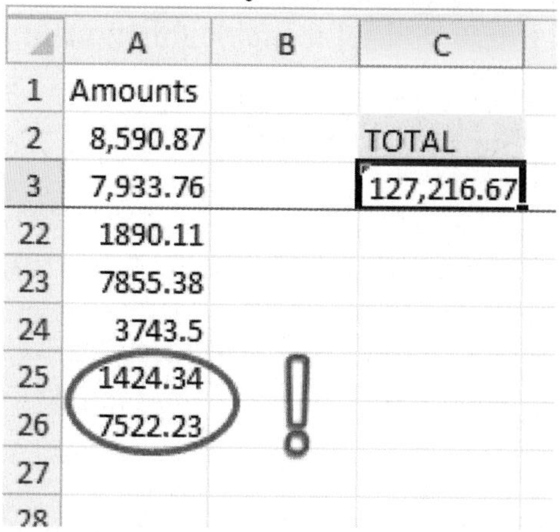

Figure 188 The last two numbers are past the sum range and are not included.

One solution is to put a warning in cell A25 reminding yourself to rewrite the formula.

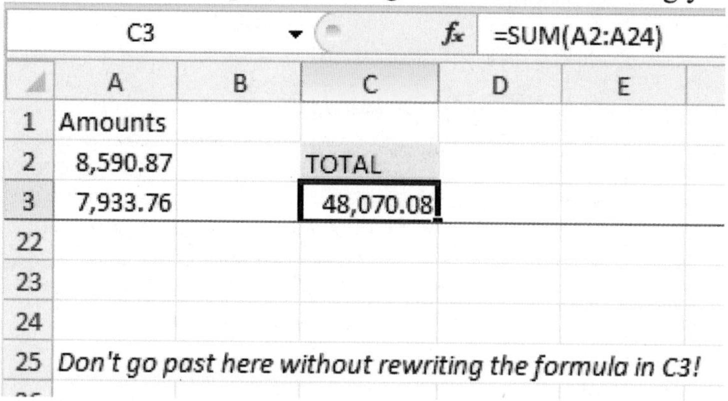

Figure 189 Leave a note to remind yourself to rewrite the formula.

Another way to go is to put the note in the last cell of the sum range, telling people to insert new rows above this cell. As you insert new rows anywhere within the sum range, the sum range will expand.

C3			f_x	=SUM(A2:A24)	
	A	B	C	D	E
1	Amounts				
2	8,590.87		TOTAL		
3	7,933.76		48,070.08		
22					
23					
24	*Insert new rows above this line so the total updates!*				

Figure 190 Ask people to insert new rows above the last cell in the sum range.

The above methods are all fairly easy. Excel gurus used to invent insane formulas using a combination of OFFSET, COUNT, and SUM to try to have the sum range automatically expand. These are not necessary given the new functionality available in Excel 2007 and newer.

Note: The following method requires that you are using Excel 2007 or newer and that you are not in compatibility mode. i.e. you cannot be using an .xls file.

Excel 2007 introduced some interesting Table functionality. While your manager may not like the unusual formula syntax that is used with tables, this method gets all the benefits of the table functionality without using the new syntax. Make sure to follow these steps exactly:

1. Build the SUM function to include only the numbers currently in the column.
2. Select a cell in the original range and press Ctrl+T.
3. Make sure the range is correct in the Create Table dialog. Click OK. As you can see in Figure 193, the formula in C3 stays the same even though it is now pointing at a table.
4. When you type a new value immediately below the table, the table definition expands to include the new cell. Magically, the formula in C3 is also rewritten to include the new cell!

C3			f_x	=SUM(A2:A6)	
	A	B	C	D	E
1	Amounts				
2	8,590.87		TOTAL		
3	7,933.76		30,132.09		
4	2,137.73				
5	1,525.41				
6	9,944.32				
7					

Figure 191 Build the formula pointing to the exact range.

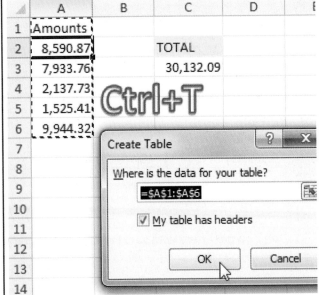

Figure 192 Define the formula as a table.

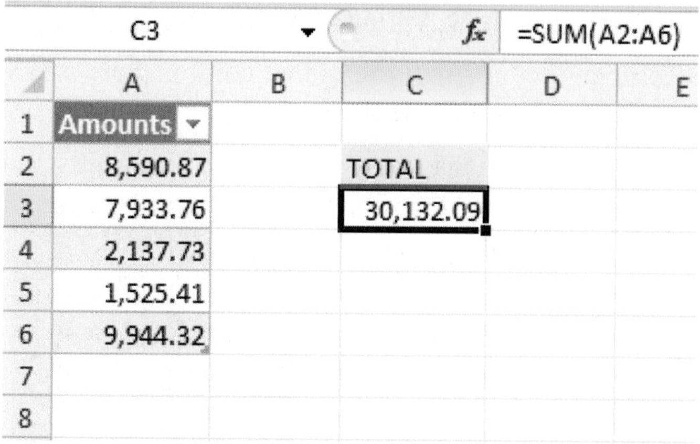

	C3		▼	⊜		f_x	=SUM(A2:A6)

◢	A	B	C	D	E
1	Amounts ▼				
2	8,590.87		TOTAL		
3	7,933.76		30,132.09		
4	2,137.73				
5	1,525.41				
6	9,944.32				
7					
8					

Figure 193 The existing formula still uses the normal formula syntax.

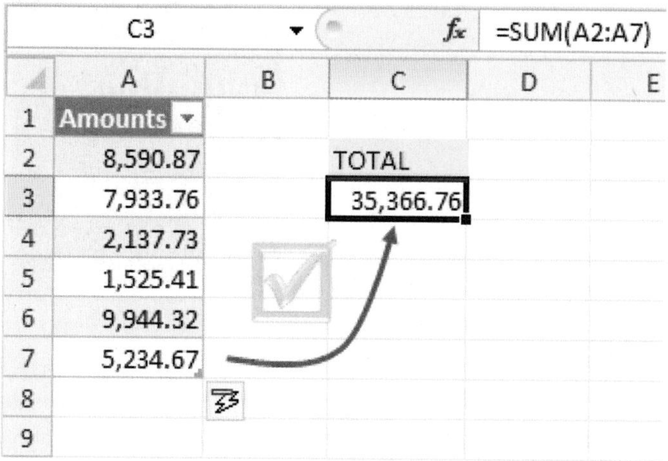

	C3		▼	⊜		f_x	=SUM(A2:A7)

◢	A	B	C	D	E
1	Amounts ▼				
2	8,590.87		TOTAL		
3	7,933.76		35,366.76		
4	2,137.73				
5	1,525.41				
6	9,944.32				
7	5,234.67				
8					
9					

Figure 194 Type new numbers just below the table. The formula in C3 expands to include the new value.

Provided you always keep typing the new number in the blank cell below the table (and never leave a blank cell), the formula in C3 will continue to expand forever. In the figure below, the function has expanded all the way down to row 93.

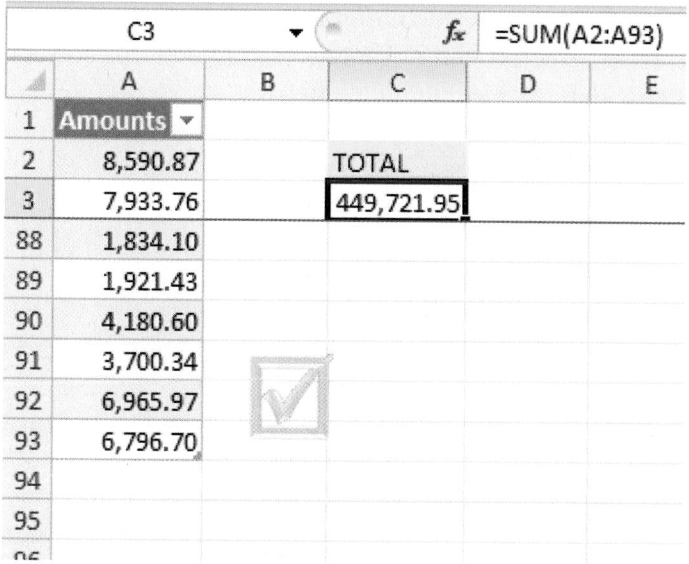

	C3		▼	⊜		f_x	=SUM(A2:A93)

◢	A	B	C	D	E
1	Amounts ▼				
2	8,590.87		TOTAL		
3	7,933.76		449,721.95		
88	1,834.10				
89	1,921.43				
90	4,180.60				
91	3,700.34				
92	6,965.97				
93	6,796.70				
94					
95					

Figure 195 The formula keeps expanding.

Caution: If you enter the formula after defining the range as a table, the formula will be =SUM(Table1[Amounts]). While this formula will work, it might confuse co-workers who prefer to see =SUM(A2:A93).

How Can I Add up Numbers in One Column Depending on What Is in Another Column?

With a list of text items in one column and their accompanying numbers in another column, here's how you can add up only the numbers that are associated with a particular text item.

Suppose the owner of a fruit stand wants to know how many bananas were sold today. The fruit stand sells many different kinds of fruits, and the list of sales is recorded similar to the following figure. For now, the owner only wants to know how many bananas were sold.

E1		fx =SUMIF(A2:A15,D1,B2:B15)			
	A	B	C	D	E	F
1	**Product**	**Sold today**		**Bananas**	96	
2	Apples	18				
3	Oranges	32				
4	Bananas	22				
5	Apples	12				
6	Oranges	38				
7	Pears	85				
8	Apples	47				
9	Bananas	48				
10	Oranges	53				
11	Pears	99				
12	Apples	46				
13	Bananas	26				
14	Pears	59				
15	Oranges	34				

> If you use SUMIF, you will eventually need to test for 2 conditions, check Excel Help for SUMIFS

Figure 196 The SUMIF function in cell E1 adds up numbers in column B where Bananas are found in column A.

Notice in the figure, range A2:A15 holds the names of fruits that were sold, and their accompanying numbers of how many were sold are in range B2:B15. Notice further that the word "Bananas" is in cell D1.

A function called SUMIF is a good way to add up the numbers in column B where "Bananas" exists in that same row in column A. In the figure, cell E1 is selected, and it displays the number 96. You can see in the Formula Bar immediately above that area that the formula in cell E1 is:

```
=SUMIF(A2:A15,D1,B2:B15)
```

Here's a breakdown of the formula:
- It starts with the equals sign as all formulas do.
- You type the name of the function, which as you can see is SUMIF.
- Inside the parentheses are three pieces of information you tell Excel:
  1. The range holding the names of the fruits being sold. In this case, that range is A2:A15.
  2. The cell address holding the criteria (in this case cell D1 for "Bananas") that you want to find in range A2:A15.
  3. The range holding the numbers you want to sum, which in this case is B2:B15.

Note: If you prefer, you can avoid using a criteria helper cell such as this example used with cell D1. The formula could have been written as =SUMIF(A2:A15,"Bananas",B2:B15) and gotten the exact same result.

Taking a quick look for verification purposes, the word "Bananas" appears in cells A4, A9, and A13. In cell B4 is the number 22, in cell B9 is the number 48, and in cell B13 is the number 26. Adding 22, 48, and 26 together equals 96, which the SUMIF formula correctly calculated in cell E1.

You Did What?

My Numbers Aren't Adding Up!

Mark recalls back to when his company got their first computer, which was running a spreadsheet called VisiCalc. His manager sat down to enter some numbers. When he totaled the column, the total did not work.

I can remember sitting through Mrs. Marhefka's typing class back in 1983. We were using electric typewriters which seemed so cool compared to the manual Royal typewriter that I had at home. The typewriter did not bother to have a numeral "1" key – you were supposed to type a lower-case "L" when you needed a 1.

=SUM(C2:C4)

C	D
Amounts	
2345.67	
4321.43	
9874.32	
12219.99	

Figure 197 9+4+2 should be at least $15K, not $12K.

Since VisiCalc came out in 1979, this certainly would have been the era where people were used to typing the lowercase letter "L" when they meant to use a number "1".

I've revealed the problem with that left-justified 4321.43 in the figure here. Using the =UPPER function, you see that the number contains the letter L instead of a 1.

=UPPER(C3)

C	D
Amounts	
2345.67	
4321.43	432L.43
9874.32	
12219.99	

Figure 198 The UPPER function reveals that what should be the number 1 is really a lower case "L".

Note: For those of you who are annoyed when Excel keeps telling you that you have a number stored as text, you will see that using 432L.43 does not cause the warning to appear. (NOT that I am recommending you start using L…)

To fix the problem: Choose the range of numbers. Press Ctrl+H to display the Find and Replace dialog. Change the lower case L to the number 1. Click Replace All.

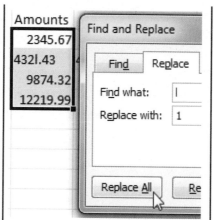

Figure 199 Replace the lower case L with 1.

The total is now correct.

Amounts
2345.67
4321.43
9874.32
16541.42

Figure 200 During the Replace, the second number becomes numeric and right justified.

You Did What?

Why Isn't AutoSum Working?

Patricia received a call from a co-worker. For some reason, the AutoSum icon was not recognizing the range of numbers. When the co-worker tried manually typing a SUM function, the answer was zero.

	E8			f_x	=SUM(E4:E7)
	A	B	C	D	E
1	Time Log				
2					
3	Activity				Hours
4	Collate and copy client report				2.5
5	G/L Journal Entries for payroll				3.7
6	Proofing spreadsheet with calculator				14.5
7	Reducing blueprint paper on copier				0.8
8					0

Figure 201 The AutoSum isn't working.

Can you see the problem above? It would be difficult to recognize the problem initially. Here is another clue – look in the Formula Bar. If you select cell A4 and look in the Formula Bar, you might notice a stray 2.5 pretty far to the right.

Collate and copy client report				2.5	
	A	B	C	D	E
1	Time Log				
2					
3	Activity				Hours
4	Collate and copy client report				2.5
5	G/L Journal Entries for payroll				3.7
6	Proofing spreadsheet with calculator				14.5
7	Reducing blueprint paper on copier				0.8
8					0

Figure 202 Look at the right side of the Formula Bar. What is that 2.5 doing there?

The problem with spaces is that they are generally invisible. It is really tough to see a space or a whole bunch of spaces. The figure below shows the worksheet after I used Find and Replace to change every space to a period.

	A
1	Time Log
2	
3	Activity Hours
4	Collate.and.copy.client.report...........................2.5
5	G/L.Journal.Entries.for.payroll.........................3.7
6	Proofing.spreadsheet.with.calculator...............14.5
7	Reducing.blueprint.paper.on.copier...................0.8

Figure 203 Changing the spaces to a period, you can see the problem.

Patricia's coworker had used multiple spaces in order to move out towards column E and then typed the number. The number is not really in column E – the number is really part of column A.

Why is this bad? First, it is difficult to get numbers lined up this way. With all fonts except Courier, each letter takes up a proportional amount of space. You are going to have to experiment with the right number of spaces just to get it lined up. Second, when the number is part of a cell containing text, it becomes nearly impossible to do any math with the number.

To fix this, make column A wider. Type the tasks in A, type the numbers in B. The AutoSum will now work.

=SUM(B4:B8)

	A	B
1	Time Log	
2		
3	Activity	Hours
4	Collate and copy client report	2.5
5	G/L Journal Entries for payroll	3.7
6	Proofing spreadsheet with calculator	14.5
7	Learned a Cool Trick in Excel	0.1
8	Reducing blueprint paper on copier	0.8
9		21.6
10		

Figure 204 Text in A, numbers in B.

Tab Tab Tab Tab Tab Tab. Shift-Tab Shift-Tab Shift-Tab Shift-Tab Shift-Tab Shift-Tab

Mark remembers a co-worker who had really long text to put in column A with some numbers that had to appear to the right of the text.

The co-worker decided that the text would roughly fill columns A through F. The co-worker would type the long text in column A, then press the Tab key six times to move over to column G. He typed the number in G, went down a row, then pressed Shift-Tab six times to go back to column A.

	A	B	C	D	E	F	G
1	Lorem ipsum dolor sit amet, consectetur adipiscing elit.						2,260.11
2	Sed eu nisl sed felis viverra adipiscing.						77,208.31
3	Mauris sit amet enim vitae risus dignissim vestibulum.						76,454.23
4	In eu sapien nec augue tristique mollis a ut nulla.						43,424.35
5	Ut pharetra euismod magna, a vulputate nulla varius eget.						72,630.04

Figure 205 Four tabs down, two more to go.

Why is this the wrong way to go?
- You have to press Tab or Shift Tab way too many times.
- What will you do when a sentence covers part of column G? Move everything over?
- With the intervening blank columns, you cannot use the AZ or ZA quick sort buttons.

To fix this, choose column A. On the right of the Home tab, open the Format dropdown and choose AutoFit Column Width.

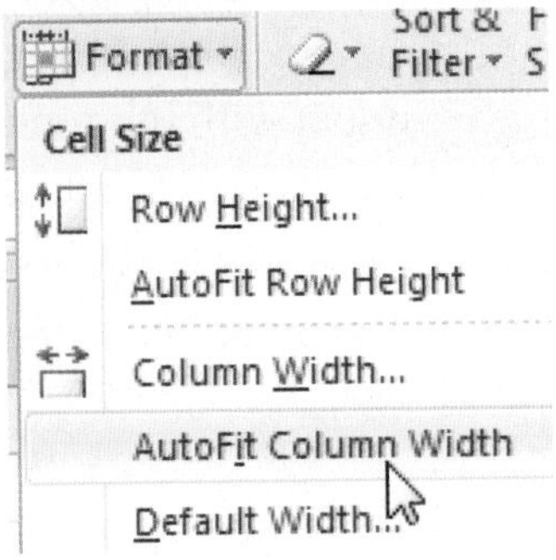

Figure 206 Choose all of column A before using AutoFit.

Column A will become wide enough to hold all of the text. You can then type your numbers in B.

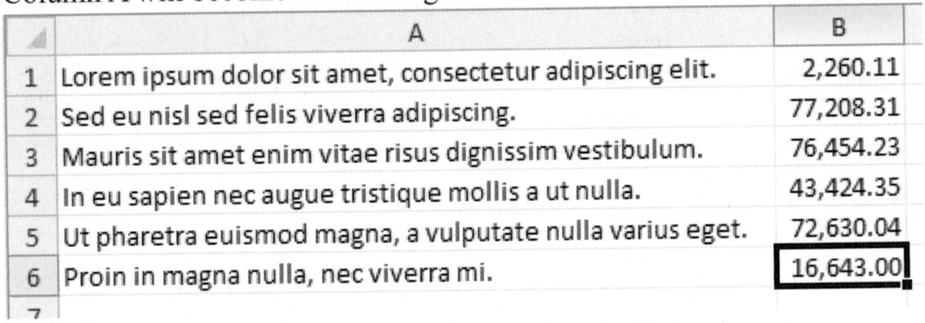

	A	B
1	Lorem ipsum dolor sit amet, consectetur adipiscing elit.	2,260.11
2	Sed eu nisl sed felis viverra adipiscing.	77,208.31
3	Mauris sit amet enim vitae risus dignissim vestibulum.	76,454.23
4	In eu sapien nec augue tristique mollis a ut nulla.	43,424.35
5	Ut pharetra euismod magna, a vulputate nulla varius eget.	72,630.04
6	Proin in magna nulla, nec viverra mi.	16,643.00
7		

Figure 207 Sorting and filtering will work better without the blank columns.

How Can I Use Excel as a Calculator?

I can't find my calculator. I just have to do some simple math. When I go to Excel and type 14215469+71077345, it does not calculate anything. Can't Excel do simple math like a .99-cent calculator?

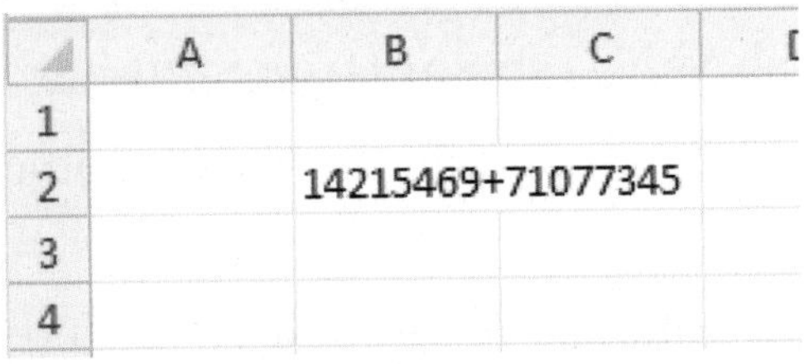

	A	B	C	D
1				
2		14215469+71077345		
3				
4				

Figure 208 Forget the leading equals sign and Excel will not calculate anything.

Yes, Excel can do everything that your .99-cent calculator can do. Before you treat it like a calculator, you have to type an equals sign.

Select any blank cell. Type =14215469+77177345 and press Enter. You will see the answer in the cell and the formula in the Formula Bar.

B2			f_x	=14215469+71077345		
	A	B	C	D	E	F
1						
2		85292814				
3						

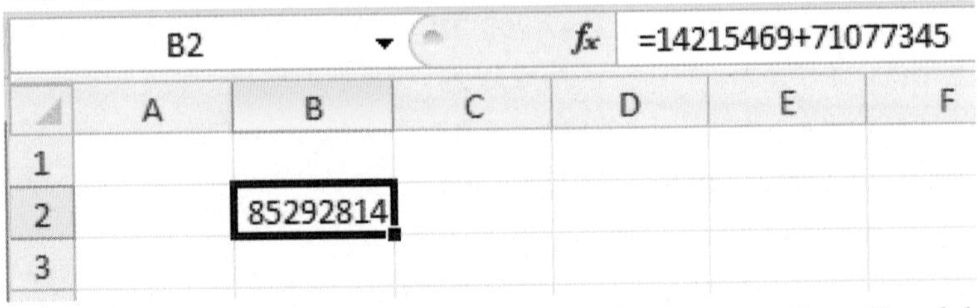

Figure 209 Use an equals sign. Excel shows the answer in the cell and the formula in the Formula Bar.

Tip: If you type the calculation and forget to put the equals sign, you do not have to retype the calculation. Select the cell. Press F2 to put the cell in edit mode. Press the Home key to move to the beginning of the cell. Type the equals sign and press Enter. Excel will now perform the calculation.

Here are some other calculator formulas that you can use:
- To multiply, use the asterisk: =4*56
- To divide, use the forward slash: =56/7
- To do a square root, use the carat and .5: =64^.5
- To do a percentage, use the % symbol: =1234*50%
- You can add parentheses: =(123+456-78)*2

Note: Before pressing Enter, you can press F9 to perform the calculation and show the answer in the Formula Bar. You can then press the Esc key to clear the entry.

How Do I Write Equations Using Different Numbers in Different Cells?

How can I make Excel solve equations across cells?

Placing formulas in cells that work with numbers from other cells—that's what Excel is all about!

The figure below shows examples of formulas that refer to numbers located in other cells. As you can see, there are numbers in cell A1, A2 and A3. The formulas in cells C1, C2 and C3 refer to those numbers in various mathematical ways.

The formula in cell C1 is:

```
=A1+A2+A3
```

it simply adds 5, 3, and 8 and returns the number 16.

The formula in cell C2 is:

```
=(A1+A2)/A3
```

this formula adds 5 and 3 (which equals 8) and divides that number by 8, returning the number 1.

The formula in cell C3 is:

```
=(A1*A2)-A3
```

this formula multiplies 5 times 3 (which equals 15) and subtracts 8, returning the number 7.

◢	A	B	C	D	E	F	G
1	5		16	Formula in C1 is =A1+A2+A3			
2	3		1	Formula in C2 is =(A1+A2)/A3			
3	8		7	Formula in C3 is =(A1*A2)-A3			
4							

Figure 210 Examples of how to construct simple equation formulas by referring to numbers in other cells.

 You Did What?

Using the QuickSum Instead of AutoSum

Kevin sent in this true story. Kevin works for a help desk. A temp worker over in accounting called Kevin to ask for some help with VLOOKUP. Kevin heads over to her desk. The temp was just finishing up a worksheet, so Kevin watched her for a few moments. She had to add a numbers that were in two different ranges.

Somehow, she had discovered that if she selected all of the cells in the range, the total would appear in the status bar. She did not know to hold down the Ctrl key to add a second range to the selection, so the best she could do was to get the totals for half the data at once.

Of course, you can see the total in the status bar. But when you click somewhere else to enter the total, the total disappears. So, the co-worker would repeat the total aloud three times so it would stick in her head.

She would then choose a blank cell and type the total that she had just said aloud.

She repeated this for the other half of the data.

Now, with two subtotals keyed into the spreadsheet, she used a calculator to total those two numbers.

Why this is bad: Kevin said that he saw the lady transpose the numbers as she typed them.

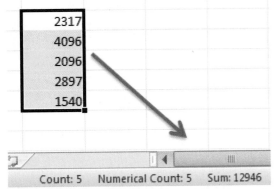

Count: 5   Numerical Count: 5   Sum: 12946

Figure 211 Select the cell, see the total.

To sum non-contiguous ranges, you would type =SUM(, then use the mouse to select the first range. Type a comma, then use the mouse to select the next range. Continue in this fashion, with a comma between each range. When you are done type the closing parenthesis and press Enter.

	A	B	C	D	E	F	G
1	Invoice	Qty	Amount		Invoice	Qty	Amount
2	1001	128	1280		1008	125	1250
3	1002	125	1250		1009	110	1100
4	1003	155	1550		1010	195	1950
5	1004	141	1410		1011	122	1220
6	1005	198	1980		1012	168	1680
7	1006	158	1580		1013	162	1620
8	1007	194	1940		1014	145	1450
9							
10			=sum(C2:C8,G2:G8)				

Figure 212 It is easy to sum non-contiguous ranges.

Is There a Difference between Typing in the Cell Itself and Typing in the Formula Bar?

My co-worker types everything in the Formula Bar. I type everything right in the cell. Is there any difference?

Most of the time, there is no difference at all.

When spreadsheets were invented, everything was typed in the Formula Bar. Back in the mid-1990's, Excel introduced the ability to enter directly in the cell. This way is clearly easier.

At least, it is easier if your text or formula doesn't go past the edge of the screen. There are some formulas which might take hundreds of characters. A cell can contain up to 4096 characters. If you find yourself entering more than 100 characters, it might be easier to work in the Formula Bar.

Although the Formula Bar starts out one row tall, you can use the arrow at the right side of the Formula Bar to open the Formula Bar to three rows. You can then use the bar at the bottom of the Formula Bar to make the Formula Bar even taller.

I am not sure who would ever use all 4096 characters in a single cell, but if you find yourself getting close, using the Formula Bar might be an easier way to go.

When you edit a formula, you can either click in the Formula Bar, double click the cell, or choose the cell and press F2.

In the figure below, the formula is edited in an expanded Formula Bar. The formula refers to cell E3 and you can still see that cell.

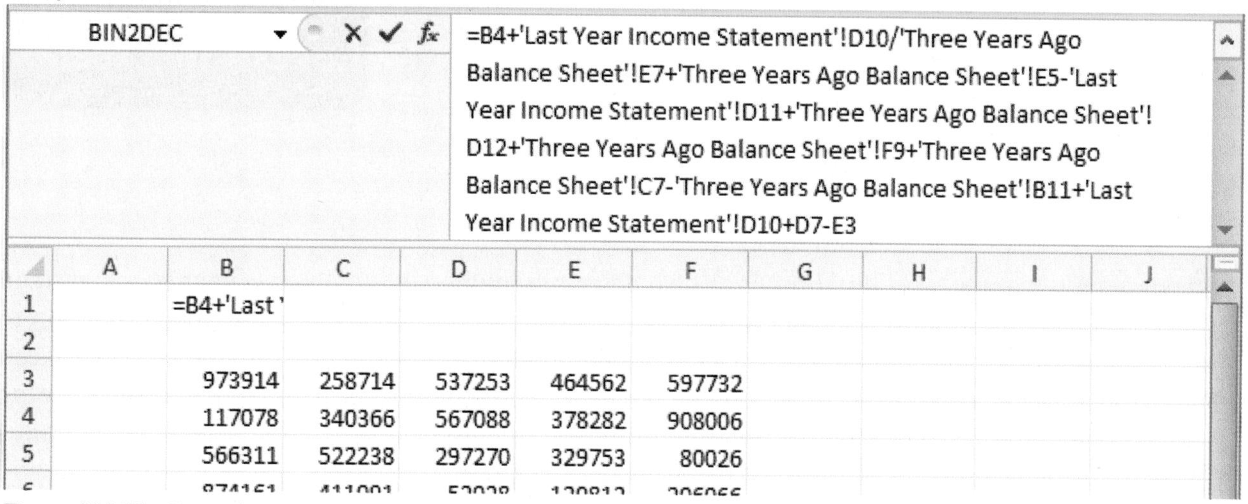

Figure 213 The Formula Bar expands and the worksheet starts lower.

In the figure below, the cell is being edited. The formula is so long, it is covering up important parts of the worksheet.

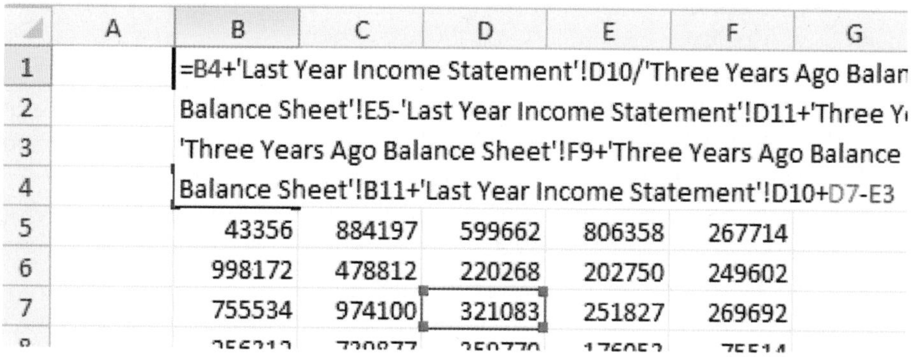

Figure 214 When editing in the cell, the formula might cover up important parts of the worksheet.

How Do I Build a Formula?

I've entered some data into my spreadsheet and now I want to add some additional values based on the data already entered. I've heard I can do this with formulas. How do I build a formula?

A formula is one of the most powerful tools at your disposal. Learning how to build a formula will allow you to fully realize Excel's potential. For example, you can sum or average a column of numbers, calculate percentages, and project future cash flow. The possibilities are virtually endless. Formulas use two basic Excel elements: cell references and functions. A cell reference is simply a reference to one or more cells on a worksheet. A function takes constants and cell references and produces some result. For example, the function SUM adds the values passed to it and produces the total sum of all those values.

Before building a formula, select a cell to contain the formula and display its result. To start building a formula, type an equal sign. Notice that Excel places the equal sign in the cell with the cursor immediately following and displays a possible function choice in the Functions drop down menu in the Formula Bar. In the case below, Excel has chosen to display the function POISSON. DIST – a function that we will not be using anywhere in this book.

40% of people using Excel have never entered a formula; learn formula creation to become a solid Level 3 in Excel

	A	B	C	D
1	Name	Job Title	Salary	
2	Sue Smith	President	150,000	
3	Janet Jones	Vice President	125,000	
4	Bob Green	Programmer	100,000	
5	Kevin Young	Exel Guru	160,000	
6	Sally Johnson	Marketer	120,000	
7			=	
8				

Figure 215 Start a new formula in a cell.

Depending on what you want the formula to calculate, you might want to enter a function, a constant, or a cell reference. Using the example in the image above, we're going to use the SUM function to sum the salaries of all the employees. You can type the function name directly into the cell or you can select the function from the list of functions presented in the Functions drop down menu. When doing the latter Excel will help you find the function you need to complete your task so let's try that now. Clicking the menu displays a short list of the last used functions.

POISSON.DIST ▼ ✕ ✓ fx =

POISSON.DIST	B	C	D
FREQUENCY	tle	Salary	
SUM	ent	150,000	
AVERAGE	resident	125,000	
IF	immer	100,000	
HYPERLINK	uru	160,000	
COUNT	ter	120,000	
MAX		=	
SIN			
SUMIF			
More Functions...			
10			

Figure 216 Using the Functions drop down to select a function.

In the example above, Excel has included the SUM function in the short list. But let's select More Functions anyway to see how Excel can help you further. The Insert Function dialog box is displayed:

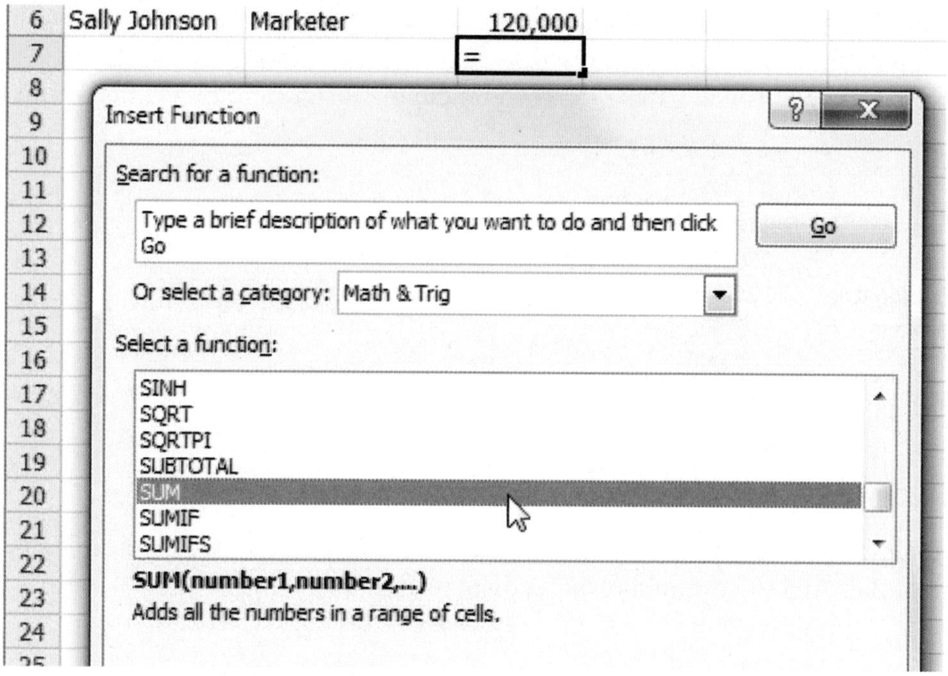

Figure 217 The Insert Function dialog box.

From within the Insert Function dialog box you can select a function category and then a specific function. In the above example we have selected Math & Trig for the category and SUM in the list of functions. Notice that Excel displays the function's description and the functions parameters at the bottom of the dialog. You can also search for a function by typing some search words in the text entry box at the top of the dialog. With the desired function selected you can click OK to open the Function Arguments dialog box.

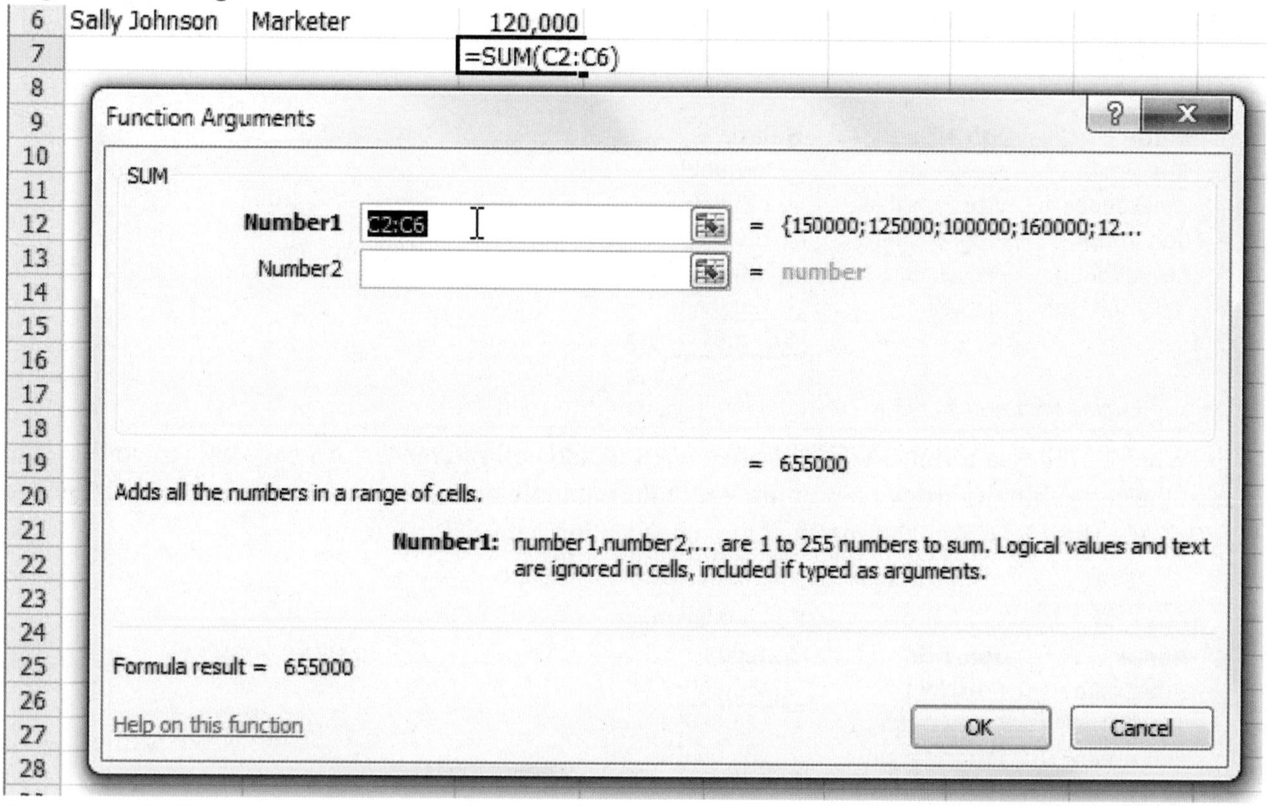

Figure 218 The Function Arguments dialog box.

Notice that Excel was smart enough to guess the cells we want to sum and it placed the cell range in the text entry box for the first parameter! Also notice that Excel has already entered the proposed formula in the cell we chose to hold the formula. Click OK to complete the formula and view the results.

C7		f_x	=SUM(C2:C6)	

	A	B	C	D
1	**Name**	**Job Title**	**Salary**	
2	Sue Smith	President	150,000	
3	Janet Jones	Vice President	125,000	
4	Bob Green	Programmer	100,000	
5	Kevin Young	Exel Guru	160,000	
6	Sally Johnson	Marketer	120,000	
7			655,000	
8				

Figure 219 Our worksheet with our first formula.

Notice that the cell we chose to hold the formula is still selected and the formula we entered is displayed above in the Formula Bar. And the formula result is displayed in the cell!

Using the Formula Bar:

You can also enter a formula using the Formula Bar. In fact, you may have noticed that as you typed in the cell the same text in the cell was displayed in the Formula Bar. You can just as easily work in the Formula Bar as you can in the cell being edited. Both techniques work exactly the same way and produce exactly the same results.

While editing a formula, there are three buttons displayed to the left of the formula entry box in the Formula Bar: an "X", a check mark, and an "fx". Clicking the fx opens the Insert Function dialog box. Clicking the check mark accepts the formula and closes the cell. Clicking the X cancels the edits made and returns the formula to its form before you started editing it.

SUM		X ✓ f_x	=SUM(C2:C6)	

	A	B	C	D
1	**Name**	**Job Title**	Enter **Salary**	
2	Sue Smith	President	150,000	
3	Janet Jones	Vice President	125,000	
4	Bob Green	Programmer	100,000	
5	Kevin Young	Exel Guru	160,000	
6	Sally Johnson	Marketer	120,000	
7			1(C2:C6)	
8				

Figure 220 Using the Formula Bar to edit formulas.

Tip: When building a formula you will often want to add cell references. An easy way to do this is to select the cells with the arrow keys or mouse. In the example below we have reset the cell reference to exclude the president from the sum function by selecting cells C3 to C6.

SUM		X ✓ f_x	=SUM(C3:C6)	

	A	B	C	D
			SUM(number:	
1	**Name**	**Job Title**	**Salary**	
2	Sue Smith	President	150,000	
3	Janet Jones	Vice President	125,000	
4	Bob Green	Programmer	100,000	
5	Kevin Young	Exel Guru	160,000	
6	Sally Johnson	Marketer	120,000	
7			1(C3:C6)	
8				

Figure 221 Using the arrow keys or mouse to insert cell references.

Is There a Way to Do Exponents in Excel?

I need to figure out 1.07 raised to the power of 5. Can Excel do Exponents?

Yes – use the carat symbol (^ - often found as Shift+6) to do exponents. Use =1.07^5.

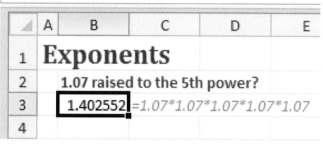

Figure 222 Use the ^ for exponents.

Square roots are related to exponents. Although Excel offers the =SQRT function to calculate square roots, you can also calculate the Nth root of any number by raising the number to the (1/N) power. In the figure below, the square root formula can be:

```
=SQRT(A4),  =A4^(1/2),  or =A4^.5
```

All three produce the same answer.

	A	B	C	D
1	**Roots**			
2	*Since 8*8 is 64, the square root of 64 is 8.*			
3	**Number**	**Square Root**	**Formula in B**	
4	64	8	*=SQRT(A4)*	
5	64	8	*=A5^(1/2)*	
6	64	8	*=A6^0.5*	
7				
8	**Number**	**Cube Root**		
9	125	5	*=A8^(1/3)*	
10				
11	**Number**	**Fifth Root**		
12	1.402552	1.07	*=A11^(1/5)*	
13	1.402552	1.07	*=A12^.2*	
14				

Figure 223 Raise a number to a fraction to find any root.

The raising to a fraction trick comes in handy when you have to calculate the third root, fourth root, fifth root or any root. The seventeenth root of 131072 is 131072^(1/17).

Note that you can replace the fraction with its decimal equivalent if the fraction does not result in a repeating decimal.

- =64^(1/2) is the same as =64^.5
- =81^(1/4) is the same as =81^.25
- =1000^(1/10) is the same as =1000^.1

Because 1/3 is a repeating decimal, it is easier to use =125^(1/3) instead of 125^0.3333

Why Doesn't the COUNT Function Count All Non-Blank Cells?

In the figure below, there are 10 non-blank cells, yet the COUNT function returns 2.

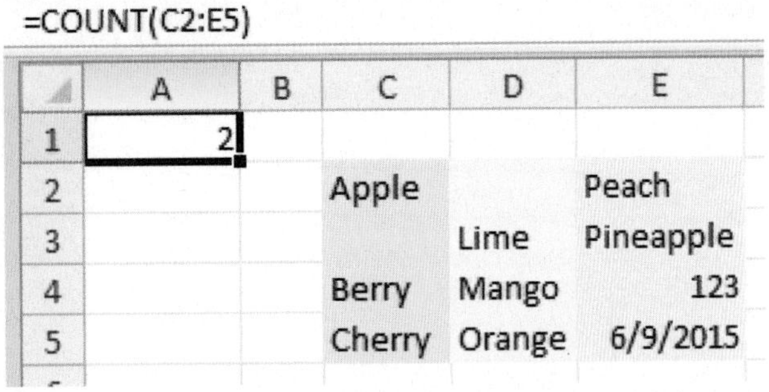

=COUNT(C2:E5)

	A	B	C	D	E
1	2				
2			Apple		Peach
3				Lime	Pineapple
4			Berry	Mango	123
5			Cherry	Orange	6/9/2015

Figure 224 Excel offers COUNT, COUNTA, and COUNTBLANK.

The COUNT function only counts cells that are numeric, date, or time. To count all non-blank cells, use the COUNTA function.

CHAPTER 4 - MORE ADVANCED TOPICS

What Are Some Useful Shortcut Keys?

The Ribbon can be a little cumbersome at times, especially when I know exactly what I want to do. Also, I often find my task requires a lot of keyboard entry and moving between the keyboard and mouse seems to slow me down. Are there some shortcut keys that will make my tasks easier?

There are a number of shortcut keys that you can use to do various common tasks with workbooks, worksheets, cells, and formulas. Below are some of the more useful shortcut keys.

Working with Workbooks

Display the Open dialog box: Ctrl+O

Create a new, blank workbook: Ctrl+N

Switch to the next workbook window: Ctrl+F6

Switch to the previous workbook window: Ctrl+Shift+F6

Save the selected workbook: Ctrl+S

Close the selected workbook: Ctrl+F4 or Ctrl+W

Display the Save As dialog box: F12

Minimize the selected workbook window: Ctrl+F9

Restore the size of the selected workbook window: Ctrl+F5

Toggle the maximized window state of selected workbook window: Ctrl+F10

Move the selected workbook window using arrow keys: Ctrl+F7

Resize the selected workbook window using arrow keys: Ctrl+F8

Working with Worksheets

Move to the next sheet in the selected workbook: Ctrl+PgDn

Move to the previous sheet in the selected workbook: Ctrl+PgUp

Display the Print Preview window: Ctrl+F2

Insert a new worksheet: Shift+F11 or Alt+Shift+F1

Working with Cells, Rows, and Columns

Display the Insert dialog box to insert blank cells, rows, or columns: Ctrl+Shift+Plus

Display the Delete dialog box to delete the selected cells, rows, or columns: Ctrl+Minus

Hide the selected rows: Ctrl+9

Hide the selected columns: Ctrl+0 (the number zero)

Selecting

Select the entire column: Ctrl+SpaceBar

Select the entire row: Shift+SpaceBar

Select the current region around the active cell (the current region is a data area enclosed by blank rows and blank columns): Ctrl+A or Ctrl+Shift+* (asterisk)

Select the entire worksheet: Ctrl+A (twice if the current region is selected)

Extend the current selection one cell/row/column: Shift+Arrow

Move the selection to the last nonblank cell in the same column or row as the active cell: Ctrl+Arrow

Extend the selection to the last nonblank cell in the same column or row as the active cell: Ctrl+Shift+Arrow

Extend the selection to the last used cell on the worksheet (lower-right corner): Ctrl+Shift+End

Extend the selection to the beginning of the worksheet: Ctrl+Shift+Home

Turn extend mode on or off ("Extended Selection" appears in the status line and the arrow keys extend the selection): F8

Add a nonadjacent cell or range to a selection of cells by using the arrow keys: Shift+F8

With an object selected, select all objects on a sheet: Ctrl+Shift+SpaceBar

Editing

Copy: Ctrl+C

Cut: Ctrl+X

Paste: Ctrl+V

Display the Paste Special dialog box: Ctrl+Alt+V

Undo: Ctrl+Z

Add or edit a cell comment: Shift+F2

Copy the value from the cell immediately above the active cell to the active cell: Ctrl+Shift+"

Copy the formula from the cell immediately above the active cell to the active cell: Ctrl+'

Copy the value and formatting from the topmost selected cell to the selected cells below: Ctrl+D

Copy the value and formatting from the left-most selected cell to the selected cells to the right: Ctrl+R

Formatting

Applies or removes bold formatting: Ctrl+B or Ctrl+2

Apply or remove italic formatting: Ctrl+I or Ctrl+3

Apply or removes underlining: Ctrl+U or Ctrl+4

Apply or remove strikethrough: Ctrl+5

Applies the General number format: Ctrl+Shift+~

Apply the number format with two decimal places, thousands separator and minus sign (-) for negative values: Ctrl+Shift+!

Apply the currency format with two decimal places (negative numbers in parentheses): Ctrl+Shift+$

Apply the percentage format with no decimal places: Ctrl+Shift+%

Apply the scientific number format with two decimal places: Ctrl+Shift+^

Apply the date format: Ctrl+Shift+#

Apply the time format with hours, minutes, and AM/PM: Ctrl+Shift+@

Display the Format Cells dialog box with the Number tab selected: Ctrl+1 (the number one)

Display the Format Cells dialog box with the Font tab selected: Ctrl+Shift+F or Ctrl+Shift+P

Entering Values

Enter the current date: Ctrl+;

Enter the current time: Ctrl+Shift+:

Find and Replace

Displays the Find and Replace dialog box with the Find tab selected: Ctrl+F or Shift+F5

Repeat the last find action: Shift+F4

Display the Find and Replace dialog box with the Replace tab selected: Ctrl+H

Formulas

Alternate between displaying cell values and displaying formulas in cells: Ctrl+`

Displays the Insert Function dialog box: Shift+F3

Insert the argument names and parentheses when the insertion point is to the right of a function name in a formula: Ctrl+Shift+A

Cycles through all the various combinations of absolute and relative references when a cell reference is selected while editing a formula: F4

Calculations

Calculate all worksheets in all open workbooks: F9

Calculate only the active worksheet: Shift+F9

Calculate all worksheets in all open workbooks, regardless of whether they have changed since the last calculation: Ctrl+Alt+F9

Recheck dependent formulas and then calculate all cells in all open workbooks, including cells not marked as needing to be calculated: Ctrl+Alt+Shift+F9

Other

Check the spelling in the selected cells: F7

Display the print dialog or tab: Ctrl+P

Close Excel: Alt+F4

Repeat the last command or action: Ctrl+Y or F4

Display the help window or task pane: F1

Toggle Ribbon visibility (Excel 2007 and later only): Ctrl+F1

Switch between Excel and the Visual Basic Environment: Alt+F11

What Is a Simple Way to Compare Two Different Ranges of Data?

Can I compare two separate lists to see if they match?

There is an easy way to compare two different cells, to see if they contain the same value. All you need to do is use the equals sign in a formula between two cell addresses to test if one cell holds the same value as the other cell. Such a formula will produce either TRUE- indicating a match, or FALSE- indicating a difference.

For example, to test if the value in cell A1 is the same as the value in cell B1, entering the following formula in a separate cell, will display the match or difference.

```
=A1=B1
```

Suppose cell A1 holds the word Hello and cell B1 holds the word Goodbye. The formula would return FALSE because the two cells contain different values. If both cells contained Hello or both cells contained Goodbye, or if both cells contained nothing at all, the formula would evaluate to TRUE, telling you both cells hold identical values, or nothing at all.

Here is an example of testing a pair of ranges to see if they match. As you can see, in this example, most ranges do match because TRUE is returned by their formulas, but look closely and you will see a few FALSE returns, because some cells do not contain matching values.

	A	B	C	D	E	F	G	H
G4				f_x =A4=D4				
1	List 1			List 2			Test for matching	
2								
3	Employee	Age		Employee	Age		Employee	Age
4	Sue Flay	40		Sue Flay	40		TRUE	TRUE
5	Brock Lee	23		Brock Lee	47		TRUE	FALSE
6	Carrie Oakey	46		Carrie Oakey	46		TRUE	TRUE
7	Jerry Atrick	33		Jerry Atrick	33		TRUE	TRUE
8	Mike Raffone	31		Mike Raffone	31		TRUE	TRUE
9	Raynor Schein	44		Raynor Schein	35		TRUE	FALSE
10	Sarah Bellum	49		Sarah Bellum	49		TRUE	TRUE
11	Ella Vador	23		Ella Vador	23		TRUE	TRUE
12	Mae O'Nayz	38		Mae B. Soh	38		FALSE	TRUE
13	Brandi Cantor	30		Brandi Cantor	30		TRUE	TRUE
14	Lou Pohl	54		Lou Pohl	54		TRUE	TRUE
15	Paige Turner	41		Paige Turner	41		TRUE	TRUE
16	Penny Nichols	55		Penny Nichols	55		TRUE	TRUE
17	Les Moore	27		Tad Moore	27		FALSE	TRUE

Figure 225 Using a TRUE/FALSE formula to compare cells in two different lists.

What Does the Format Painter Do?

It looks like a little paintbrush in the Home tab.

There are two ways to use the Format Painter. The first method is the one that many people know and is a bit strange to use. The second one works much better.

Say that you have several identically shaped ranges in Excel. You've formatted the first range and need to format the other ranges.

	A	B	C	D	E	F	G
1	Product A				Product D		
2		List Price	Sale Price			List Price	Sale Price
3		$1,295	$1,095			995	850
4							
5	Product B				Product E		
6		List Price	Sale Price			List Price	Sale Price
7		1195	995			995	850
8							
9	Product C						
10		List Price	Sale Price				
11		1095	895				
12							

Figure 226 You want to copy the formatting to the other ranges.

Here is the common Method 1: Select the formatted range. Click the Format Painter. The marching ants appear around the original range.

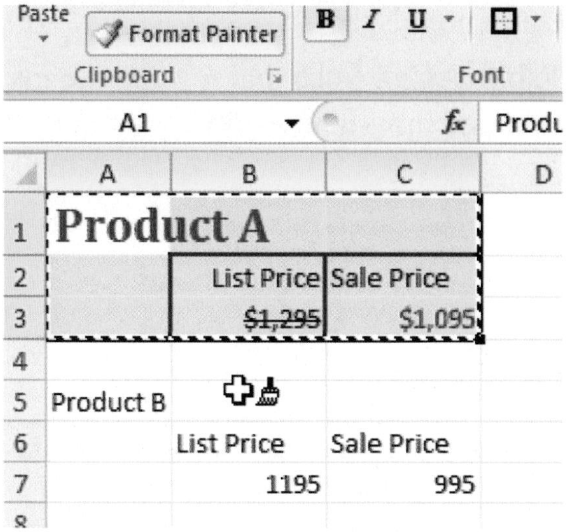

Figure 227 You've copied the formatting from this range.

You now have to immediately select the top-left corner of the next range. Don't accidentally click anywhere else. Don't do any other commands. Don't stop to jot a grocery list out to the right. Use the mouse to select B5. Both ranges are formatted the same.

Double-click the Format Painter to format many ranges

Figure 228 This is easier than re-doing the formatting step-by-step.

That is it. You've pasted the range to one place and you are done. To do the other ranges, you have to repeat everything. I am not sure why this is any better than Paste Special Formats. Well – if you copy the formats from one of more complete columns, Excel will also copy the column widths with the Format Painter, a trick that Paste Special won't do.

Method 2 is a well-kept secret and is easier to use:
1. Select A1:C3.
2. Double-click the Format Painter. You are now in Format Painter mode. You can click the top left corner of each report to format the report.
3. When you are done formatting, either press Esc or click the Format Painter to exit to regular mode.

Caution: Don't forget to press Escape, or you will be painting the format everywhere you click. I forgot to exit the Format Painter mode and accidentally formatted several blank sections before I realized what was going on. Again, to exit this mode, press Escape.

Does Splitting One Worksheet Allow Me to Use One Spreadsheet as Two?

There is a Split command on the View tab of the Ribbon. Can I use that to separate my worksheet? Perhaps I could split the worksheet to put one month on its own worksheet?

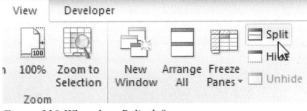

Figure 229 What does Split do?

That would be a really cool feature, but it is not built into Excel. (There is an add-in that will do this and a lot of other useful things that Excel doesn't do. Visit www.Easy-XL.com for a free trial).

Instead, the Split command lets you see the left and right edge of the spreadsheet at the same time. This is great for very wide worksheets where you need to see a total column while you are working on other columns. You can also use the split feature to see the top and bottom of the worksheet at the same time.

In the following figure, a horizontal split near the bottom of the window shows the total row. The top of the window is free to scroll through the rows near the top of the worksheet. (It is also possible to see the bottom row in the top of the window, although that is a little pointless). A vertical split near the right side shows the total in Column O.

	A	B	C	D	E	F	G	H	O
1	**Sales Forecast**								
2									
3	Region	Customer	Jan	Feb	Mar	Apr	May	J	Total
4	East	Bank of America	$0	$0	$0	$0	$0		$25,350
5	West	AT&T	$0	$0	$0	$0	$25,310		$25,310
6	Central	Wal-Mart	$0	$25,140	$0	$0	$0		$25,140
7	West	General Motors	$0	$25,080	$0	$0	$0		$25,080
8	East	Ford	$0	$0	$0	$25,060	$0		$25,060
9	West	CitiGroup	$0	$0	$0	$0	$0		$25,010
10	Central	CitiGroup	$0	$0	$24,430	$0	$0		$24,430
11	East	SBC Communic	$0	$0	$0	$0	$0		$24,420
12	West	Boeing	$0	$0	$0	$0	$0		$24,130
13	West	Wal-Mart	$0	$0	$0	$0	$0		$24,070
14	East	Bank of America	$0	$0	$0	$0	$0	$23,9	$23,990
15	Central	Bank of America	$0	$0	$0	$0	$0		$23,970
567	Total		$530,746	$555,597	$476,495	$539,300	$655,183	$419,3	$6,707,812

Pivot Table

Ready   100%

Figure 230 That's what a split does.

To set up a split, skip the icon in the Ribbon. Look at the bottom of the screen to the right of the horizontal scrollbar. There is a tiny rectangle. Grab this rectangle and drag left to set up a vertical split.

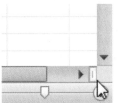

Figure 231 Drag this rectangle to the left to set up a vertical split.

There is a similar rectangle at the top of the vertical scroll bar. Drag this rectangle down to set up a horizontal split.

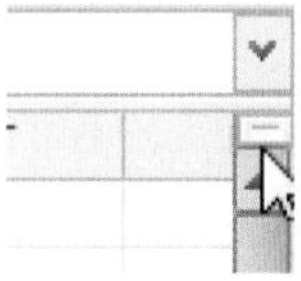

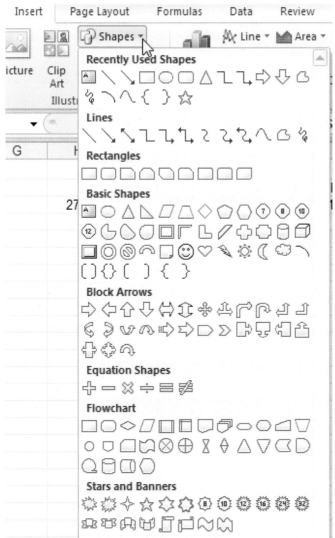

Figure 232 Drag this rectangle down to set up a horizontal split.

Note: Some people love the split feature. I am not a fan because I cannot get the hang of it. To turn off the split, click the Split icon shown in Figure 280.

Why Would I Ever Use the Shapes?

There are a whole bunch of shapes on the Insert tab. Why would I ever use Shapes in Excel?

Figure 233 A gallery of 175 shapes is available in Excel.

Each shape can contain text, so it is possible to use shapes to create eye-catching headlines, such as the starburst or cloud shown below. However, the shape that I find that I use most often is the Curve, in order to create an arrow to show the relationship between one cell that flows to another cell.

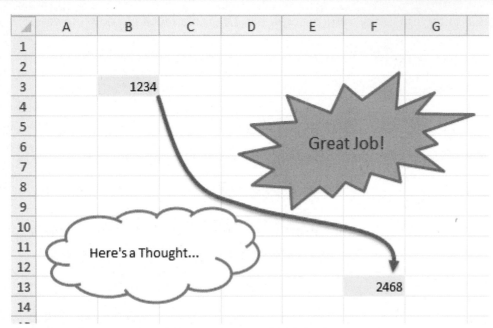

Figure 234 Three examples of what can be created with the shapes.

Here are steps to create the starburst shape shown above:

1. Open the Shapes gallery on the Insert tab. Click on the Starburst.
2. Using the mouse, click near the upper left corner where you want the shape to be. Drag towards the lower right corner. Excel will create a dark blue shape. As long as the shape is selected, you will see the Drawing Tools Format tab in the Ribbon.
3. Open the Shape Styles gallery and choose one of the Orange shapes.
4. Click the Text Box icon on the left side of the Ribbon.
5. Type some text. It will start out as boring black text left and top aligned.
6. After typing the text, press Shift+Home to select all of the text.
7. Back on the Home tab, choose the Middle Align icon and the Center icon to center the text in the shape.
8. Use the Increase Font Size icon several times until the text almost fills the shape. Don't make the text too big. It is common to see the text get truncated once you click away from the shape.

Figure 235 The text initially starts out small and left aligned.

Drawing the curved arrow requires some practice. If you can get away with a straight arrow, it is easy to select the arrow from the Shapes gallery and drag from the start point to the end point. To do a curved arrow, choose the Curve shape from the Shapes gallery. You will click four times as shown in Figure 236 and then double-click at the end.

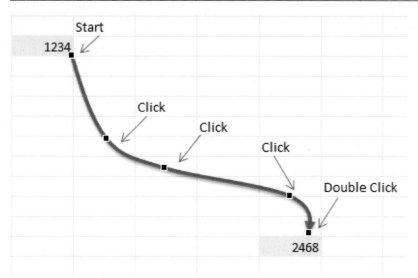

Figure 236 Click at each of the points shown.

After drawing the arrow, use the Shape Styles gallery to choose a different color and thickness. Then, open the Shape Outline menu, select Arrows and choose one of the arrows from the gallery.

If you find that the arrow doesn't follow the correct path, right-click the line and choose Edit Points. You can then drag the inflection points to help shape the curve.

How Can I Click a Cell That Has a Hyperlink, without Following the Link?

I typed something into a cell and Excel automatically made it into a hyperlink. Every time that I click on the cell to select it to get rid of the hyperlink, Excel takes me to the website specified in the hyperlink. How can I select the cell without following the hyperlink?

A quick click on the cell will follow the hyperlink.

Clicking and holding the cell will select the cell without following the hyperlink.

Once you see the pointing hand mouse pointer change to a white plus mouse pointer, you can let go of the mouse button.

	A	B	C	D
1	www.mrexcel.com			
2				
3				
4				

http://www.mrexcel.com/ - Click once to follow. Click and hold to select this cell.

Figure 237 Click the cell and hold the mouse button down to actually select this cell.

Note: To remove a hyperlink, right-click the cell. Choose Remove Hyperlink. This choice is usually near the bottom of the right-click menu. To remove all hyperlinks from a range in Excel 2010 or newer, select the entire range. Select Home, Clear, Remove Hyperlinks. This will remove all of the hyperlinks in the selection, but will not change the formatting. You will have to use the Underline and Font Color dropdowns in the Font group of the Home tab to remove the underline.

Why Is There a Green Triangle in the Top Left of a Cell?

A green triangle is appearing in the top left corner of a cell. What does it mean? How do I get rid of it?

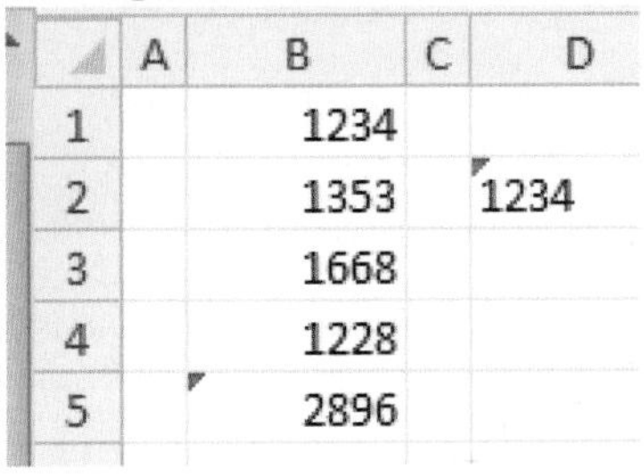

◢	A	B	C	D
1		1234		
2		1353	1234	
3		1668		
4		1228		
5		2896		

Figure 238 What do the green triangles mean?

The green triangle is alerting you to a possible problem with the cell. Before you get rid of the triangle, you should see why Excel thinks the cell is a problem. Select the cell and a tiny diagonal symbol with an exclamation point will appear next to your cell.

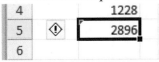

Figure 239 Select the cell with the green triangle.

When you hover over the exclamation point, a tooltip identifies the problem.

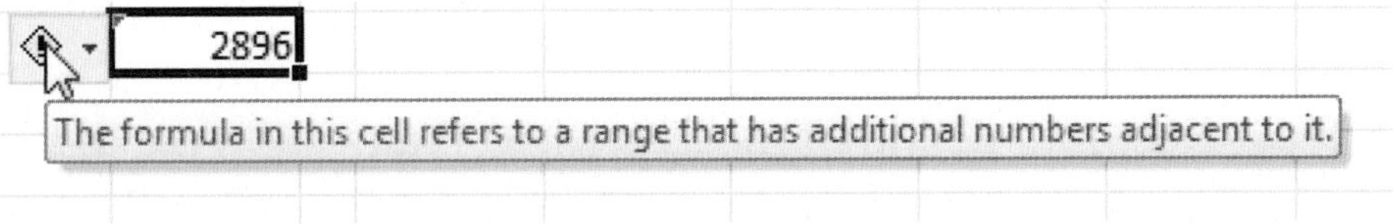

◆ ▾	2896

The formula in this cell refers to a range that has additional numbers adjacent to it.

Figure 240 Hover over the exclamation point to see the problem.

After hovering, open the exclamation point dropdown for some choices that might solve the problem. If you determine that there is not actually a problem, you can choose to ignore the error. This will make the green triangle go away.

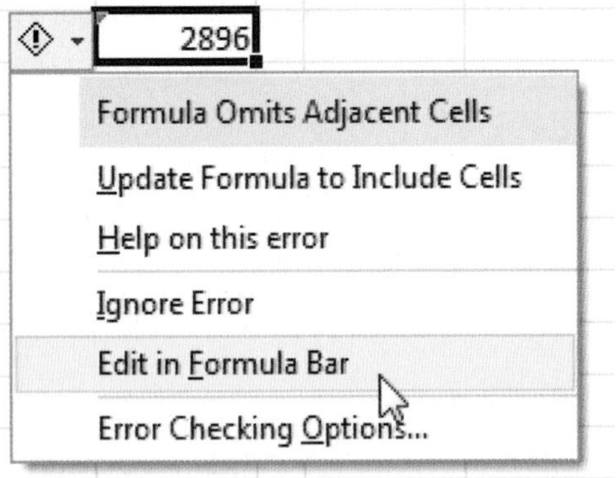

◆ ▾	2896

Formula Omits Adjacent Cells

Update Formula to Include Cells

Help on this error

Ignore Error

Edit in Formula Bar

Error Checking Options...

Figure 241 Ignore the error if you have determined there is not a problem.

The errors that cause the green triangles are of varying levels of seriousness. Any time that you store a number as text (perhaps to keep leading zeroes), you will see a green triangle letting you know that this is a number stored as text. Provided you are not planning on doing math with the numbers, it is fine for them to be stored as text.

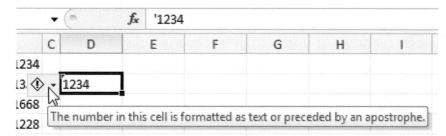

Figure 242 Any number stored as text will be marked with a green triangle.

How Can I Find or Replace an Asterisk or Question Mark on My Worksheet?

Welcome to the world of the wildcard workaround.

If you have not yet heard the term "wildcard" in your Excel travels, now's the time for a quick lesson about wildcards. In Excel, a wildcard is one of two generic characters that are utilized to represent the presence of other characters. There are two wildcard characters in Excel—the question mark "?" and the asterisk "*".

The question mark character is used as a placeholder for any single character. For example, if you want to find either "wall", "will", or "well", you could use the criteria "w?ll". If you wanted to find "stand" or "speed" you could use the criteria "s???d".

The asterisk character is a placeholder for any number of characters. If you want to find "something", "everything", "nothing", or "anything", you could use the criteria "*thing".

When you want to find an actual question mark or asterisk character, because they are wildcard characters you need to place the tilde "~" character in front of the wildcard character you are looking for. In the figure, note how "~?" is entered in the Find dialog box to locate cell A3 in the selected range, which holds the value 456?def.

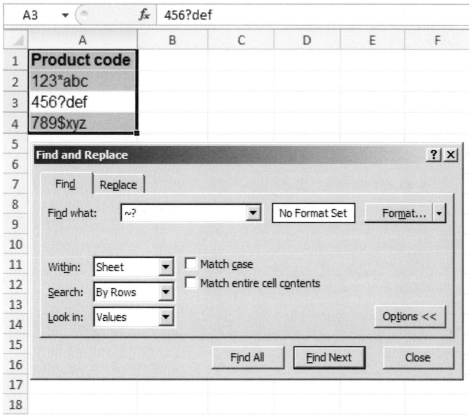

Figure 243 The Find and Replace dialog box, with the tilde character preceding the question mark character.

How Do I Make a Cell Show an Abnormality in a Spreadsheet?

Say that I am logging some quality scores. Any time that a score is below 90, I want to highlight the cell in red.

⊿	A	B	C	D	E	F
1		MON	TUE	WED	THU	FRI
2	Line 1	96	90	90	92	90
3	Line 2	93	95	97	94	88
4	Line 3	90	93	88	98	85
5	Line 4	97	95	94	92	92
6	Line 5	98	98	92	90	87
7	Line 6	88	88	100	97	88
8	Line 7	91	95	88	100	93
9	Line 8	99	96	93	95	97

Figure 244 Automatically mark any scores < 90 in red.

This feature is called conditional formatting. Highlight the range of scores. From the Home tab, choose Conditional Formatting, Highlight Cells Rules, Less Than.

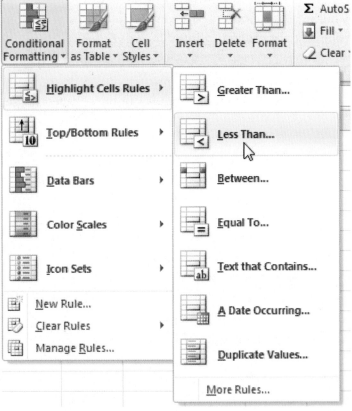

Figure 245 You want to mark any cells less than 90 so choose Less Than.

Enter the limit of 90. Excel offers a dropdown with a lame set of choices. None of these seem dramatic enough to me, so you can click Custom Format and choose a Fill Color and a Font Color.

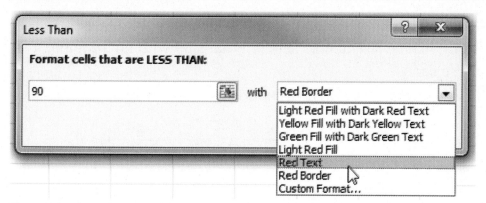

Figure 246 If you don't like this short list of formats, choose Custom Format and then use the Format Cells dialog to specify a format.

The result: any cells below 90 are marked in red.

⊿	A	B	C	D	E	F
1		MON	TUE	WED	THU	FRI
2	Line 1	96	90	90	92	90
3	Line 2	93	95	97	94	88
4	Line 3	90	93	88	98	85
5	Line 4	97	95	94	92	92
6	Line 5	98	98	92	90	87
7	Line 6	88	88	100	97	88
8	Line 7	91	95	88	100	93
9	Line 8	99	96	93	95	97
10						

Figure 247 The bright red formatting calls attention to the problem cells.

Next week, as you key in new data, the red cells will automatically move to highlight the bad ranges.

⊿	A	B	C	D	E	F
1		MON	TUE	WED	THU	FRI
2	Line 1	91	90	91	94	91
3	Line 2	89	90	93	91	93
4	Line 3	90	90	91	90	91
5	Line 4	94	93	89	93	90
6	Line 5	94	93	95	92	93
7	Line 6	95	93	92	89	93
8	Line 7	93	94	94	93	93
9	Line 8	92	93	93	89	90

Figure 248 No one wants to be in red. The quality improved already!

How Do I Undo Conditional Formatting?

I set up some conditional formatting that my manager does not want. How do I keep the formulas, values and other formatting but remove the conditional formatting?

In Excel 2007 or newer, select the range that contains the conditional formatting. On the Home tab, open the Conditional Formatting dropdown. Near the bottom, there is a flyout Clear Cells menu. Select Clear Cells, From Selected Cells.

In Excel 2003 or earlier, use Format, Conditional Formatting. Click Delete and choose which rule(s) to delete.

What Are the Auto-Fill Options?

I know you can drag the fill handle to extend a series. What's up with the little box that pops up near the end of the series?

If you select any of the cells shown in this figure and drag the fill handle, Excel will continue the series.

Figure 249 Drag the fill handle to extend the series.

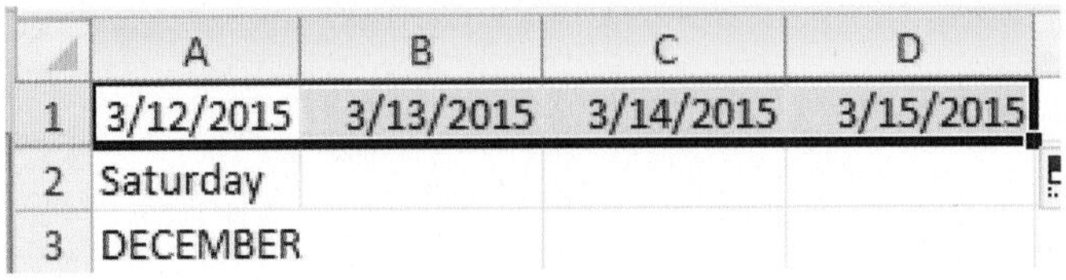

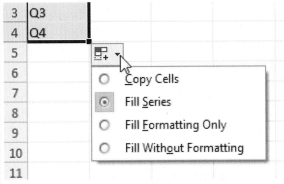

Figure 250 Excel fills the series.

By default, Excel will try to follow your lead. If you started with all caps, they will fill with all caps.

If the cell contains a date or text, Excel will choose to Fill Series. You can override the default by holding the Ctrl key while you drag in order to copy instead of filling.

If the cell contains a single number, Excel will choose to copy instead of filling. You can force Excel to fill by holding down the Ctrl key.

Beyond those choices, Excel offers a little on-grid dropdown that appears just beyond the fill area. Open this dropdown to choose between copying and filling. You can also use this to fill the formatting only or to fill without formatting.

By far, the most choices happen when you drag a date. You have the option to fill days, weekdays, months, or years. The weekdays option fills only Monday through Friday dates.

Figure 251 Open the on-grid dropdown to see more choices.

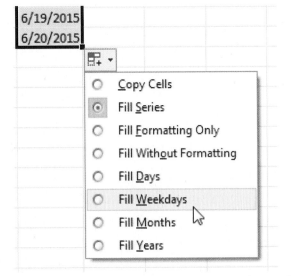

Figure 252 With dates, you can fill the same date each month, each year, or only weekdays.

Note: You can easily access these choices by right-dragging the fill handle. When you let go of the mouse button, Excel will automatically show these options.

Below are examples of filling weekdays, months, and years. Note that I selected a "difficult" choice for months and years and Excel selected dates that made sense.

	A	B	C
1	Fill Weekdays	Fill Months	Fill Years
2	Thursday, January 15, 2015	1/31/2015	2/29/2016
3	Friday, January 16, 2015	2/28/2015	2/28/2017
4	Monday, January 19, 2015	3/31/2015	2/28/2018
5	Tuesday, January 20, 2015	4/30/2015	2/28/2019
6	Wednesday, January 21, 2015	5/31/2015	2/29/2020
7	Thursday, January 22, 2015	6/30/2015	
8	Friday, January 23, 2015	7/31/2015	
9	Monday, January 26, 2015	8/31/2015	
10	Tuesday, January 27, 2015	9/30/2015	
11	Wednesday, January 28, 2015	10/31/2015	
12	Thursday, January 29, 2015	11/30/2015	

Figure 253 Fill months in B fills the last day of the month.

Most people are frustrated that Excel doesn't seem to fill numbers automatically. Select a 1 and drag the fill handle and Excel gives you 1, 1, 1, 1. The trick is either to hold down the Ctrl key while dragging, or select the 1 and the blank cell next to the 1. Alternatively, you can type the 1 and the 2, select them both, and then drag the fill handle. This last trick is a great trick when you want to fill some series other than 1, 2, 3.

> Ctrl+Drag 1 to get 1, 2, 3
>
> –Dr. Fill

	A	B	C	D	E	F	G	H	I
1	Regular		With Ctrl		Selecting Adjacent Also			Selecting First Two	
2	1		1		1			5	
3	1		2		2			10	
4	1		3		3			15	
5	1		4		4			20	
6								25	
7									

Figure 254 Various ways to make a 1 fill to 1, 2, 3.

Figure 255 shows the results of dragging the fill handle from the first cell in the column to the right. Note the last row - this is the only way to show quarters and years and have them fill.

3/12/2015	3/13/2015	3/14/2015	3/15/2015	3/16/2015
Saturday	Sunday	Monday	Tuesday	Wednesday
DECEMBER	JANUARY	FEBRUARY	MARCH	APRIL
JUN	JUL	AUG	SEP	OCT
SAT	SUN	MON	TUE	WED
4th Quarter	1st Quarter	2nd Quarter	3rd Quarte	4th Quarter
Room 101	Room 102	Room 103	Room 104	Room 105
Q415	Q116	Q216	Q316	Q416

Figure 255 Examples of using the fill handle to drag from first column across.

How Can I Hide Some Columns?

I used a couple of columns that are needed for the calculation but do not need to be in the printed report. Although my data goes from A:H, I do not need to print columns D, E, or F. How can I print the worksheet but not those columns?

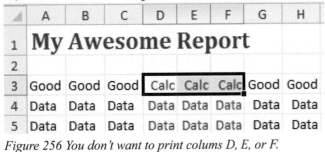

Figure 256 You don't want to print colums D, E, or F.

The best way to do this is to hide the columns. This will prevent them from being printed. Follow these steps:

1. Select one or more cells in columns D, E, and F. For example, select D3:F3.
2. There is a Format dropdown menu near the right side of the Excel 2010 Home tab. Select Format, Hide and Unhide, Hide Columns.

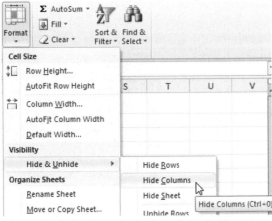

Figure 257 Choose to Hide the selected columns.

You can easily see that there are some hidden columns because the column letters skip from C to G.

	A	B	C	G	H	I
1	**My Awesome Report**					
2						
3	Good	Good	Good	Good	Good	
4	Data	Data	Data	Data	Data	
5	Data	Data	Data	Data	Data	
6	Data	Data	Data	Data	Data	

Figure 258 Columns D, E, F are still there, but are not visible and will not print.

Caution: If you send the workbook to someone else, they can easily unhide the columns. Don't forget that the hidden columns are there. Your nosy co-workers will often unhide the hidden columns to see what kind of data is in there. If you don't want anyone see what is in the columns, create a PDF of the worksheet and send the PDF. See File, Save and Send, Create PDF, Create PDF.

How Do I Unhide the Columns?

After hiding columns D:F, I need to unhide all of the columns. How do I get those columns back so I can see them again?

Select columns C through G. Use Home, Format, Hide & Unhide, Unhide Columns. To select the columns, click on the C column heading and drag the mouse over to the G column heading. The tooltip should indicate that you've selected "5C" which is shorthand for "5 columns".

Note: What if you've hidden columns A, B, and C? How can you unhide those? Click on the D column heading and slide the mouse to the left. The tooltip will indicate that you've selected four columns.

How Do I Unhide One Column but Not the Others?

I've hidden columns D:F and need to unhide only column D. Is there a way to only unhide that column? I could unhide all three columns and then re-hide the two that I don't need to be visible, but this seems crazy.

Yes – there is a cool trick to solve this. Although column D is hidden, you can use the Go To dialog to select a cell in the hidden column D before running the Unhide Column command. Follow these steps:

1. Press F5 or Ctrl+G to display the Go To dialog.
2. Type a cell address anywhere in the column that you want to unhide and click OK. You can now see in the name box that you've selected a cell in the hidden column. The Formula Bar will also show the text or formula in that cell.
3. Select Home, Format, Hide & Unhide, Unhide Columns. Only column D will be unhidden.

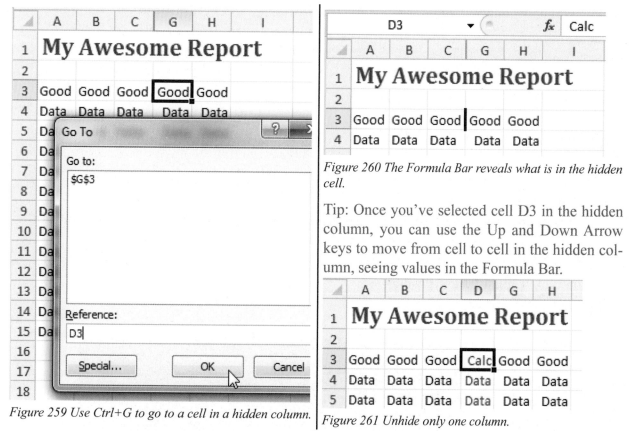

Figure 259 Use Ctrl+G to go to a cell in a hidden column.

Figure 260 The Formula Bar reveals what is in the hidden cell.

Tip: Once you've selected cell D3 in the hidden column, you can use the Up and Down Arrow keys to move from cell to cell in the hidden column, seeing values in the Formula Bar.

Figure 261 Unhide only one column.

How Can I Delete Rows with Blank Cells?

I have a range of data, and I need to delete rows where cells in a column are blank.

Sooner or later you'll encounter a range of data containing blank cells that are not supposed to be there. It won't be your fault. It can happen when data is downloaded from other programs into Excel, or when someone entered the original data in a less-than-perfect fashion.

Depending on the situation, these blank cells might mean that the row they are on should be deleted. You'll need a fast and easy way to handle the task, especially when the range of data is thousands of rows deep and there might be hundreds of blank cells to identify for row deletion. The following figure is a before-and-after example of what you have and what you want:

	A	B	C
1	Name	Birth Date	Position
2	Sue Flay	Oct 09 1958	Manager
3	Brock Lee	Mar 30 1962	Sales
4			
5	Carrie Oakey	Aug 23 1965	Support
6	Jerry Atrick	Apr 18 1971	Analyst
7	Mike Raffone	Jul 01 1982	Sales
8			
9	Raynor Schein	May 09 1980	Admin
10	Sarah Bellum	Jul 09 1963	Sales
11	Ella Vador	Nov 24 1977	Support
12	Mae O'Nayz	Sep 03 1988	Analyst
13			
14	Brandi Cantor	Apr 05 1983	Admin
15	Lou Pohl	Sep 15 1979	Manager
16			
17	Paige Turner	Jun 15 1983	Analyst
18	Penny Nichols	Feb 03 1980	Admin
19	Tad Moore	Oct 01 1986	Manager

	A	B	C
1	Name	Birth Date	Position
2	Sue Flay	Oct 09 1958	Manager
3	Brock Lee	Mar 30 1962	Sales
4	Carrie Oakey	Aug 23 1965	Support
5	Jerry Atrick	Apr 18 1971	Analyst
6	Mike Raffone	Jul 01 1982	Sales
7	Raynor Schein	May 09 1980	Admin
8	Sarah Bellum	Jul 09 1963	Sales
9	Ella Vador	Nov 24 1977	Support
10	Mae O'Nayz	Sep 03 1988	Analyst
11	Brandi Cantor	Apr 05 1983	Admin
12	Lou Pohl	Sep 15 1979	Manager
13	Paige Turner	Jun 15 1983	Analyst
14	Penny Nichols	Feb 03 1980	Admin
15	Tad Moore	Oct 01 1986	Manager
16			
17			
18			
19			

Figure 262 You are faced with blank cells in a column whose rows need to be deleted.

Follow these three easy steps to make this happen:

1. Select the column header for the column holding the blank cells, and hit the F5 key on your keyboard. In this next figure, column A is selected.

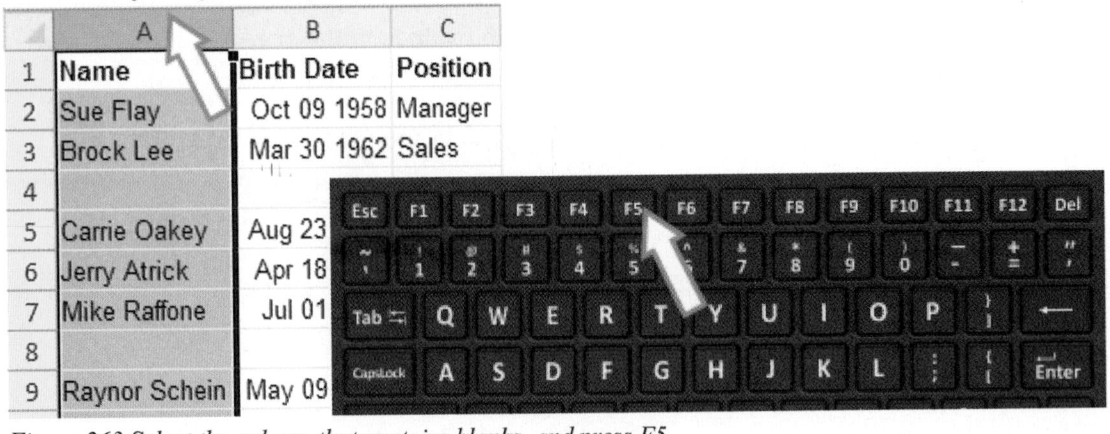

Figure 263 Select the column that contains blanks, and press F5.

2. You will see the Go To dialog box. Click the Special button. Next, select the option for Blanks and click OK.

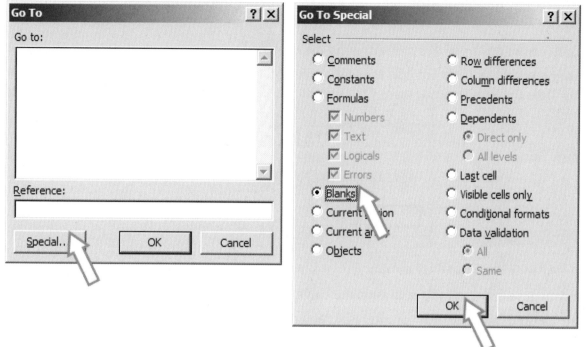

Figure 264 Click the Special button of the Go To dialog box, then select Blanks and click OK.

3. On your keyboard, press the Ctrl and minus (or hyphen) keys as shown in the next figure. This will show the Delete dialog box. Select the option for "Entire row" and click OK.

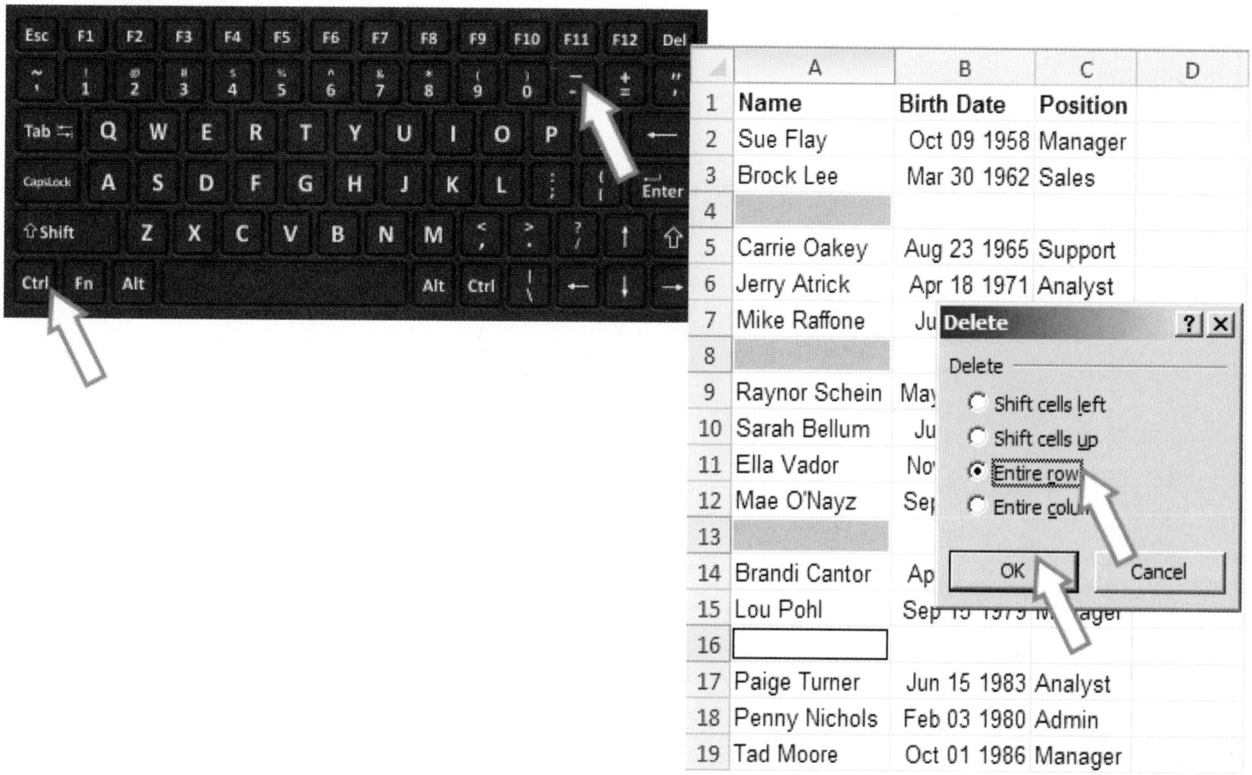

Figure 265 Press the Ctrl and minus (or hyphen), then select for Entire row and click OK.

I Need to Increase All Numbers in a Particular Column by 5?

Can I add 5 (or some other arbitrary number) to every number in a range without editing each number?

There is a clever way to solve this problem using the clipboard.

The first thing you have to do is to get the number 5 on the clipboard. Go to any blank cell in your worksheet. Type the number 5 and press Ctrl+Enter to accept the entry. Type Ctrl+C to copy the 5 to the clipboard.

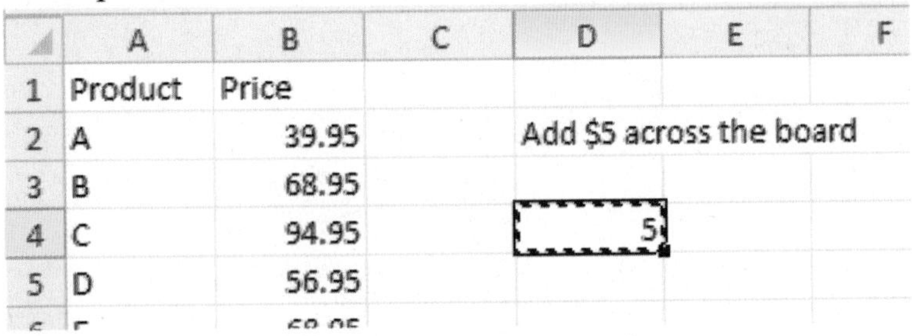

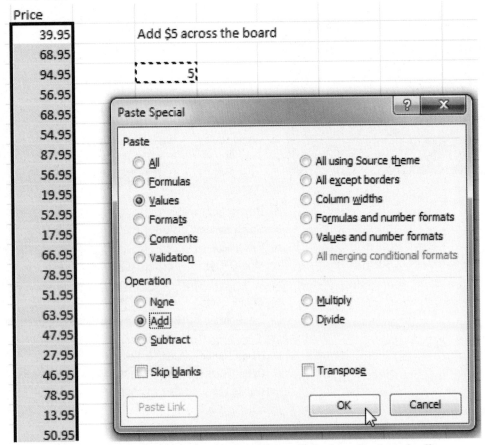

Figure 266 Put 5 in a blank cell and copy that cell.

Although you generally can't see what is on the clipboard, there is a 5 sitting on the clipboard.

Select your range of numbers that have to be increased.

Type Alt+E followed by S. Or, open the Paste Dropdown and choose Paste Special… from the bottom of the menu.

In the Paste Special dialog, choose Values from the first section and Add from the second section. Click OK.

Figure 267 Use the Add operation in Paste Special to add the 5 to all selected cells.

Excel will add five to each number in the selection.

	A	B
1	Product	Price
2	A	44.95
3	B	73.95
4	C	99.95
5	D	61.95
6	E	73.95
7	F	59.95

Figure 268 Excel added the 5 to each cell.

Tip: While the "Add" selection is the important one here, I also use Values to make sure that the general formatting from the cell that contains the 5 does not overwrite any special formatting or borders in the area where you are adding the 5.

Note: Although you generally never see what is on the clipboard, there is a way to display the clipboard. On the Home tab, click the dialog launcher in the Clipboard group.

How Do I Set the Same Page Setup for All Sheets in My Workbook?

I have twelve similar worksheets in the workbook. Do I have to set the Page Setup settings twelve times?

The solution is powerful, works for everything but the print range and print titles, but is very dangerous if you forget to reset the setting when you are done.

Powerful, but Dangerous: Group Mode.

Right-click any sheet tab. In the menu that appears, choose Select All Sheets. You have now put the workbook in Group mode. Any change that you make to the visible sheet will be made to all worksheets in the workbook. This includes typing data on the visible sheet and editing cells on the visible sheet. If you accidentally edit a number on the January worksheet while the workbook is in Group Mode, you just overwrote that cell in all of the other worksheets in the workbook.

Forget to exit Group Mode and you will quickly destroy data on the non-active worksheets

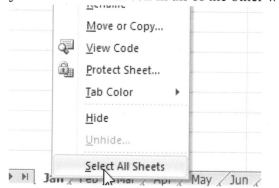

Figure 269 Selecting all worksheets puts the workbook in Group Mode.

While the workbook is in Group Mode, change anything in the Page Layout tab. Those changes will be made to all worksheets. Note that the icons for Print Area and Background are greyed out. You cannot change those settings in Group Mode. The icon for Print Titles is not greyed out, but it should be. When you click Print Titles, you are taken to the Page Setup dialog, and the settings for Rows to Repeat at Top and Columns to Repeat at Left are greyed out.

Caution: You need to remember to exit Group Mode as soon as you finish adjusting the page setup. Right-click any worksheet tab and choose Ungroup Sheets. If you forget, and start working in the visible worksheet, you will be destroying data on the other worksheets in the workbook.

Select All Sheets

Ungroup Sheets

Figure 270 Don't forget to exit group mode.

What Are Cell Comments and When Should I Use Them?

How can I use cell comments to make me more efficient?

An Excel worksheet has 17 billion cells where you can store a number or some text. Each cell is allowed to have a single note where you can type a comment about the content in the cell. This note might be to remind you of where you found the number, or a note about how the formula works, or a note telling the person who will receive the spreadsheet something about the number.

To add a comment, select the cell and make sure that you are not in Edit mode. Choose Review, New Comment. Alternatively, use Alt+I+M or right-click and choose Add Comment. The comment box will appear. Type text for your comment and then click away from the comment.

Comments do not appear in the cell. Instead, they appear as a red triangle in the top right corner of the cell. To view the comment, hover the mouse over the cell. The comment appears. When you move the mouse away from the cell, the comment is hidden again.

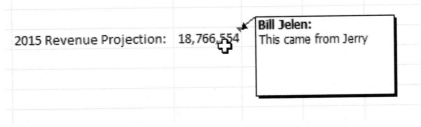

Figure 271 Hover over a cell with a red triangle to see the comment.

Tip: Be cognizant of comment limitations before you start using them. Comments generally do not print so they are good for information that is viewed on screen. You cannot sort by comment, nor can you search the comments. In Word, you can use the Reviewing Ribbon to see only comments made by a certain person. This feature is not available in Excel. Unlike Word, Excel can only have a single comment per cell. If you want to have a conversation in an Excel comment, each person will have to append their comments to the end of the previous comment.

Excel will begin each new comment with the name of the person using the computer in Bold. (To change this name, visit File, Options. At the bottom of the first page of options is a User Name field.) The name in the comment can be cleared out by backspacing through the name. Once you backspace through the name, the Bold icon will be turned on in the Home tab. Turn it off with Ctrl+B to go back to regular font.

You can change some font options while typing a comment. You can switch to Bold, Italic, or Underline for a word and then turn it back off. (Use Ctrl+B, Ctrl+I or Ctrl+U respectively). You can make the font larger for a few words or change the font name mid-comment. You can apply strikethrough to a word by selecting the word and pressing Ctrl+5. You cannot change the font color of individual words while typing, but you can change the font color and background color of the entire comment.

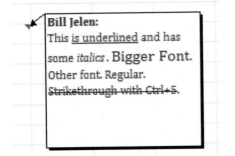

Figure 272 You can apply some simple formatting as you are originally typing the comment.

It is easy to apply formatting to a comment while you are typing the comment the first time. You might want to return to the editing mode later. If you need to change the formatting later, right-click the cell containing the comment and choose Edit Comment.

There is a frustrating distinction when editing the text in a comment or the entire comment. When a comment is selected, it will be surrounded by either diagonal lines or a series of dots. When you see diagonal lines, you are editing the text in a comment. If you were to press Ctrl+1 (the number one) while editing the text of a comment, you would get a Format Cells dialog with a single tab. This tab lets you change font characteristics, but not the fill color and many other comment settings. To get to the better Format dialog box, you need to return to the comment. With your mouse, carefully click on the diagonal lines surrounding the comment. This will change the diagonal lines to dots. Press Ctrl+1 (the number one) and you will have access to tabs for Alignment, Colors, Size, Protection, Properties, Margins and Alternative Text.

To delete a comment, right-click on the cell and choose Delete Comment.

Can I Resize a Comment?

If I type too much in a comment, the text will scroll beyond the size of the comment. But then when I hover over the cell to display the comment, I cannot see the text that extended below the bottom of the comment.

Comments start out large enough to display five short lines of text. If you see that you've typed too much in a comment, you should resize the comment. You can do this as soon as you finish typing the comment, while the comment is still in edit mode. Using the mouse, click on the bottom right resize handle and drag to make the comment taller and/or wider. The size that you make the comment when you are editing the comment is the size that the comment will appear when you hover over the cell.

Use Visible Comments to Guide the Person Using Your Worksheet

It is possible to make one comment or all comments permanently visible. This means that you will see the comment even when you aren't hovering above the cell. Since comments generally don't print, the comments are a good place to provide guidance for the person filling out a worksheet that you designed. The comments will appear on the screen as they type, but they will not print.

To show all comments, use the Show All Comments command on the Review tab of the Ribbon. This will show all comments. If there are a couple of comments that you want to then hide, select the cell containing that comment and choose Show/Hide Comment.

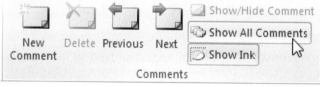

Figure 273 Choose Show All Comments to display all comments.

Once you show all comments, you might realize that some are appearing on top of each other. To move a comment, click the comment, then drag the border to a new location.

Tip: I've seen a few worksheets where the worksheet designer used color in the comments. People in Marketing were supposed to pay attention to the blue comments. People in Sales should use the yellow comments, and so on. To change the color of a comment, edit the comment, click on the diagonal lines surrounding the comment to change them to dots. Then use Ctrl+1 (the number one) and the Colors and Lines tab in the Format Comment dialog. The Color: dropdown in the Fill section will change the background color of the comments.

Can I Change the Default Color of All Future Comments?

Yes, but don't. The settings are not in Excel. You have to change some settings in the control panel for the computer. Changing the setting for the comment color will also change the colors of tool tips and many other Windows elements. I did this once and hated how this change (designed to change the comment) ended up rippling throughout my copy of Windows. It also seemed that I could never get back to the right tooltip color. Trust me, it is not worth it.

Track Changes - What Does It Do, What Does It Not Do?

How useful is Track Changes REALLY?

While the Track Changes feature is great in Word, you should consider it practically non-existent in Excel.

In order to track changes, you have to create a Shared Workbook. When you share a workbook, Excel turns off dozens of features, including common tasks like inserting a row. If you need to truly share a workbook, save it the SkyDrive and access it with the Excel Web App.

> Track changes is very limited in Excel, particularly because of the functionality that you lose when you share the workbook

You can use track changes to log details about workbook changes every time you save a workbook, but be aware of what is not recorded.

Track changes helps you keep abreast of changes made to a shared workbook. You can see the changes that were made directly on the worksheet or on a separate history worksheet.

You can highlight changes such as new data entry, data deletions, edits, or row and column insertions. You can also approve or reject changes that were made by others.

There are some actions that track changes does not monitor and hence does not record. Examples include:

- Changed sheet names.
- Inserted or deleted worksheets.
- Formatted cells or data.
- Hiding or un-hiding of rows or columns.
- Additional or changed comments.
- Cells that change because a formula calculates a new value.
- Unsaved changes.

There are some features in Excel that are not supported in shared workbooks, hence not recorded for track changes. This is important to note because the only time track changes is used is in a shared workbook. These features include:

- Insert or delete blocks of cells.
- Merge cells or split merged cells.
- Add or change conditional formats.
- Add or change data validation.
- Create or change charts or PivotCharts.
- Insert or change pictures or other objects.
- Insert or change hyperlinks.
- Use drawing tools.
- Assign, change, or remove passwords.
- Protect or unprotect worksheets or the workbook.
- Create, change, or view scenarios.

- Group or outline data.
- Insert automatic subtotals.
- Create data tables.
- Create or change Pivot Tables.
- Write, record, change, view, or assign macros.
- Add or change Microsoft Excel 4.0 dialog sheets.
- Change or delete array formulas.

Caution: Be aware that when you turn off track changes or stop sharing the workbook, all change history is permanently deleted!

Tip: If you really need to see what changed in a workbook, you should consider buying a third-party solution such as those offered by Litera.com.

Can I Require a Password to Open an Excel File?

I want to mark a workbook as private and require a password for someone to open it.

Open the Excel file. In Excel 2010, click on the File menu to open the Backstage view.

There are several choices along the left edge of the window. Make sure Info is selected.

Click the Protect Workbook dropdown and choose Encrypt With Password.

Figure 274 This setting is found in the File menu.

You will have to type the same password twice.

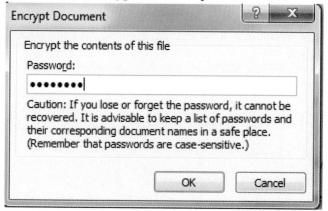

Figure 275 Type the password here and on the next dialog.

Save the workbook. When you go to open the workbook, Excel will ask for the password.

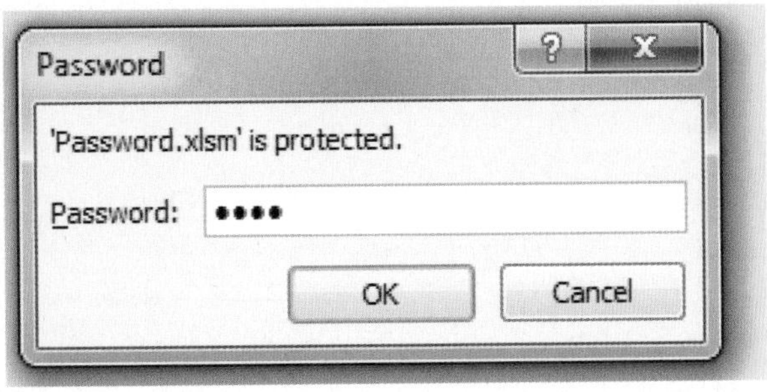

Figure 276 Before you can open the file, you will have to type the password.

If the password is incorrect, Excel will tell you to check your Caps Lock key.

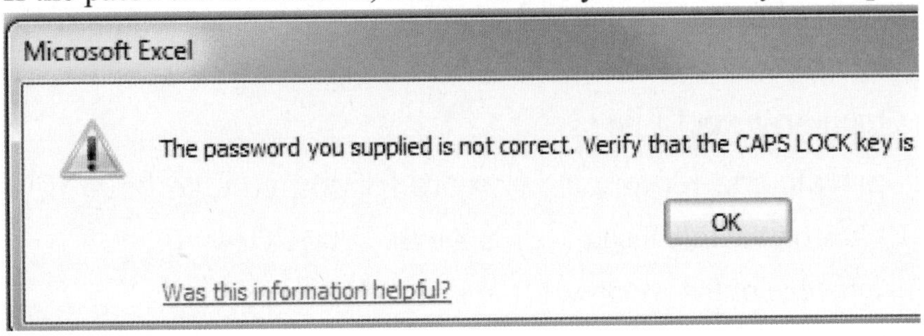

Figure 277 Don't forget the password.

Tip: If you do forget the password, go to your favorite Internet search engine and search for Excel Password. Various security companies offer the ability to recover your password for a fee.

What to Do If I Forgot My Password for a Secured Workbook?

I saved my workbook with a password and now, I cant remember it. What pray tell am I to do?

When you lock your keys in the car, you have to hire a locksmith who has special tools to get you into the car. Upon arriving, that locksmith is going to size you up, to make sure that you aren't trying to steal the car. Similarly, there are services out there that can get you into a locked workbook. Depending on the service, you might have to convince them that you are a legitimate owner of the workbook. To find such a service, search the Internet for Excel Lost Password.

How Do I Make My Workbook Read Only So It Can't Be Changed?

I have a worksheet that I spent a lot of time creating and I want people to use it but I don't want anyone to make changes to it. How do I protect it from changes?

To make a workbook read only so that no one can modify it, you have to use the file manager on your computer (Explorer on Windows) and turn on the file's read-only attribute. On Windows you will right-click on the workbook file and select Properties. You can also select the file and choose Properties from the File menu. Check the Read-only checkbox.

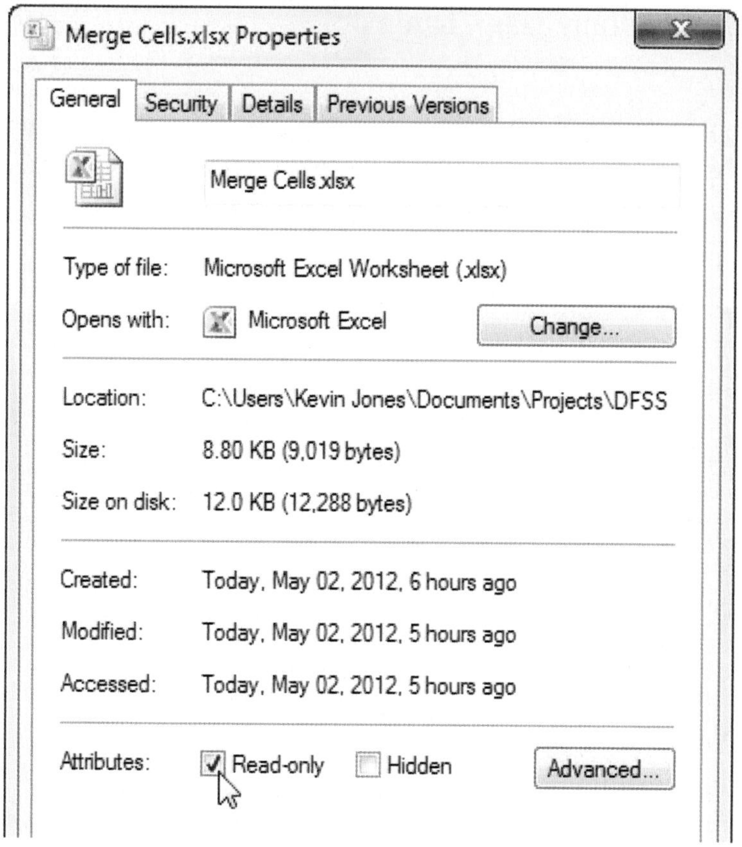

Figure 278 The Windows Properties dialog box.

When this property is set for a workbook, Excel will always open the workbook in read-only mode. You can tell when a workbook is open in read-only mode by looking at the window title for the text "[Read-Only]" at the end of the workbook file name as shown below:

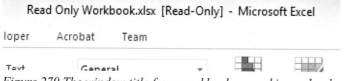

Figure 279 The window title for a workbook opened in read-only mode.

If you try to save the workbook, Excel will display a warning and offer to save the workbook with a different name.

Figure 280 The warning displayed when trying to save a read only workbook.

When working in read-only mode, if you want to save the workbook anyway, you have to save the workbook with a new file name and then, using your file manager, delete the original and rename the new workbook file to the old name.

Note: While you think you might be able to trick Excel into saving the workbook over the old one using the Save As dialog, Excel will prevent you from doing so and will insist that you use a new file name. If you will be making a lot of changes to a workbook currently set to be read-only, you will be best served by turning off the read-only attribute for the workbook file at least while you are making the changes.

Why Does Excel Ask Me to Save When Nothing Has Changed?

Save changes? Save *what* changes?!

Has this ever happened to you? You open a workbook, maybe you look at it but you do not make any changes and you do not even select any cells. You just open the workbook and immediately close it.

That should be the end of the story, right? Except that the workbook does not close -- Excel shows you this message, asking if you want to save your changes.

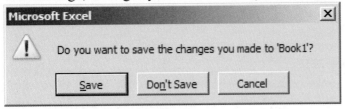

Figure 281 Prompt to save changes.

OK, what gives?

If the workbook was created in any prior version of Excel and you are opening it in any newer version of Excel, you will get this message.

Likely, your workbook contains a volatile function in one of its formulas. A volatile function in a formula makes that cell be always recalculated at each recalculation.

You might wonder what can possibly be recalculating if all you did was open and close your workbook. The most common volatile functions are the TODAY and NOW functions. These functions measure the current time, and especially, the passage of time. In this case, some small amount of time, even a split second or less has passed between when you opened your workbook and when you attempted to close it.

Here is a list of common volatile functions that, if they are present in any formulas in your workbook, may be the reason you see the prompt to save even if you have made no changes.

TODAY, NOW, AREAS, CELL, RAND, INDIRECT, OFFSET, COLUMNS, ROWS, INFO

There are possibilities other than volatile functions causing a prompt to save. They include dynamic named ranges, a chart or Pivot Table that is sourced externally. But the first place to look is at your worksheet formulas for any of the above functions.

What Is a Macro?

I hear my coworkers talking about macros. What is a macro? What would I use one for?

A macro is a way to repeat a set of identical steps. This can be a huge time saver if you have to do the same steps over and over hundreds or thousands of times.

It takes a good intuition to select which tasks should be macro-ized. I often find that if there is a ten-step process to producing a report, there are one or two steps that are tedious and take the longest amount of time. If you can get someone to macro-ize those one or two steps, you might be able to cut the time to produce the report down by 80%.

Say that you have a manual process that takes one minute. It probably would take ten minutes for someone efficient at macros to write a macro for that process. So, if you have to do this three times a year, it does not make sense to do a macro to automate that step. But if you have to do the step 100 times a day every weekday, then investing ten minutes or even an hour to create a macro would be an excellent use of your time.

How do you create macros? The best way at first is to find someone to help. If you work in a medium or large company, there is probably one person up in accounting that is really good at writing macros.

Each company seems to have one person who can knock out macros. Make friends with that person. Take them to lunch. Buy them some maple cream sticks from Krispy Kreme.

What if you work for a small company? Then head out to the MrExcel Message board and post a new topic. Explain what your data looks like and the steps you are manually doing to solve it. Explain that you have to do this hundreds of times a day and that your manager drives you crazy wanting you to do it faster. If it is macro-able, someone there will let you know and will probably even knock out the code if it is something that can be done in ten minutes.

What if you want to create your own macros?

There is a Macro Recorder (View, Macros, Record Macro), but it is very difficult to use correctly. There are several undocumented rules that you must follow to get macros that will work. You could also learn how to write code in Visual Basic for Applications. My LiveLessons Power Macros and VBA DVD-ROM from QUE will explain the undocumented macro recorder rules and help you get started writing your own macros.

What Is an Add-In?

I keep hearing my co-workers talk about add-ins and how useful they are. What is an add-in and where can I get mine?

Excel offers a lot of functionality. But it doesn't offer every bit of functionality. People are always coming up with ideas that would make Excel easier to use. Whenever I encounter a great idea, I pass it along to the project managers on the Excel team. Unfortunately, they have to prioritize what they have time to do for this version. While I might think I have the greatest idea ever, there might be better ideas that get in and my idea isn't included. Microsoft provides development tools that let me extend Excel. I can write a program that works with Excel and lets me do things that Excel normally wouldn't do.

I might write this program just for my use.

But, I might feel like this program could help a lot of other people. At that point, if it took me an hour to write, I would probably offer the add-in for free on my site (Mr.Excel.com). However, if I had invested hundreds of hours in developing the add-in, I might ask people to buy the add-in.

There are hundreds of Excel add-ins out there, some free and some for sale.

Can You Set up Data to Auto-Delete after a Certain Amount of Time Has Passed?

I can make my PDF files expire after a certain date. Can I do the same thing with Excel?

Not really. At least not easily.

There are good articles on the web that suggest a lot of ways to force Excel to delete data after a certain date. (For a start, go to Chip Pearson's excellent site: http://www.cpearson.com/Excel/workbooktime-bomb.aspx). However, for these to work, the person has to have macros enabled. Since macros are disabled by default, the scheme won't work for most people.

The next step is a macro to keep the data hidden until someone enables macros. OK – that adds a layer of complexity and is possible, but anyone who knows VBA can defeat it. In fact, anyone who sets their system clock back can defeat it.

You could password-protect the VBA code so no one can see the code. But there are plenty of unscrupulous utilities on the Internet that will hack the password for $39 or so.

At best, you will spend a lot of effort and keep the honest people from seeing the data after the date. If someone really wants to keep the data after the date, they will be able to do so.

I think you misunderstood my question. Deleting the data will actually help me. I will be happy to enable macros if it will prevent me from having to go through and manually choose rows to delete.

Oh. Sorry.

Yes. It is easy to do if you find someone who can write a quick macro for you.

Can Excel Talk?

Yes - Excel can read you the contents of the cells. This feature was probably added to assist in proofing numbers after keying them from paper. As Excel reads the cells that you typed, you can keep your eye on the paper. You can either have Excel repeat the cells as you enter them, or read a selected range.

Excel can speak what you type

To set up the Speech capabilities, right-click the Quick Access Toolbar and choose Customize Quick Access Toolbar. In the left dropdown, choose All Commands. Scroll down to Speak Cells. There are five icons for Speech. Add them all to your Quick Access Toolbar.

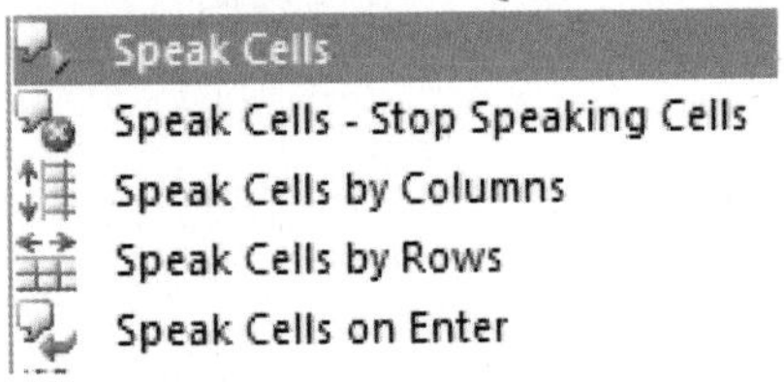

- Speak Cells
- Speak Cells - Stop Speaking Cells
- Speak Cells by Columns
- Speak Cells by Rows
- Speak Cells on Enter

Figure 282 Excel will speak the contents of cells.

Select a range of cells and choose Speak Cells. Excel will read the cells. To have Excel repeat everything that you type, toggle on Speak Cells on Enter. When this gets annoying, click the same icon to toggle off the feature.

Note: The voice you hear is dependent on the operating system. Windows XP featured Microsoft Sam. Vista and newer offers Microsoft Anna. While Sam was choppy and clearly computer generated, the voice for Microsoft Anna is more realistic.

CHAPTER 5 - CHARTS

How Do I Convert My Data into a Chart?

You have a range of data that you want to visually represent in a chart. No problem!

One of Excel's truly remarkable features is its ability to represent data in charts whose quality rivals that of any chart software anywhere. It's easy and free: all chart-making tools come with Excel.

After you have set up your data with header labels and no empty rows or columns inside the range you want to chart, click the Insert tab on the Ribbon and select your desired chart type. For example, the following figure shows range A3:E6 selected, and on the Insert tab, a Clustered Column type chart is being chosen.

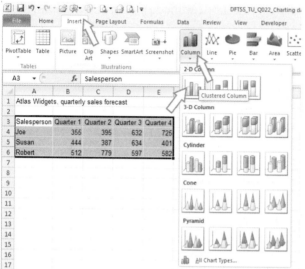

Figure 283 Select your range of data, and choose your chart type from the Chart section of the Insert tab.

Here is an example of how that chart looks on your worksheet after you selected your chart type:

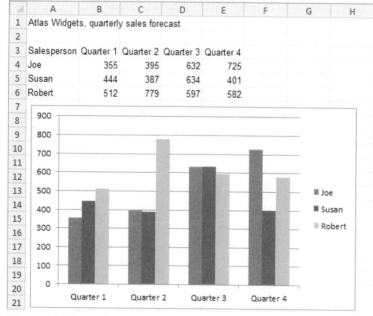

Figure 284 Example of a Clustered Column type chart.

Tip: A really fast way to create a chart and put it on its own sheet, (called a chart sheet) is to select any cell in your data range and press the F11 key. In Excel 2007 or newer, you can create a default chart on the current worksheet using Alt+F1.

How Do I Go about Setting up a Chart and a Table Simultaneously?

I don't want to have to do the work twice.

You have to set up a table in Excel in order to create a chart.

Once you create a chart, you can either:

- Arrange the chart and the data range in the worksheet, or
- Use Chart Tools Layout, Data Table, Show Data Table to add a table below the chart.

Personally, I prefer to place a chart above the data used to create the chart. There are plenty more formatting options for worksheet cells. You can add borders, number formats, colors, cell styles and more.

Excel offers two choices for a table integrated with a chart, either with legend keys or without. But you will find that you do not have much control over the appearance of the table within the chart.

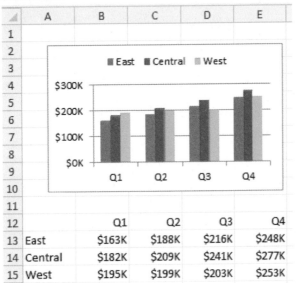

Figure 285 Here is a chart placed above the data used to create the chart.

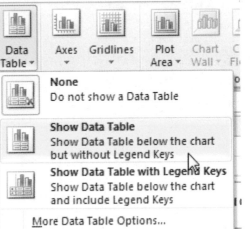

Figure 286 Choose between these options found on the Chart Tools Layout Ribbon.

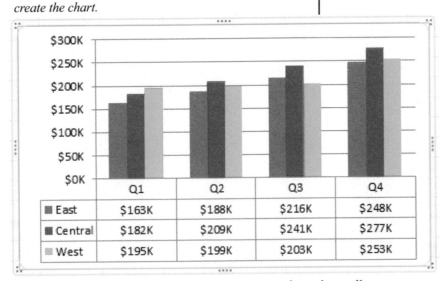

Figure 287 This Integrated Data table incorporates a legend as well.

CHAPTER 6 - FORMULAS II

I Typed 12-13 in a Cell and Excel Changed It to December 13?

My friends twisted my arm to stop doing my budget on a yellow tablet using a calculator and I reluctantly opened Excel to begin re-entering all the stuff on my yellow pad in Excel. The topmost item was a column header that said 12-13 (since it is a budget for 2012-2013). I typed 12-13, pressed Enter, and Excel changed it from 12-13 to 13-Dec! What the heck is this??? That's it. I am done with Excel. If it randomly changes entries, why would I trust it to add a column of numbers. I will keep my yellow pad and my calculator.

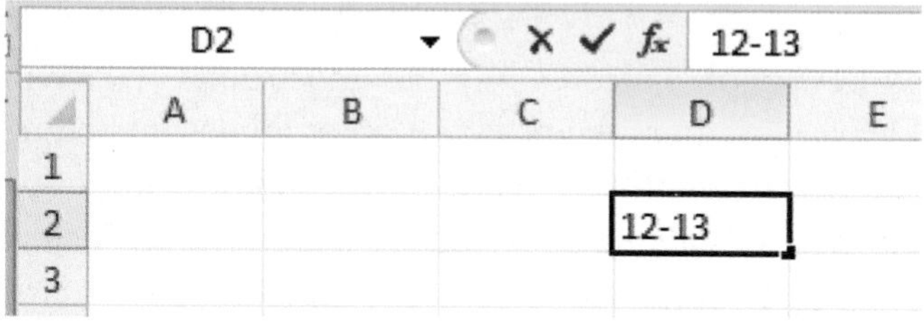

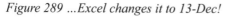

Figure 288 Type 12-13…

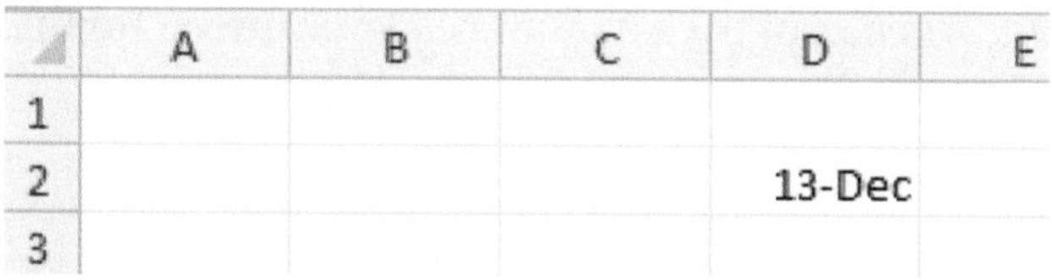

Figure 289 …Excel changes it to 13-Dec!

This was a very unfortunate first experience with Excel. It is, unfortunately, true. To this day, John (his real name) is still using the yellow pad and a calculator because of this one cell.

Had John gone back to the cell he entered and looked in the Formula Bar, he would see that Excel changed his entry to 12/13/2012 (which was December 13 of the current year). Excel is just trying to be helpful… it allows you to enter dates using dozens of shorthand notations. If you are trying to enter a date for the current year, you are not required to enter the year. You could enter 12/13, 12-13, Dec 13, 13 Dec, and Excel would figure that you meant to enter December 13 of the current year

Think about the unfortunate person who has to do a lot of data entry, entering fifty records a day, each with a date. Being able to enter 6/15 instead of 6/15/2015 would save massive amounts of time..

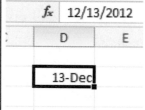

Figure 290 In the Formula Bar at the top of this figure, you can see that Excel is storing 12/13/2012. Dates can be displayed in dozens of different ways. The 13-Dec format just happens to be the one that Excel chooses when you enter a date without a year.

So, you are telling me that it is impossible to put 12-13 in a box and have Excel keep it as 12-13?

No, it is possible. You can use a formatting command to mark a cell or a range of cells as an area that should hold text. When you type 12-13 in a cell marked as text, Excel will keep it as 12-13. But I don't want you to use that formatting command.

The formatting command to specify text is a bit of a hassle and requires a few mouse clicks. Excel is really built to help the people who have to do a lot of text entry. Excel has a shortcut method for marking a cell as text and entering the value all at once. If you want to keep 12-13 displaying as 12-13, simply type an apostrophe before the value. Type '12-13 and press Enter. Excel will display 12-13 in the cell. It will display the apostrophe in the Formula Bar at the top of the worksheet. This lets you know that you or someone used the apostrophe shortcut to tell Excel that this entry should be treated as text.

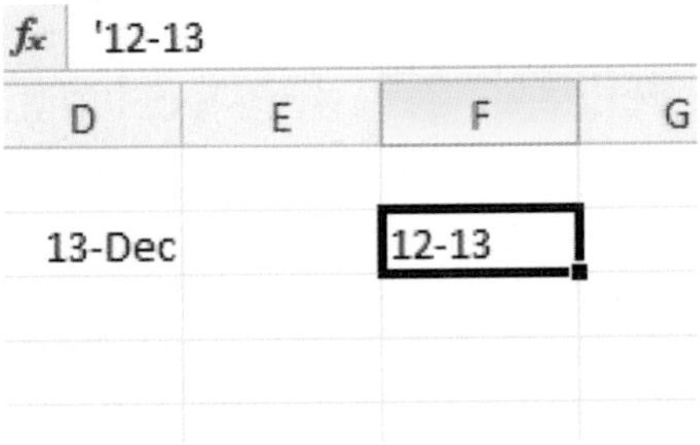

Figure 291 Putting an apostrophe at the beginning of a cell tells Excel not to reformat your entry.

An apostrophe? That is completely unintuitive! How was I supposed to know that?

You weren't. Excel is filled with tiny little arcane keyboard shortcuts like the apostrophe. You will learn some of them by reading this book. You will learn a lot more when a co-worker comes up behind you and watches what you are doing for thirty seconds. They will say, "Hey – did you know there is a faster way to do that?" Expect it. Don't be offended. Don't think the co-worker is a know-it-all. Thank them. That is how all of us learned to use Excel. Frankly, I could take three pages and tell you a bunch of shortcut keys, but it would not sink in. These are best-learned one at a time, as you are painfully doing something the long way. When someone shows you a cool trick and makes your fifteen minute task into a twelve minute task, you are much more likely to remember that shortcut key.

I don't have any co-workers. I am it.

OK – take two minutes each weekday and watch the MrExcel Podcast (posted most mornings to www.YouTube.com/bjele123). You will learn little tips and tricks, a few each day.

What if I want a cell to start with an apostrophe?

Put two apostrophes.

What other things is Excel going to change on the fly?

Many things that look roughly like a date. Many things that look roughly like a time. There is a list of hundreds of common misspellings that Excel will automatically correct for you. To see the complete list, go to Excel and press Alt+T followed by A.

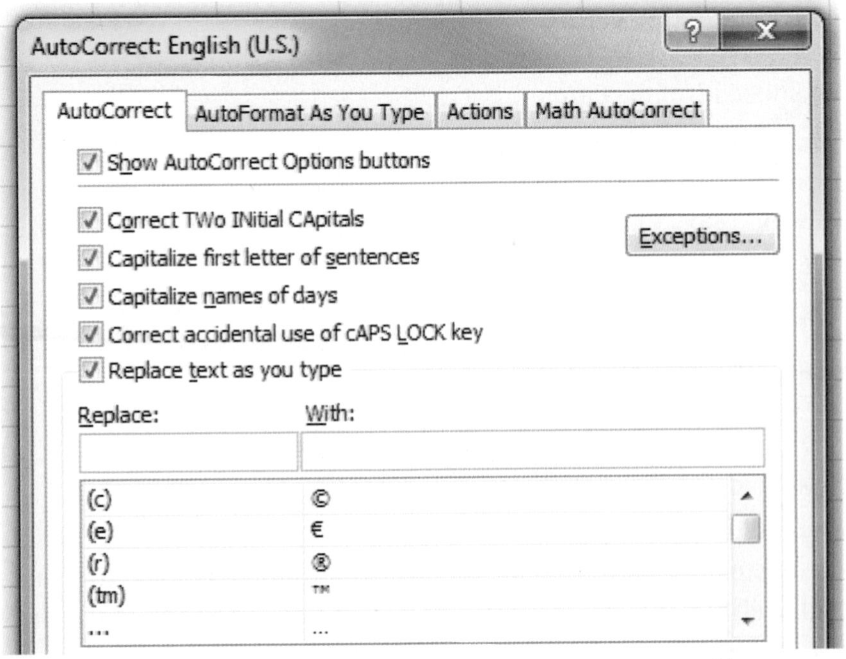

Figure 292 The complete list of AutoCorrect options. You can even add your own.

Alt+T A? Where did you learn that?

It goes way back to Excel 2003 when Alt+T would open the Tools menu and A would choose AutoCorrect Options. Today, the same command is in File, Options, Proofing, AutoCorrect Options. Alt+T A is one of a dozen commands stuck in my head. It is just easier than using the mouse.

If you enter 00123, it will change it to 123. If you enter 123.000, Excel will keep 123. You can always get the extra zeroes to appear using a number format.

OK, I guess I will try Excel one more time to do the budget. Will you show me how to set up the budget worksheet?

Yes. See the next topic.

I Want to Move to Level 3

Show me how to build the budget worksheet that you mentioned in the last topic.

In the Level 2 case study on page 29, you learned how to enter text, use Cell Styles and formatting to set up a simple form. Re-read that section and you should be able to easily build this starting budget worksheet. The only thing new in the report below is that cells A4, A9, and A14 use a cell style called Heading 3.

Case Study 2

Follow the steps to build simple formulas

	A	B	C	D	E	F
1	**Budget Worksheet**					
2						
3			12-13	13-14	% Change	
4	Income	Collections	554123			
5		Grants	100000			
6		Donations	50000			
7		Total				
8						
9	Expenses	Salary	84123			
10		Utilities	85000			
11		Prop Taxes	3500			
12		Total				
13						
14	Net Income					
15						

Figure 293 This is all text and numbers, there are no formulas yet.

Add Totals Using AutoSum

To total each section of the budget, use the AutoSum button. In the image below, select cell C7. On the Formulas tab, choose the big Greek E called a Sigma.

File	Home	Insert	Page Layout	Formulas	Data	Review

Insert Function | AutoSum | Recently Used | Financial | Logical | Text | Date & Time | Lookup & Reference | Math & Trig | Fu

Function Library

C7   *fx*

	A	B	C	D	E
1	**Budget Worksheet**				
2					
3			12-13	13-14	% Change
4	Income	Collections	554123		
5		Grants	100000		
6		Donations	50000		
7		Total			
8					
9	Expenses	Salary	84123		
10		Utilities	85000		
11		Prop Taxes	3500		
12		Total			
13					
14	Net Income				
15					
16					

Figure 294 Go below your numbers and click AutoSum.

Excel proposes a formula. Make sure that the flashing lines are around the data you want to total. Press Enter.

12-13
554123
100000
50000
=SUM(C4:C6)

Figure 295 Make sure this data is the correct range to be totaled.

Excel will insert the total for you, without you ever touching a calculator!

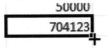

50000
704123

Figure 296 If any numbers above change, this formula will automatically update!

Copy cell C7 and paste to D7. The formula will now total column D income instead of column C.

Use the AutoSum button in C12 to total the Expenses section of the report. Copy C12 to D12.

You now need to calculate Total Income from Total Expenses and put the result in C14. Start in cell C14. Type an equals sign to tell Excel that you are doing a formula.

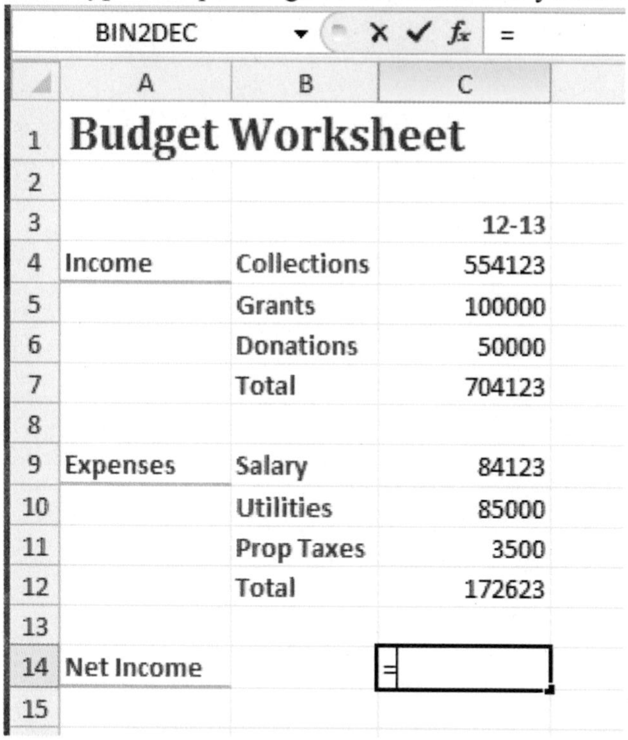

	A	B	C
1	**Budget Worksheet**		
2			
3			12-13
4	Income	Collections	554123
5		Grants	100000
6		Donations	50000
7		Total	704123
8			
9	Expenses	Salary	84123
10		Utilities	85000
11		Prop Taxes	3500
12		Total	172623
13			
14	Net Income		=
15			

Figure 297 All formulas start with an equals sign.

Using the mouse or the arrow keys, select the total income cell C7. The formula now says =C7.

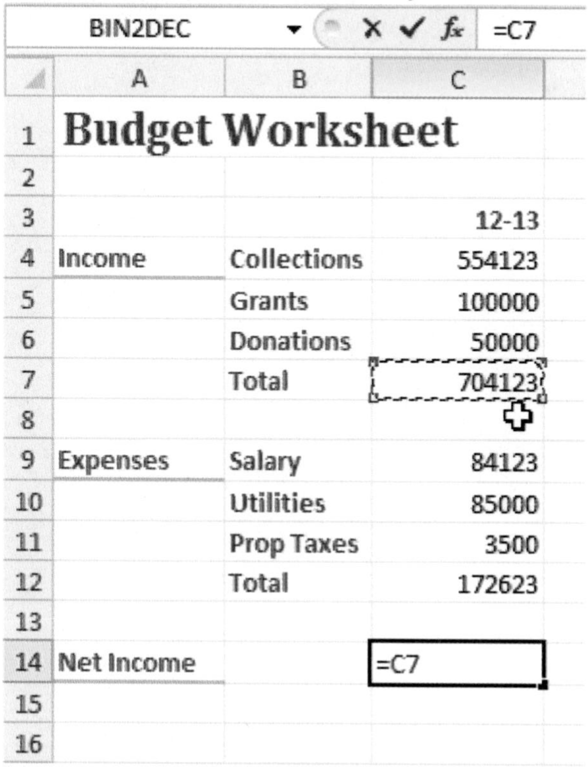

	A	B	C
1	**Budget Worksheet**		
2			
3			12-13
4	Income	Collections	554123
5		Grants	100000
6		Donations	50000
7		Total	704123
8			
9	Expenses	Salary	84123
10		Utilities	85000
11		Prop Taxes	3500
12		Total	172623
13			
14	Net Income		=C7
15			
16			

Figure 298 The Formula now says =C7.

Type a minus sign. The formula now says =C7-.

=C7-

Figure 299 Press the minus button on the keyboard and Excel adds it to the formula.

Using the mouse or arrow keys, click on total Expenses in C12.

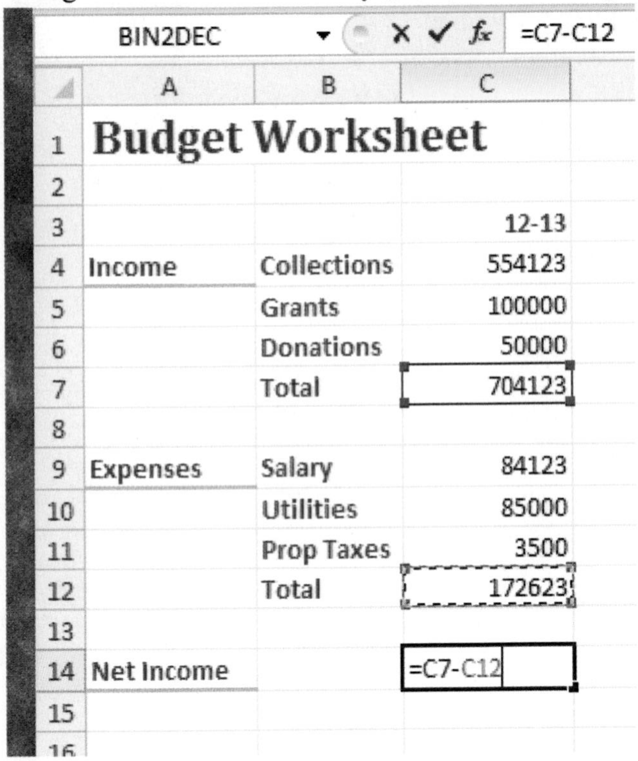

	A	B	C	
	BIN2DEC	▼	× ✓ ƒx	=C7-C12
1	**Budget Worksheet**			
2				
3			12-13	
4	Income	Collections	554123	
5		Grants	100000	
6		Donations	50000	
7		Total	704123	
8				
9	Expenses	Salary	84123	
10		Utilities	85000	
11		Prop Taxes	3500	
12		Total	172623	
13				
14	Net Income		=C7-C12	
15				
16				

Figure 300 Click on the next cell in the formula.

You could build a larger formula by continuing in this fashion. Click an operator (+-*/^&) and then click another cell. You can even click cells in other worksheets and have this formula refer to those other sheets!

When you are done entering the formula, press Enter. Copy C14 to D14.

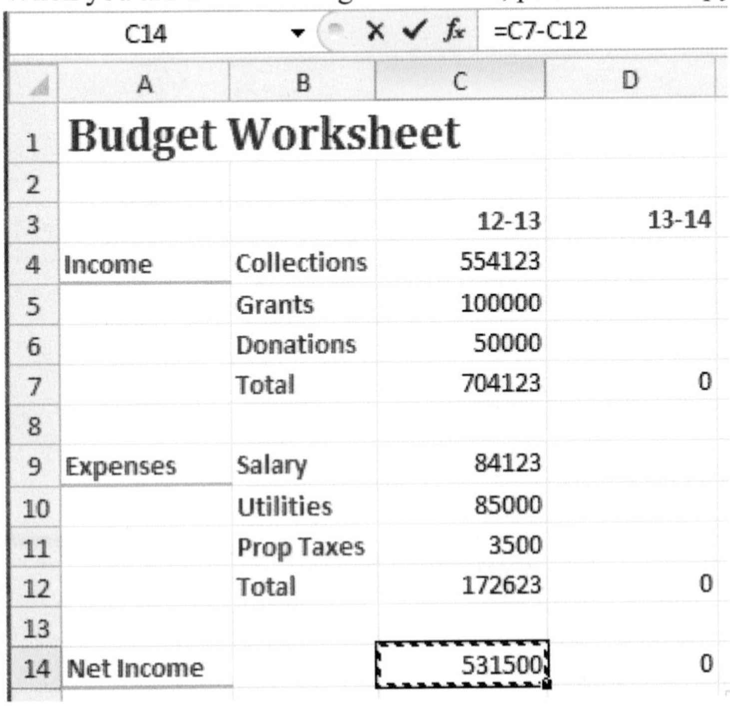

	A	B	C	D
	C14	▼	× ✓ ƒx	=C7-C12
1	**Budget Worksheet**			
2				
3			12-13	13-14
4	Income	Collections	554123	
5		Grants	100000	
6		Donations	50000	
7		Total	704123	0
8				
9	Expenses	Salary	84123	
10		Utilities	85000	
11		Prop Taxes	3500	
12		Total	172623	0
13				
14	Net Income		531500	0

Figure 301 The result of the formula is shown in C14. The formula you built is shown in the Formula Bar at the top of the worksheet.

Go to the first cell of the % Change column. Type an equals sign. Click on D4 and type a divide sign which is the forward slash (/).

	12-13	13-14	% Change
⊕	554123	575000	=D4/
	100000	95000	

*Figure 302 Use / for divide, * for multiply, and ^ for exponents.*

Click on C4. Type -1.

| BIN2DEC | ▼ | ✕ ✓ fx | =D4/C4-1 |

	A	B	C	D	E	F
1	**Budget Worksheet**					
2						
3			12-13	13-14	% Change	
4	Income	Collections	554123	575000	=D4/C4-1	
5		Grants	100000	95000		
6		Donations	50000	10000		

Figure 303 Here is the formula before pressing Enter.

The result of the formula is not formatted as a percentage. It is the right answer, but it looks bad.

L4	% Change
00	0.037675751
00	
00	

Figure 304 Right answer, but wrong format.

Click the % icon and the Increase Decimal icon.

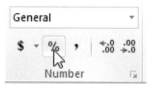

Figure 305 Percentage.

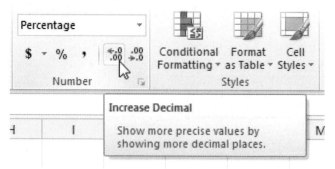

Figure 306 Increase decimal.

You now have a better looking result.

13-14	% Change
575000	-3.8%
95000	
10000	
680000	

Figure 307 The revenue is budgeted to be down 3.8% next year.

That first row looks good with the -3.8%. For lines that went up, the formula and formatting will say something like 5.0% instead of +5%. For budget worksheets, it is nice to show the + for positive variances. Here is how to do it:

Select the cell containing your first formula.

Press Ctrl+1 (the number one) to open the Format Cells dialog.

If it is not selected, choose the Numbers tab from along the top of the dialog.

Choose Custom in the Category list.

The type box currently contains 0.0%. There is a way to specify a different format for positive, negative and zero. Separate each zone with a semi-colon. Type =0.0%;-0.0%;0.0% and click OK.

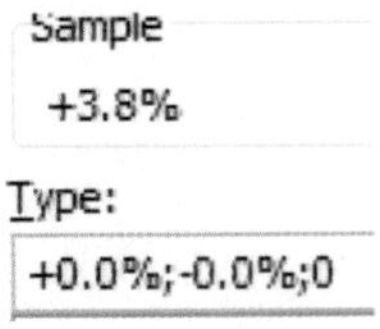

Sample

+3.8%

Type:

+0.0%;-0.0%;0

Figure 308 This is a cool formatting trick – different formats for positive and negative. The third zone is for those items where the change calculation is exactly 0.

Here is another Level 3 trick: get the formula correct and the cell formatted before copying it. Now that cell E4 is correct, copy it and paste to E5:E7. Paste again to E9:E12. Paste again to E14.

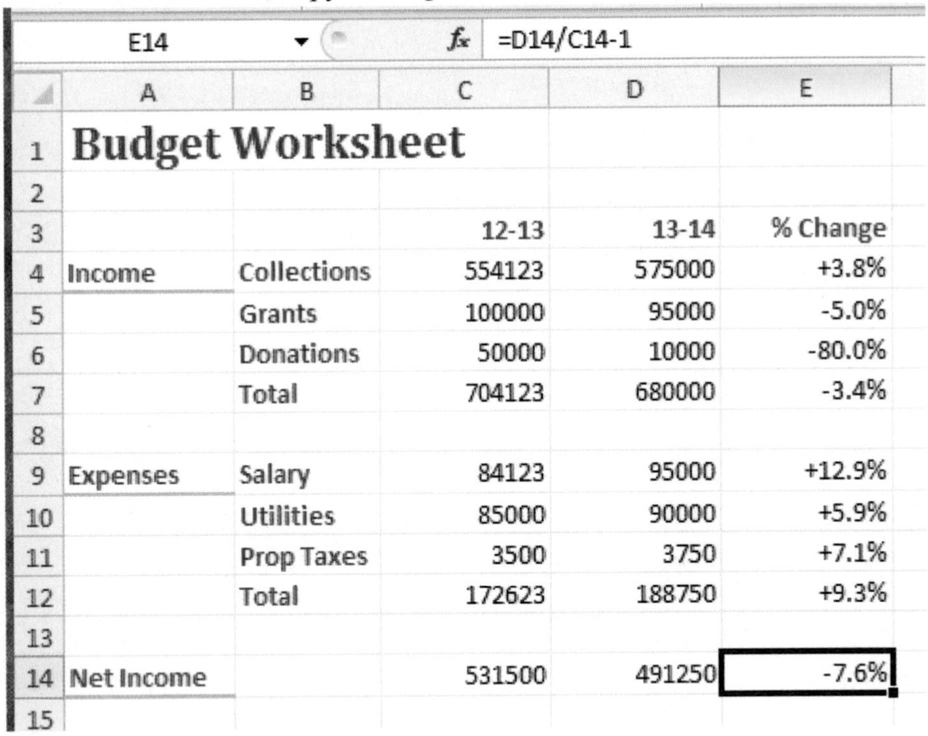

E14			*fx*	=D14/C14-1	
◢	A	B	C	D	E
1	**Budget Worksheet**				
2					
3			12-13	13-14	% Change
4	Income	Collections	554123	575000	+3.8%
5		Grants	100000	95000	-5.0%
6		Donations	50000	10000	-80.0%
7		Total	704123	680000	-3.4%
8					
9	Expenses	Salary	84123	95000	+12.9%
10		Utilities	85000	90000	+5.9%
11		Prop Taxes	3500	3750	+7.1%
12		Total	172623	188750	+9.3%
13					
14	Net Income		531500	491250	-7.6%
15					

Figure 309 A completed budget worksheet.

Tell me again why this is better than using a calculator and a yellow pad?

Say that you decide to change the budget in cell D11.

You can do calculations on the fly. Type =1.1*C11 in the cell and press enter. Excel will calculate a 10% increase for you.

9	Expenses	Salary	84,123	95,000	+12.9%
10		Utilities	85,000	90,000	+5.9%
11		Prop Taxes	3,500	=1.1*C11	+7.1%
12		Total	172,623	188,750	+9.3%
13					
14	Net Income		531,500	491,250	-7.6%

Figure 310 Do calculations in Excel.

Further, all of the other formulas that depend on this cell will automatically update!

◢	A	B	C	D	E
1	**Budget Worksheet**				
2					
3			12-13	13-14	% Change
4	Income	Collections	554,123	575,000	+3.8%
5		Grants	100,000	95,000	-5.0%
6		Donations	50,000	10,000	-80.0%
7		Total	704,123	680,000	-3.4%
8					
9	Expenses	Salary	84,123	95,000	+12.9%
10		Utilities	85,000	90,000	+5.9%
11		Prop Taxes	3,500	3,850	+10.0%
12		Total	172,623	188,850	+9.4%
13					
14	Net Income		531,500	491,150	-7.6%

Figure 311 The totals updated as well.

(For the final case study, see page page 196).

How Can I Make Excel Round Numbers?

I have to increase last year's rates by 3.5%. I keep getting values that have fractions of values. Can I force Excel to round to the nearest penny or dollar?

`=B2*1.035`

◢	A	B	C
1	Product	Rate	New Rate
2	A	216.20	223.767
3	B	368.11	380.9939
4	C	122.26	126.5391
5	D	157.77	163.292
6	E	109.31	113.1359

Figure 312 Force column C to round to two decimal places.

Caution: Although using the Decrease Decimal icon will make it look like column C is rounded, any future formulas that refer to C will be using the non-rounded version of column C.

`=D3*C3`

▲	A	B	C	D	E
1	Product	Rate	New Rate	Units	C*D
2	A	216.20	223.77	100	22376.7
3	B	368.11	380.99	100	38099.385
4	C	122.26	126.54	100	12653.91
5	D	157.77	163.29	100	16329.195
6	E	109.31	113.14	100	11313.585
7	F	149.34	154.57	100	15456.69
8					
9		⁺.₀ .₀₀ Conditional Format Ce			Fixing C with
10		Formatting ▾ as Table ▾ Style Styles			Decrease Decimal may look right
11		Decrease Decimal			but future calcs
12		Show less precise values by showing fewer decimal places.			are wrong!
13					

Figure 313 Using Decrease Decimal appears to work, but future calculations show that Column C is still storing all of the decimals.

The solution is to wrap the column C formula in the ROUND function. You specify any calculation and then the number of decimals. As shown below, the result of:

`=ROUND(B2*A2,2)`

actually rounds to dollars and cents. The formula in E which multiplies C times 100 is producing the correct result.

`=ROUND(B2*1.035,2)`

▲	A	B	C	D	E
1	Product	Rate	New Rate	Units	C*D
2	A	216.20	223.77	100	22377
3	B	368.11	380.99	100	38099
4	C	122.26	126.54	100	12654
5	D	157.77	163.29	100	16329

Figure 314 Using the ROUND function to eliminate any fractional cents.

Tip: To round to the nearest dollar, specify 0 as the second argument in ROUND. To round to the nearest thousand dollars, specify -3 as the second argument in ROUND.

`=ROUND(A9,B9)`

▲	A	B	C
1	Original Number	# Digits	Round
2	123456.454545	4	123456.4545
3	123456.454545	3	123456.455
4	123456.454545	2	123456.45
5	123456.454545	1	123456.5
6	123456.454545	0	123456
7	123456.454545	-1	123460
8	123456.454545	-2	123500
9	123456.454545	-3	123000

Figure 315 Rounding to a negative number of decimal places will round to nearest 10, 100, 1000 and so on.

I Have to Divide This Row by the Mean of All Rows

It is going to be painful to enter the similar formula over and over.

```
=B2/AVERAGE(B2:B11)
```

◢	A	B	C
1	Product	Score	Score vs Average
2	A	67.6	83.3%
3	B	71.8	
4	C	95.7	
5	D	79.4	
6	E	67.3	
7	F	75.3	
8	G	93.6	
9	H	96.7	
10	I	66.7	
11	J	97.1	
12			

Figure 316 You need to enter a similar formula for each row.

If you copy that formula down to the other rows, the B2 in the numerator will change, which is great.

Unfortunately, you want the B2:B11 in the denominator to stay the same as you copy it down. Here is the formula after it has been copied to B3:

```
=B3/AVERAGE(B3:B12)
```

◢	A	B	C	D
1	Product	Score	Score vs Average	
2	A	67.6	83.3%	
3	B	71.8	=B3/AVERAGE(B3:B12)	
4	C	95.7	114.0%	
5	D	79.4	96.5%	
6	E	67.3	81.3%	
7	F	75.3	87.7%	
8	G	93.6	105.7%	
9	H	96.7	111.4%	
10	I	66.7	81.4%	
11	J	97.1	100.0%	
12				
13				

Figure 317 The range in the denominator keeps shifting down.

Tip: Learning the solution to this problem will make you better at Excel than 60% of the population of people using Excel.

Change the formula to:

```
=B2/AVERAGE($B$2:$B$11)
```

Do you see the difference? A reference of B2:B11 is called a relative reference. As you copy the formula, the reference will change. A reference of $B$2:$B$11 is called an "Absolute Reference." When you copy a formula containing this reference, the reference will always point to B2:B11!

```
=B2/AVERAGE($B$2:$B$11)
```

◢	A	B	C
1	Product	Score	Score vs Average
2	A	67.6	83.3%
3	B	71.8	
4	C	95.7	
5	D	79.4	

Figure 318 Add dollar signs to the range in the denominator.

> Understanding when to put $ in your cell references is the single most important concept in using formulas

When you copy this formula, the denominator range will stay constant.

	A	B	C	D
1	Product	Score	Score vs Average	
2	A	67.6	83.3%	
3	B	71.8	88.5%	
4	C	95.7	118.0%	
5	D	79.4	97.9%	
6	E	67.3	83.0%	
7	F	75.3	92.8%	
8	G	93.6	115.4%	
9	H	96.7	119.2%	
10	I	66.7	82.2%	
11	J	97.1	=B11/AVERAGE($B$2:$B$11)	

Figure 319 Even at the bottom of the range, the denominator is still pointing to B2:B11.

Tip: There is a great shortcut for adding the dollar signs. If you use the mouse to select B2:B11, press the F4 key after selecting the range and before typing more of the formula. Excel will add all four dollar signs.

Note: Each dollar sign freezes the column letter or row number that follows the dollar sign. There are situations where you want to freeze only the column $B2 or only the row B$2. My friend Mike Girvin (see ExcelisFun on YouTube) teaches his college students to only use the dollar signs that you need. Mike would say that since you never expect to copy the formula across, you only need two dollar signs: =B2/AVERAGE(B$2:B$11). While Mike is correct, either formula works.

How Can I Run Several Different Versions of a Calculation?

What if I am trying to figure out a formula, but I want to include several different numeral amounts? Is there a way to do that without having to re-enter all of the data?

Excel is great at What-If analysis. While there are all sorts of formal tools like Scenario Manager and Data Table and Goal Seek, you need just good, old-fashioned Excel to run several options.

You've built the perfect model in B3:B7. Copy those cells.

=PMT(B5/12,B4,-B3)

	A	B
1	**Buy a Car!**	
2		
3	Price	12500
4	# Months	48
5	Rate	4%
6		
7	Payment	$282.24

Figure 320 Use the PMT function.

	A	B	C
1	**Buy a Car!**		
2			
3	Price	12500	
4	# Months	48	
5	Rate	4%	
6			
7	Payment	$282.24	
8			

Figure 321 Copy the original model.

Now – select several cells along the top row of your model. In this case, C3:H3.

	A	B	C	D	E	F	G	H
1	**Buy a Car!**							
2								
3	Price	12500						
4	# Months	48						
5	Rate	4%						
6								
7	Payment	$282.24						

Figure 322 Selecting six cells will make six copies of your model for a total of seven.

Press Ctrl+V to paste.

You now have seven copies of the model. In the next figure, I added headings to name each possible choice. You might have a red Chevy in B, financed over 48 months and the same red Chevy in C, financed over 60 months. In each column, change only the relevant numbers that vary for that choice. You will quickly end up with the same calculation for seven different scenarios.

	A	B	C	D	E	F	G	H
1	**Buy a Car!**							
2		Red Chevy	Red Chevy	Blue Ford	Blue Ford	Mustang	Junker	Mom's Car
3	Price	12500	12500	9995	9995	28500	2100	5000
4	# Months	48	60	48	60	72	12	12
5	Rate	4%	4.25%	4%	4.25%	4.5%	8%	0%
6								
7	Payment	$282.24	$231.62	$225.68	$185.20	$452.41	$182.68	$416.67

Figure 323 Car payments for seven different scenarios.

Tip: Here is a cool bonus tip that uses a different kind of conditional formatting. Choose the cells that have the car payment calculation – B7:H7. Select Home, Conditional Formatting, Color Scale. Choose the second icon that has the red on top.

Excel will automatically format the cells from green for low payments to bright red for high payments.

Figure 324 This will help you to visualize the range of car payments.

	A	B	C	D	E	F	G	H
1	**Buy a Car!**							
2		Red Chevy	Red Chevy	Blue Ford	Blue Ford	Mustang	Junker	Mom's Car
3	Price	12500	12500	9995	9995	28500	2100	5000
4	# Months	48	60	48	60	72	12	12
5	Rate	4%	4.25%	4%	4.25%	4.5%	8%	0%
6								
7	Payment	$282.24	$231.62	$225.68	$185.20	$452.41	$182.68	$416.67

Figure 325 No offense, Mom, but your deal is one of the higher payments.

How Can I Strip Away the Left or Right Part of a Cell?

How do I remove unwanted data from a cell and keep only what I want?

There are many times when you'll come across cells that contain a value of some kind, and you'll want another cell to show only a portion of that value. Examples may include:

- A cell contains an Excel file name such as Budget.xlsx and you want only the word Budget in another cell.
- A cell contains a sentence and you want only the first word of that sentence in another cell.
- A cell contains a decimalized number such as 534.26 and you want only the whole number 534 in another cell.

The good news is there are formulas that can easily do the job in these cases. See the next three examples:

Example 1:

In the following figure, cell C2 is selected and contains the value "Budget". You can see in the Formula Bar (above column B) that the formula in cell C2 is:

`=LEFT(A2,LEN(A2)-5)`

This formula looks at what is in cell A2, which at the moment happens to be "Budget.xlsx", and displays all but the five left-most characters of that value. The reason for the number 5 is, in this example you want to show Budget.xlsx (or whatever Excel workbook name happens to be in cell A2) without the last five characters of the extension ".xlsx".

C2 ▼	f_x =LEFT(A2,LEN(A2)-5)	
	A	B	C
1	Original Values	What you want	Formula Solution
2	Budget.xlsx	File name without last 5 characters ".xlsx"	Budget
3	Excel is your friend	First word	Excel
4	534.26	The whole number without the decimal	534

Figure 326 The formula in cell C2 returns whatever is in cell A2 except for the last five characters.

Example 2:

In the next figure, cell C3 is selected and contains the word "Excel". In the Formula Bar is C3 formula, which is:

`=LEFT(A3,FIND(" ",A3)-1)`

This formula may look strange at first, but all it's doing is finding (with the FIND function) the first space (that is what " " means) in cell A3, and displaying everything to the left of that, using the LEFT function.

Note: The "-1" part of the formula simply addresses the fact that you probably want just the first word of what's in cell A3 (Excel in this case), and not the first word and the first spacebar character that comes after Excel.

C3 ▼	f_x =LEFT(A3,FIND(" ",A3)-1)	
	A	B	C
1	Original Values	What you want	Formula Solution
2	Budget.xlsx	File name without last 5 characters ".xlsx"	Budget
3	Excel is your friend	First word	Excel
4	534.26	The whole number without the decimal	534

Figure 327 The formula in cell C3 returns the first word from cell A3.

Example 3:

In this last example, the decimalized number 534.26 is in cell A4. Cell C4 displays 534 which is returned by the formula:

```
=INT(A4)
```

The INT function returns just the whole integer portion of a number, without the decimal portion if there is one.

C4	▼	f_x	=INT(A4)	

	A	B	C
1	**Original Values**	**What you want**	**Formula Solution**
2	Budget.xlsx	File name without last 5 characters ".xlsx"	Budget
3	Excel is your friend	First word	Excel
4	534.26	The whole number without the decimal	534

Figure 328 The formula in cell C4 uses the INT function to give you the whole integer portion of a decimalized number.

How Can I Separate People's First and Last Names?

From a list of people's first and last names in a cell, I need to put the first name in one cell and the last name in another cell.

When a list of people's names is created, such as for a company's names of its employees, the best method from the get-go is to enter the last name in one column and the first name in another column. Unfortunately, you might inherit a list where first names and last names are all in one cell, and you need to put the last names in one column and the first names in another column.

In the next figure, a before-and-after comparison shows the original list on the left, and the result you want on the right. There could be thousands of cells in column A that need their first and last names separated, so you will need a quick and easy way to get this done.

	A	B
1	**Name**	
2	Sue Flay	
3	Brock Lee	
4	Carrie Oakey	
5	Jerry Atrick	
6	Mike Raffone	
7	Raynor Schein	
8	Sarah Bellum	
9	Ella Vador	
10	Mae O'Nayz	
11	Brandi Cantor	
12	Lou Pohl	
13	Paige Turner	
14	Penny Nichols	
15	Tad Moore	

	A	B
1	**Name**	
2	Sue	Flay
3	Brock	Lee
4	Carrie	Oakey
5	Jerry	Atrick
6	Mike	Raffone
7	Raynor	Schein
8	Sarah	Bellum
9	Ella	Vader
10	Mae	O'Nayz
11	Brandi	Cantor
12	Lou	Pohl
13	Paige	Turner
14	Penny	Nichols
15	Tad	Moore

Figure 329 At left, a list with first and last names in column A. At right, first and last names placed in separate cells.

An easy way to accomplish this task is seen in the three following steps:

1. Select the list as you see was done for the names in column A. Then, click the Data tab on the Ribbon (or if you are using version 2003, the Data item on the Menu Bar) and select Text to Columns.

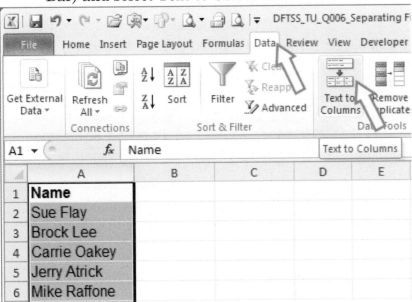

Figure 330 Select the list and click Data , Text to Columns.

2. You will see the Text to Columns Wizard. As shown in the next figure, select the option for Delimited and click the Next button.

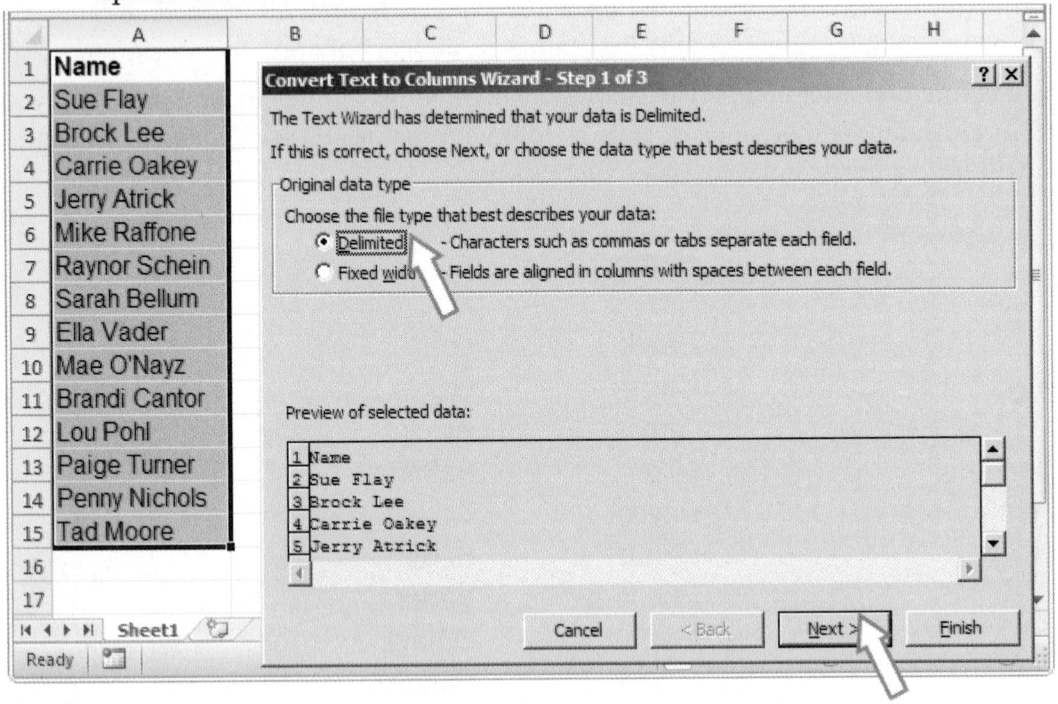

Figure 331 In the Text to Columns Wizard, select Delimited and click Next.

3. As seen in the next figure, click the tiny white box to the left of Space (which will put a checkmark in that box), and click the Finish button.

Note: In this example, you select Space because it's a space (as opposed to a comma or some other character) that separates the first and last names in the cells of the original list.

Caution: If your data includes Mary Ellen Walton, the text will split to three columns instead of the expected two columns. Go to cell C1 and press Ctrl+Down Arrow to find if anything is split to three columns.

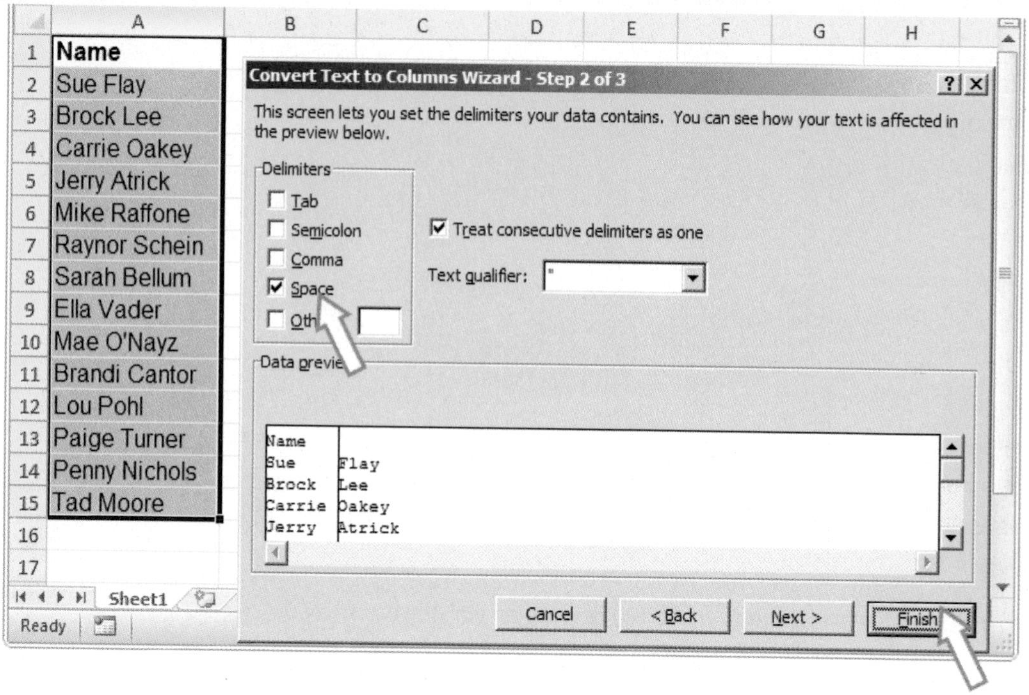

Figure 332 Indicate Space as your delimiter and click Finish.

How Can I Fill Empty Cells with the Entry from Above?

There's got to be an easy way to fill in these empty cells!

Sometimes you have a column that contains some data, along with a lot of empty cells to represent whatever text was in the last non-empty cell above it. This first figure shows a "before and after" example for the empty cells in column A to be filled in with whatever clothing item existed in the cell above it.

	A	B			A	B
1	Items sold	Month		1	Items sold	Month
2	Sweaters	January		2	Sweaters	January
3		February		3	Sweaters	February
4		March		4	Sweaters	March
5	Hats	April		5	Hats	April
6		May		6	Hats	May
7		June		7	Hats	June
8		July		8	Hats	July
9		August		9	Hats	August
10	Winter coats	September		10	Winter coats	September
11		October		11	Winter coats	October
12		November		12	Winter coats	November
13		December		13	Winter coats	December
14				14		

Figure 333 At left, you have empty cells in a column. At right, the cells are filled in.

For this example, select from cell A1 to the cell in column A that's on the same row as the last text item in column B. In the next figure, range A1:A13 is selected because cell B13 holds the last text item "December" in column B. After you've selected the range, press the F5 key on your keyboard.

	A	B
1	Items sold	Month
2	Sweaters	January
3		February
4		March
5	Hats	April
6		May
7		June
8		July
9		August
10	Winter coats	September
11		October
12		November
13		December

Figure 334 Select the cells in the column of interest, and then press the F5 key on your keyboard.

After you press the F5 key, you will see the Go To dialog box. Click the Special button as shown in Figure 335. After you click the Special button you will see the Go To Special dialog box. Select the option for Blanks, and click the OK button as shown in Figure 336.

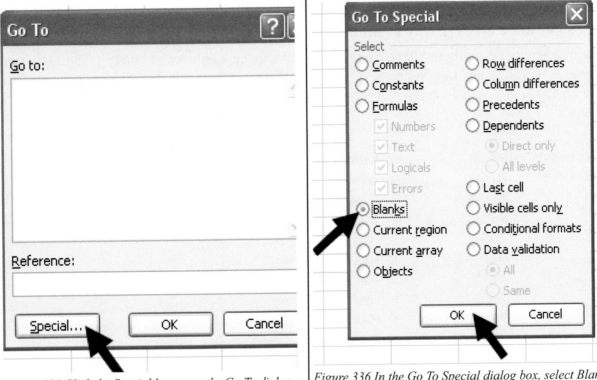

Figure 335 Click the Special button on the Go To dialog box.

Figure 336 In the Go To Special dialog box, select Blanks and click OK.

In the next figure, the image at the left shows that only the blank cells are selected in column A. So far so good. At this point, you can see that the active cell is A3 because it is part of the selection, but not dark. Also, in what's called the *name box* located immediately above column A, you can see the cell reference "A3", which is Excel's way of telling you the active cell's address for any selection.

Because cell A3 is the first selected blank cell, that must mean cell A2 (directly above cell A3) is not blank. Therefore, you can simply type the formula =A2 (but don't hit Enter!). Instead of typing the formula, you could type the equals sign, the up arrow, then Ctrl+Enter.

	A3	▾				SUM	▾	✗ ✓ ƒx	=A2

	A	B
1	**Items sold**	**Month**
2	Sweaters	January
3		February
4		March
5	Hats	April
6		May
7		June
8		July
9		August
10	Winter coats	September
11		October
12		November
13		December
14		

	A	B
1	**Items sold**	**Month**
2	Sweaters	January
3	=A2	February
4		March
5	Hats	April
6		May
7		June
8		July
9		August
10	Winter coats	September
11		October
12		November
13		December
14		

Figure 337 With the blank cells selected, type the formula =A2.

Here's the trick! From your keyboard, hold down the Ctrl key while you press the Enter key. When you do that, the formula will only be applied to the selected blank cells, which will fill them all in with the value from the cells above them!

What Are Your Favorite Excel Functions?

Excel offers lots of functions…which ones do you like the best?

Ask 1000 people to tell you what their favorite movie is, or their favorite make of an automobile and you will receive 1000 different answers. Current versions of Excel come with some 400 functions, and almost anyone you talk to will tell you a different set of which functions they use every day.

Note: Here are lists from a few different people using Excel:
- Kevin Jones: SUMPRODUCT, SUMIFS, COUNTIFS, AVERAGEIFS, MATCH with INDEX, AND and OR used in arrays.
- Mike Girvin: INDEX, MATCH, AGGREGATE, NPV, XNPV, IF, AVERAGE, STDEV.S and SUMPRODUCT.
- Bill Jelen: RANDBETWEEN, ROUND, INDEX, VLOOKUP and COUNTA
- Tom Urtis: COUNTA, INDEX, ISNUMBER, LEN, LOOKUP, MATCH, MAX, MIN, SUM, SUMIF, and SUMPRODUCT.
- Tyler Nash: SUM, IF, AND, OR (for my math class). VLOOKUP sounds interesting from what I've read.
- Worldwide, the most frequently used Excel functions are: SUM, IF, AND, VLOOKUP, ROUND, AVERAGE, OR, SUMIF, INT, MOD, COUNTIF, NOW, TODAY, and DATE.
- The functions that made it into this book are: CHOOSE, CONCATENATE, COUNT, COUNTA, DATE, DAY, FIND, HLOOKUP, IF, IFERROR, INDEX, INT, LEFT, LEN, MOD, MONTH, NOW, OFFSET, PMT, ROW, SUBTOTAL, SUM, SUMIF, SUMPRODUCT, TEXT, TODAY, UPPER, VLOOKUP, WEEKDAY and YEAR

For someone like me who builds workbooks for data analysis, I cannot imagine a few basic functions not being a part of every workbook project. Those functions are SUM, AVERAGE, SUMPRODUCT and CONCATENATE but using the ampersand character "&" to supplant the actual CONCATENATE function.

The following figure shows examples of each of the four functions I mentioned. The formula for the SUM function at the top left is:

```
=SUM(B2:B9)
```

The formula for the AVERAGE function at the top right is:

```
=AVERAGE(B2:B9)
```

The formula for the SUMPRODUCT function at the lower left is:

```
=SUMPRODUCT(B2:B5*C2:C5)
```

The formula for CONCATENATING, (joining) cell values together using the ampersand "&" character at the lower right is:

```
=A2&" "&B2
```

B10	fx	=SUM(B2:B9)
	A	B
1	Monthly Expense	Cost
2	Rent	$1,600
3	Utilities	$ 50
4	Internet	$ 75
5	Telephone	$ 100
6	Cell phone	$ 45
7	Auto payment	$ 165
8	Insurance	$ 127
9	Food	$ 500
10	Total	$2,662

B10	fx	=AVERAGE(B2:B9)
	A	B
1	Student Name	Test Score
2	Sue Flay	85
3	Brock Lee	92
4	Carrie Oakey	91
5	Jerry Atrick	78
6	Mike Raffone	76
7	Sarah Bellum	94
8	Ella Vador	68
9	Paige Turner	86
10	Average Score	83.75

C6	fx	=SUMPRODUCT(B2:B5*C2:C5)
	A	B	C
1	Item	Count	Price
2	Widgets	492	$ 103
3	Wombats	267	$ 56
4	Wallets	379	$ 80
5	Whistles	105	$ 22
6	Total Count times Price		$ 98,284

C2	fx	=A2&" "&B2
	A	B	C
1	First Name	Last Name	Full Name
2	Sue	Flay	Sue Flay
3	Brock	Lee	Brock Lee
4	Carrie	Oakey	Carrie Oakey
5	Jerry	Atrick	Jerry Atrick
6	Mike	Raffone	Mike Raffone

Figure 338 Examples of functions for SUM, AVERAGE, SUMPRODUCT, and CONCATENATING using the ampersand "&" character.

Why Don't the Formulas in My Workbook Re-calculate?

I have a worksheet with formulas that show calculated results using other cells as input values. I made some changes (deleted some rows and changed some values) but the calculated results were not updated to reflect those changes. What is wrong?

The problem is most likely that Excel has been instructed to not calculate the formulas on the worksheet. This situation can occur for a couple of different reasons (discussed later). The important thing to remember is that Excel determines whether or not to automatically calculate the formulas on a worksheet based on a single setting called the calculation mode. The calculation mode is an option that has three settings:

- Automatic – Excel recalculates all dependent formulas every time you make a change to a value, formula, or name.
- Automatic Except for Data Tables – The same as Automatic, but data tables are not calculated. This option makes calculations a little faster if your workbook contains large data tables.
- Manual – Excel only calculates formulas when you instruct it to do so.

To set the calculation mode navigate to the Formulas tab and click the Calculation Options menu in the Calculation group to view the three calculation mode options. The current mode is checked:

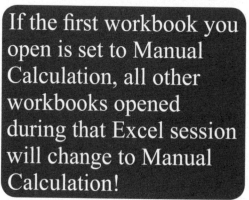

Figure 339 The Calculation Mode menu.

Select the desired mode to change it. Unless you specifically do not want formulas to calculate when you make changes, select Automatic.

Note: You might be wondering why Excel offers the option to not automatically calculate formulas. The reason is that some workbooks can get rather large and complex with a lot of formulas and the time it takes to recalculate all the formulas affected by a single change can take a while; sometimes so long that it makes the process of making changes annoying. By allowing you to turn off automatic calculations on such a workbook, you can do so and then make multiple edits to the workbook without waiting for Excel to calculate the entire workbook every time you make a single change. When finished, you can turn automatic calculations back on to refresh all the formulas. Or you can leave automatic calculations disabled and recalculate the workbook manually.

If the first workbook you open is set to Manual Calculation, all other workbooks opened during that Excel session will change to Manual Calculation!

When working in a workbook with automatic calculations disabled (manual calculation mode,) you can recalculate the entire workbook by clicking Calculate Now in the Calculation group on the Formulas tab. You can recalculate just the worksheet by clicking Calculate Sheet in the Calculation group on the Formulas tab.

Note: You might be also be wondering how the calculation mode can be set to manual. There are a few ways this can occur. The most common way is you or someone else specifically changed the calculation mode to manual and left it that way when the workbook was last saved. Another way it can be set to manual is if the first workbook opened had its calculation mode set to manual; every workbook opened after the first was opened will also be in manual calculation mode. And, if you save any workbook while Excel is in manual calculation mode, that workbook will default to manual calculation mode when opened in the future! Yet another way a workbook's calculation mode can be changed is if a macro (programming code written in Visual Basic for Applications) changes it; the macro may or may not reside in the workbook. It is also possible that a single worksheet in a workbook has been instructed to not calculate automatically; this is done by changing the sheet's Enable Calculation property using the VBE (Visual Basic Environment) to False. How this is done is beyond the scope of this book.

Is There a Way to Find the Value of Data or Numbers in Several Different Spreadsheets?

How can I write a formula on one worksheet that can display what's in a cell on another worksheet?

An Excel workbook can hold many worksheets. In fact, when creating your workbooks, it is a wise design practice to avoid cramming everything onto a single worksheet. Workbooks are best organized when their worksheets have some kind of theme or purpose to them.

For example, if you are developing a budget workbook for your business, you may want to organize your income and expenses on twelve different worksheets, one for each month of the year. Then, on a thirteenth worksheet that might be a summary of all twelve months' worksheets, you can enter formulas to pull in whatever data from each (or all) of those individual month sheets.

Here are a few examples. Suppose you are on your Summary worksheet and you want to show what is in, say, cell K32 of the worksheet named January. This formula would display that information:

```
=January!K32
```

If your other worksheets are named January, February, March and so on through December, the following formula on your Summary sheet will sum numbers for a particular cell (A5 in this example) for all those worksheets.

```
=SUM(January:December!A5)
```

As a final example, this formula adds up the numbers in a range of cells for a worksheet named Quarter4:

```
=SUM(Quarter4!A2:F2)
```

Excel Doesn't Recognize My Dates?

I pasted dates from an e-mail. Excel is not recognizing my dates. What can I do?

Excel can accept an amazing variety of dates. Whether the month is spelled out, abbreviated, with spaces or without, Excel can often figure out the date.

Valid	Valid	Not Valid
March 31, 2015	2015/03/31	March 32, 2015
Mar 31, 2015	2015-03-31	2015-03 31
31 Mar 2015	2015-03/31	03-31-2015 11:30AM
31Mar2015	03-31-2015 11:30 AM	03-31-2015 11:30 AM EST
31-Mar	03-31-2015 17:30	July 4, 1776

It always surprises me that Excel handles all of the dates that it does. For example, I wouldn't expect it could handle a mix of slash and dash in Mar-31/2015, but it does.

However, there are a few things that will always cause problems when Excel tries to recognize dates:

- If the text contains an invalid date, such as April 31 or March 32, Excel will not recognize the date. This also includes dates before 1900.
- Date and time are OK, but you must have a space between the time and AM or PM. Otherwise, Excel will not recognize the date.
- Time Zones such as EST, EDT, PST, CST will cause the date to go unrecognized.

The most common problem here is the absence of a space before the AM or PM. Try pasting your data in Notepad. You can then use the Edit, Replace command to change "AM" to " AM" and "PM" to " PM". Copy the fixed data from Notepad and paste to Excel. The dates should be recognized.

If the time zones are a problem, use Notepad's Replace tool to remove all EST, EDT, CST, and so on before pasting to Excel.

Is It Possible to Make Excel Auto-Date?

For example: if I need to enter today's date in a row or column, instead of doing so everyday, can I set Excel up to automatically fill in the date?

Yes - but first, a couple of cool date tricks.

Select any cell. Press Ctrl+;. Excel will insert the current date in the cell.

Select another cell. Press Ctrl+:. Excel will insert the current time in the cell.

Tip: To remember those shortcuts, think about a time, like "10:23". There is a colon in the time. Press Ctrl+Colon to insert the current time. To put the date instead of time, use the same key, but don't press shift.

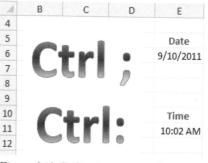

Figure 340 Ctrl+; for current date.

But...here is the bad part. The date and time inserted by Ctrl+; and Ctrl+: is a static date or time. It will always represent the date and time when you pressed the shortcut. It will not automatically update to show the current date or time.

To have Excel always show the current date, type a formula of =TODAY().

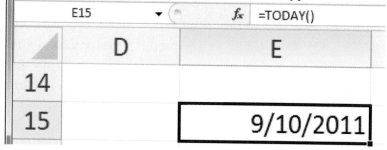

Figure 341 Use =TODAY() for a date that changes to the current day.

When you use this formula and open the workbook on another day, Excel will display the current date.

That's a good formula. Is there a function to display the current time?

The NOW function will return the current date and time, although you can format it to show time.

1. Go to any cell. Type =NOW() and press Enter to accept the formula. Excel will display the current date and time.

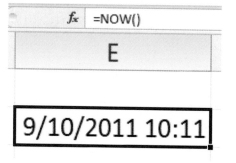

Figure 342 Now shows today + time.

2. Select the cell that contains your formula. On the Home tab, go to the dropdown in the Number group and choose Time.

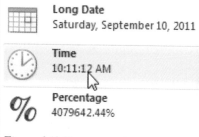

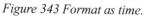

Figure 343 Format as time.

Excel will now display the time as 10:11:12 AM. This is an insanely geeky way to display time. Press Ctrl+1 (the number one) to display the Format Cells dialog. Because the current cell is formatted as time, you will automatically go to the Number tab and the Time category will be selected. You can see several different time samples available. Choose one of the less geeky times, perhaps 1:30 PM. Click OK.

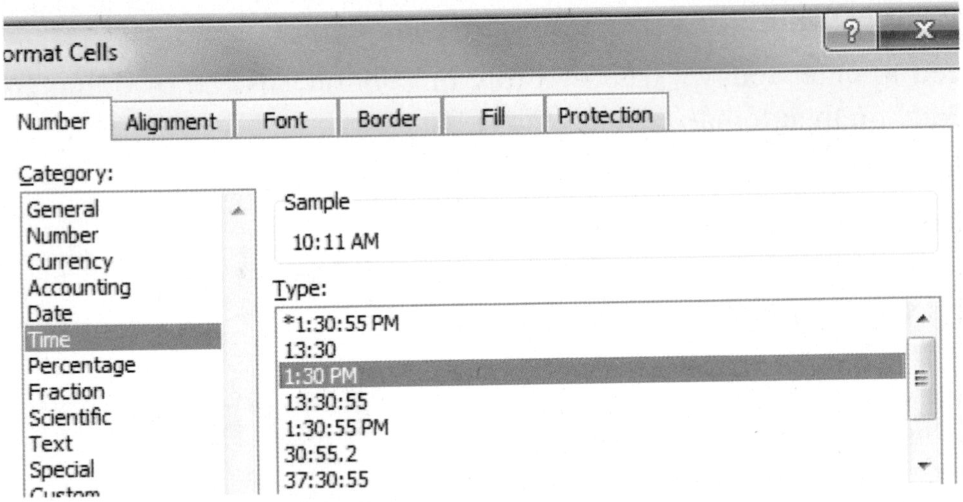

Figure 344 Or choose a different format.

Gotcha: the result of NOW() does not update every minute. You can stare at the spreadsheet for ten minutes and the time will never change. To get the time to change, you have to do something to cause Excel to recalculate the spreadsheet. There are a lot of ways to have this accidentally happen. Some ways that it will happen are:

- Enter a value or a formula in another cell.
- Select the time cell, press F2 to edit, then Enter to accept the unchanged formula.
- Click the vertical line between any two column letters as if you were about to resize the column.
- Close and open the workbook (this seems like overkill, doesn't it?)
- Press F9. This is the "official way". Microsoft expects you to remember to press F9 in order to update the results of all formulas.

How Can I Set up Dates to Display the Way I Want after Importing?

I imported some dates and they are all showing up as 23-Jan-2015. Can I display the dates as 1/23/2015?

Select the range of dates. On the Home tab, find the large dropdown at the top of the Number group. This dropdown offers a Short Date and a Long Date. The Short Date is the format that you want. There are more options than just the two in the dropdown. Select the date range then press Ctrl+1 (the number one) to reach the Format Cells dialog.

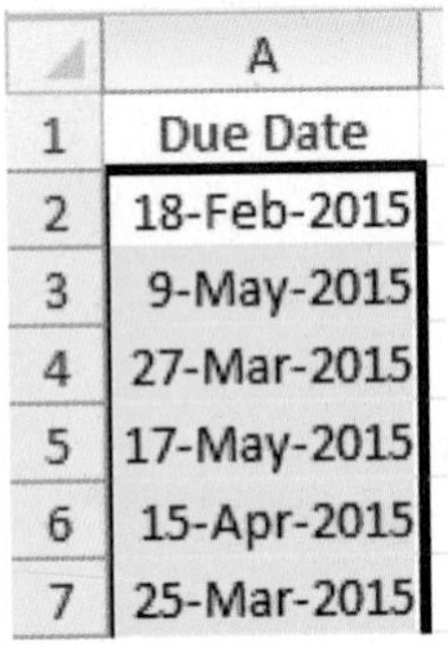

Figure 345 The default Excel format for dates.

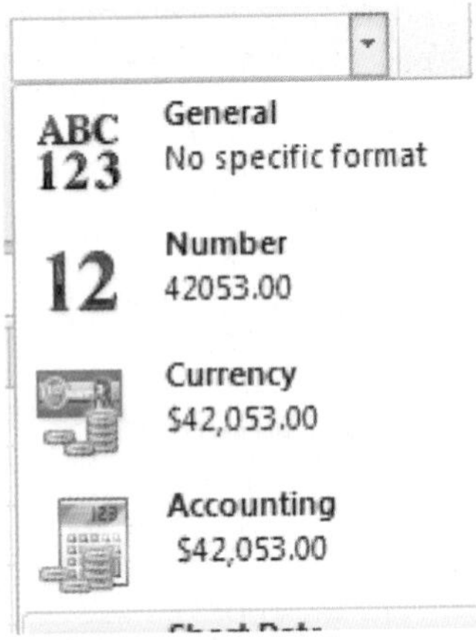

Figure 346 Short date uses slashes and no leading zero for months with one digit.

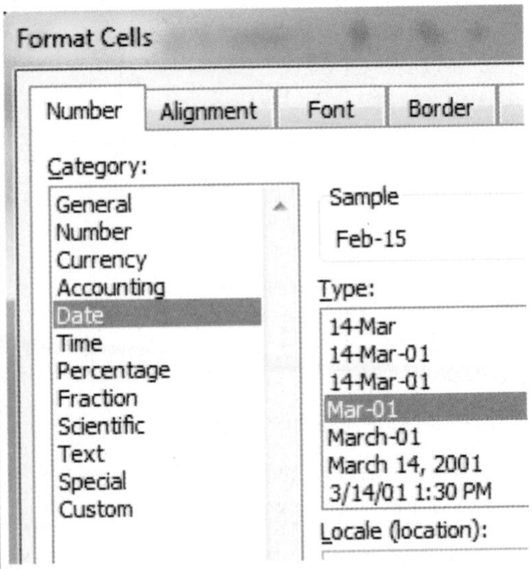

Figure 347 Excel offers many built-in date formats.

Choose Number across the top, and then Date from the Category list. There are various options listed in the Type box. As you select an option, the Sample shows how the active cell would look. In Figure 347, "Feb-15" is referring to February 2015, which seems very ambiguous.

Don't be surprised if you don't find your desired format in the list. Most of those choices were designed before 2000 when it was common to use two-digit years. Only four choices in the list offer a four-digit year.

The solution is to choose the Custom category from the Format Cells dialog. You can then type a custom format in the Type box. As shown below, "ddd, mmm d, yyyy" will display a date as "Wed, Feb 18, 2015":

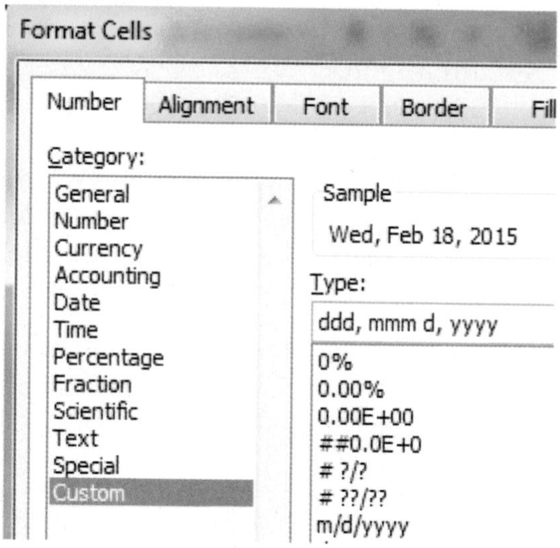

Figure 348 You have more control using a custom number format.

Custom number formats for dates can use any combination of spaces, commas, dashes, slashes, and the format codes shown below:

Custom Format	Displays As
M/D/YYYY	1/23/2015
D	23
DD	23
DDD	Fri
DDDD	Friday
M	1
MM	01
MMM	Jan
MMMM	January
MMMMM	J
YY	15
YYYY	2015
MMMM D	January 23
MMMM YYYY	January 2015

Figure 349 String together any combination of these codes to build a date format.

How Can I Combine a Date with Words in a Cell, and Make It Look like a Date?

How can I combine a date with text in Excel, and have it appear as a date?

If you have ever tried to enter a formula to combine a date with text in the same cell, you may have seen a curious result. The date does not look like a date, but rather a number, such as seen in C1.

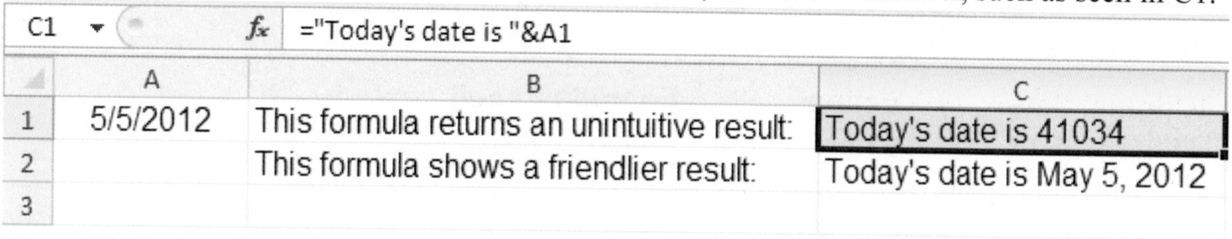

Figure 350 The formula in cell C1 returns a combination of text and an unfamiliar-looking date reference.

To Excel, a date is nothing more than a five-digit serial number. For example, in the figure, cell A1 contains the date of May 5, 2012. True, A1 is formatted to look like 5/5/2012 but what is really happening behind the scenes is, Excel looks at that date and regards it as serial number 41034. If the date were May 6, 2012, Excel would see it as 41035, and so on.

The formula in cell C1 that attempts to combine (using the ampersand character) the date in cell A1 with some preceding text is: `="Today's date is "&A1`

You can see that the result is not very intuitive. Nobody—including the most hardcore Excel power wizards—would know that 41034 means May 5, 2012.

To adjust the above formula for user friendliness, you can use the TEXT function to specify your desired format for a more readable date when it's combined with text. In the next figure, cell C2 is selected, and its formula is: `="Today's date is "&TEXT(A1,"MMM D, YYYY")`

| C2 ▾ | f_x | ="Today's date is "&TEXT(A1,"MMM D, YYYY") |

	A	B	C
1	5/5/2012	This formula returns an unintuitive result:	Today's date is 41034
2		This formula shows a friendlier result:	Today's date is May 5, 2012
3			

Figure 351 The formula in cell C2 uses the TEXT function to help show a recognizable date.

Note: The second argument in the formula above is any combination of the number formatting codes from Figure 349.

How Can I Add or Subtract Days, Months, or Years from a Date?

I heard that date math in Excel is easy! How so?

When you have a date in one cell and you want to add or subtract a period of time from it, there's a simple process that works in most cases. Excel regards dates as numbers. The way dates are formatted in a cell does not change the fact that to Excel, a date is nothing more than a five-digit number which you can work with mathematically just like you can work with any other kind of number.

The most useful tip to remember is, Excel works with dates based on their three basic components, in this order: Year, Month, and Day. For example, to Excel, the date of May 15, 2012 is Year number 2012, Month number 5, and Day number 15. As you will see, this comes into play by using Excel's DATE function.

Here are three examples of mathematical operations upon the date of May 15, 2012. Take a look at all three formula examples and you will get the gist of how to add or subtract years, months, and days from a date.

Example 1-

In the following figure, cell C2 displays May 15, 2013, which is the date of May 15, 2012 plus one year. The formula in cell C2 is:

`=DATE(YEAR(A2)+1,MONTH(A2),DAY(A2))`

| C2 ▾ | f_x | =DATE(YEAR(A2)+1,MONTH(A2),DAY(A2)) |

	A	B	C
1	**Original date**	**Action**	**Formula Result**
2	May 15, 2012	Add a year	May 15, 2013
3		Subtract 6 months	November 15, 2011
4		Add 3 days	May 18, 2012

Figure 352 The formula in cell C2 adds a year to the date in cell A2.

Example 2-

This next figure shows how to operate on the Month component of your original date. Cell C3 is selected, showing November 15, 2011, which equals the date of May 15, 2012 minus six months. Here's the formula:

`=DATE(YEAR(A2),MONTH(A2)-6,DAY(A2))`

C3 ▾		f_x	=DATE(YEAR(A2),MONTH(A2)-6,DAY(A2))	
	A		B	C
1	**Original date**		**Action**	**Formula Result**
2	May 15, 2012		Add a year	May 15, 2013
3			Subtract 6 months	November 15, 2011
4			Add 3 days	May 18, 2012

Figure 353 The formula in cell C3 subtracts six months from the date in cell A2.

Example 3-

When working with days, the task is even simpler. Just add (or subtract) the number of days from the original date, as shown in cell C5 which adds three days to arrive at May 18, 2012 with the formula:

=A2+3

C4 ▾		f_x	=A2+3	
	A		B	C
1	**Original date**		**Action**	**Formula Result**
2	May 15, 2012		Add a year	May 15, 2013
3			Subtract 6 months	November 15, 2011
4			Add 3 days	May 18, 2012

Figure 354 The formula in cell C4 adds 3 days to the date in cell A2.

Is It Possible to Find the Date for a Particular Day in Excel?

Can I find the date for seventeen weeks from Friday? Or – can I figure out what day of the week January 23, 2016 falls on?

Excel's date handling is fairly cool. Each day counts as the number 1. Thus, to go out 17 weeks, you would add 17*7 to a starting date.

Here are the steps for finding the date for 17 weeks from Friday:
1. Go to a blank cell (say B1) and type Ctrl+; to enter today's date.
2. Select the cell, open the dropdown in the Number group of the Home tab and choose Long Date. You will see that today is a Monday or whatever day you happen to be reading this.
3. In your head, calculate that Friday is four days away.
4. In the cell below today's date, enter =B1+4. The new cell will pick up the format from the first cell and it will show Friday, May 04, 2012.
5. Go to cell B3, enter =B2+7*17. There are 7 days in a week and you want to go out 17 weeks. 17 times 7 is the number of days away. The result will show the date 17 weeks away.

B2	▾	f_x	=B1+4
	A	B	C
1	Today:	Monday, April 30, 2012	
2	Friday:	Friday, May 04, 2012	
3			
4			

Figure 355 Add a few days to get to Friday.

B3	▾	f_x	=B2+7*17
	A	B	C
1	Today:	Monday, April 30, 2012	
2	Friday:	Friday, May 04, 2012	
3	17 Weeks later:	Friday, August 31, 2012	
4			
5			

*Figure 356 Add 17*7 to go out 17 weeks.*

To find the day of the week for a particular date, you can enter that date in a cell and format the cell as a Long Date. Excel will show you the day of the week. Open the dropdown in the Number group of the Home tab to choose Long Date (or, as you can see below in the figure shows you that the date is a Saturday).

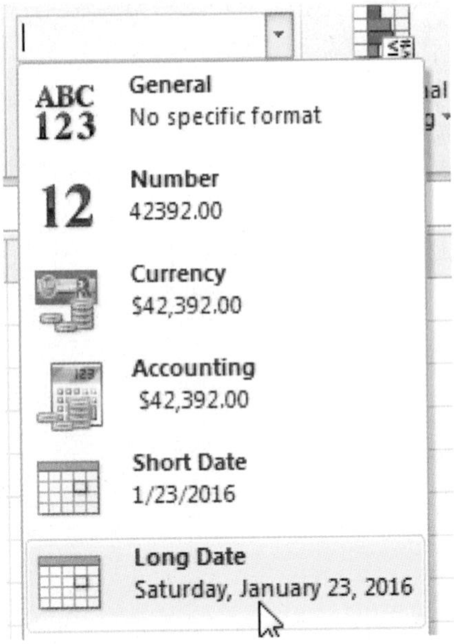

Figure 357 Format the date as a Long Date to see the day of the week.

You didn't ask, but another cool thing you can do with dates is to show every bi-weekly pay day. Enter the next pay day in a cell and then use a formula such as =14+B8 copied down to several rows.

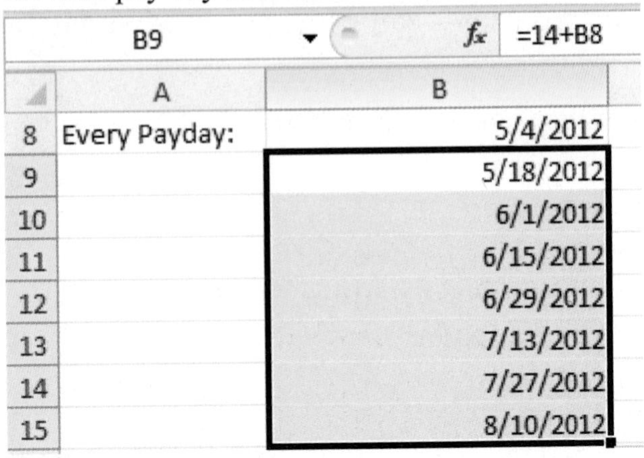

B9		f_x =14+B8
	A	B
8	Every Payday:	5/4/2012
9		5/18/2012
10		6/1/2012
11		6/15/2012
12		6/29/2012
13		7/13/2012
14		7/27/2012
15		8/10/2012

Figure 358 Add 14 to the cell above to show the next pay date.

Wait a second, those steps work fine for one date, but I have to do this calculation for a whole column of dates! Don't you have anything better than mentally calculating that Friday is four days away from Monday?

Oh. Sorry.

To automate finding your way to the next Friday, you would use a combination of WEEKDAY and CHOOSE. The WEEKDAY function will return a 1 for Monday through 7 for Sunday. The CHOOSE function then converts the 1 from a Monday to a 4. It converts the 4 from Thursday to a 1. Adding the result of the CHOOSE gets you to the next Friday and then the 7*17 gets you out 17 weeks. The formula is:

```
=A2+CHOOSE(WEEKDAY(A2,2),4,3,2,1,0,7,6,5)+7*17.
```

```
=A2+CHOOSE(WEEKDAY(A2,2),4,3,2,1,0,7,6,5)+7*17
```

	A	B	C	D
1	Order Date	Promise Date		
2	Fri 1/2/2015	Fri 5/1/2015		
3	Fri 2/20/2015	Fri 6/19/2015		
4	Wed 5/6/2015	Fri 9/4/2015		
5	Tue 3/24/2015	Fri 7/24/2015		
6	Thu 4/16/2015	Fri 8/14/2015		
7	Mon 7/20/2015	Fri 11/20/2015		

Figure 359 This fairly complicated formula replicates the five steps from the beginning of this section.

To find the weekday for a series of dates, use:

```
=TEXT(A2,"DDDD")
```

as shown in Figure 360.

```
=TEXT(A2,"DDDD")
```

	A	B
1	Order Date	Day of Week
2	Fri 1/2/2015	Friday
3	Fri 2/20/2015	Friday
4	Wed 5/6/2015	Wednesday
5	Tue 3/24/2015	Tuesday
6	Thu 4/16/2015	Thursday
7	Mon 7/20/2015	Monday

Figure 360 The TEXT function displays a value or a date using a specific number formatting code.

To show the month name instead of weekday, use:

```
=TEXT(A2,"MMMM").
```

How Can I Calculate Time and Show a Result That Makes Sense?

Adding and subtracting times can show strange results. How can I make the results look right?

In the first figure, the formula in cell B3 is:

```
=B2-B1
```

which returns the elapsed time in hours and minutes between the Start time and the End time. You want the visual value 6:45 (meaning six hours and forty-five minutes), but instead Excel gives you an elapsed time that looks like a time of day, in this example 6:45 AM.

B3	▼	*fx*	=B2-B1

	A	B	C
1	Start time	9:00 AM	
2	End time	3:45 PM	
3	Elapsed time	6:45 AM	
4			

B3	▼	*fx*	=B2-B1

	A	B	C
1	Start time	9:00 AM	
2	End time	3:45 PM	
3	Elapsed time	6:45	
4			

Figure 361 A comparison of Excel's default result when working with times, and how you really want it to look.

Dates and times in Excel are numbers, so the underlying numeric value in cell B3 is in fact what you want. All that's needed is to format cell B3 for the kind of appearance that makes visual sense. Right-click cell B3, and select Format Cells.

In the Format Cells dialog box, take these steps as shown in Figure 362.

1. Select the Number tab.
2. Select the Custom item in the Category pane.
3. In the Type field, enter [h]:mm.
4. Click the OK button.

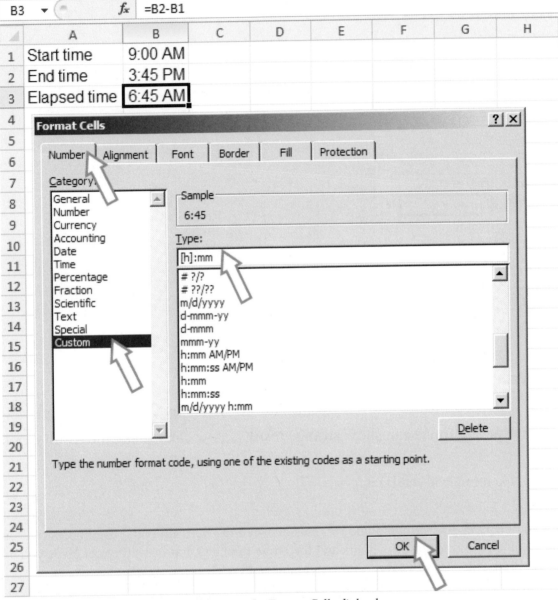

Figure 362 Apply the custom format [h]:mm in the Format Cells dialog box.

The square brackets around the h are the key to seeing times in excess of 24 hours

CHAPTER 7 - OTHER APPLICATIONS

Can I Transfer Excel Files from Excel 2003 to Excel 2010?

Will I Encounter Problems? Is there a way to save the file differently to prevent this?

Some things to know:

Excel 2003 supported 65 thousand rows. Excel 2007 supports a million rows.

Excel 2003 supported 56 colors. Excel 2007 supports 16 million colors.

Excel 2007 introduced Tables and made improvements in Conditional Formatting.

When you have an Excel 2003 file, it is stored with a .xls extension. When someone opens an xls file in Excel 2010, the title bar says that they are in Compatibility Mode. In this mode, Excel will not let you access any of the rows from 65537 to 1048576. They figure that you might be sending the workbook back to the person with Excel 2003 and they don't want you using parts of the spreadsheet that the other person won't be able to see.

What if you never plan on returning the file to the person with Excel 2003? You can upgrade the file to unlock all of the new features. In the File menu, choose Convert.

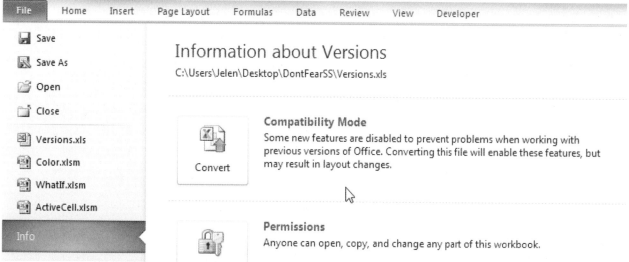

Figure 363 If the file is never going back to Excel 2003, use Convert to unlock all features.

What if I created the file in Excel 2010 and I need to send it to someone who has Excel 2003?

When you use File, Save As, choose to save the file in Excel 97-2003 format. Excel will bring up a Compatibility Checker. This tool categorizes all of the problems into one of two categories:
- Significant Loss of Functionality – pay attention to these. It means that something will not calculate correctly in Excel 2003.
- Minor Loss of Fidelity – you can usually ignore these. It means that a color is going to shift to a nearby shade.

How Do I Import Files into Excel?

I have some data that was given to me that I have to import into Excel so that I can clean it up and present it to others. How do I import the data into a worksheet so I can get started?

The most common format used to distribute data has been and continues to be the text file which is also known as the flat file, tab delimited file, comma delimited file, or print file. There are others such as XML but here we will be discussing just the text file formats.

A text file consists of one line per record where a record is a set of values and all records in the file contain the same fields. There may or may not be a header row or rows. The fields are separated by a tab, comma, or, in the case of a print file, a series of spaces in order to space out the fields so they line up when printed using a mono-spaced font.

To import a text file into Excel, navigate to the Data tab and click From Text in the Get External Data group.

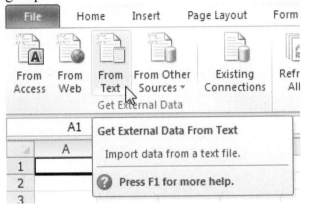

Figure 364 Starting the import process.

The Excel Open dialog box is displayed. Use the dialog to find and open the desired text file. Once open, Excel then displays Text Import Wizard dialog box.

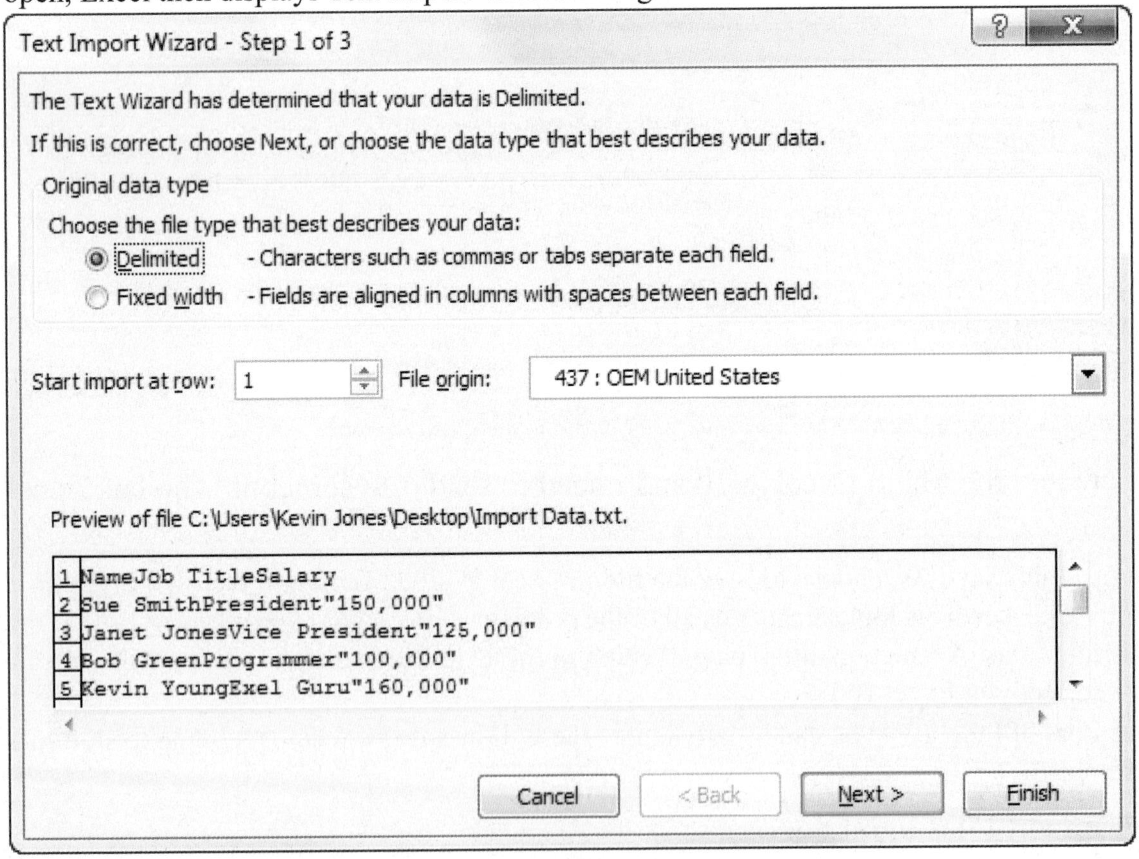

Figure 365 "Text Import Wizard" dialog box – step 1 of 3.

If the import file is a print file select Fixed Width. If the import file has one or more header rows then change the Start Import at Row to reference the first data row. Click Next to continue to the next step.

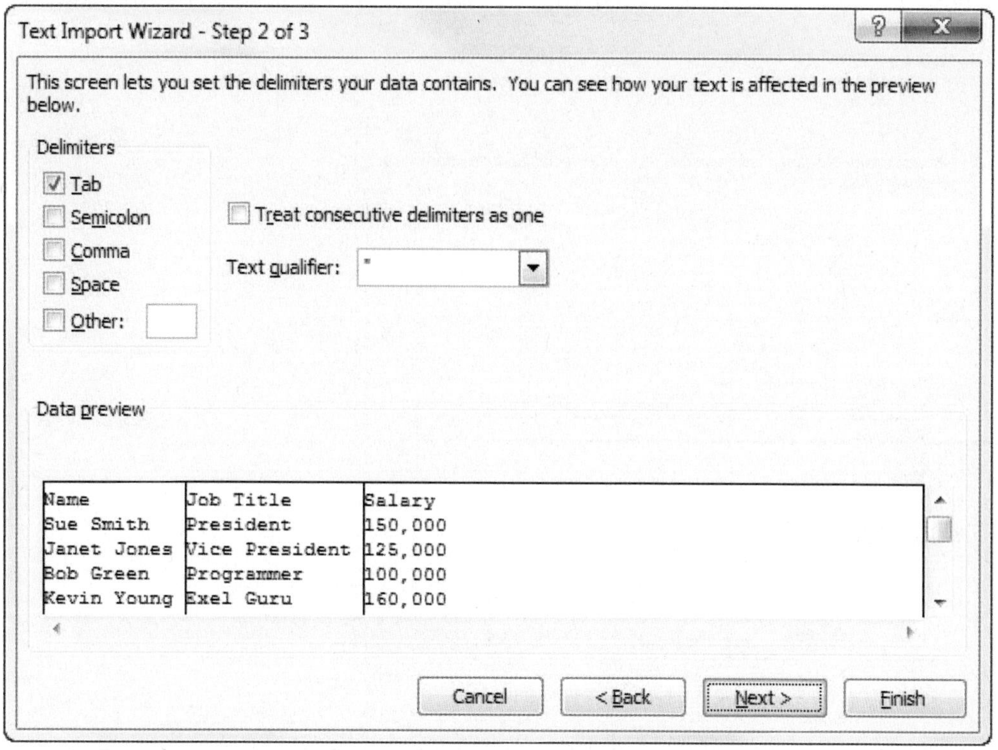

Figure 366 Text Import Wizard dialog box – step two of three illustrating importing a tab or comma delimited file.

On this dialog you can select the delimiters used to separate the fields in each record. Select Tab if a tab delimited file. Select Comma if a comma delimited file.

Caution: Note that you can select more than one delimiter. It is recommended that you not do this unless you are sure you need to, as most text files will use only one delimiter.

If you selected Fixed Width in step one above then the second step presents a different dialog that allows you to specify where each field starts and ends.

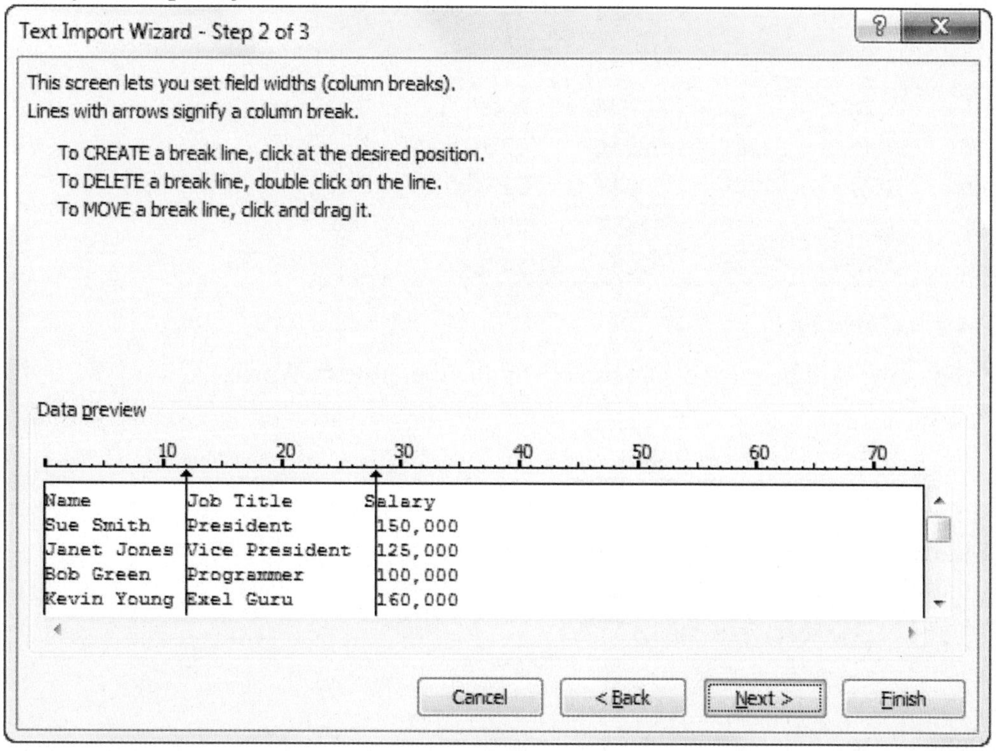

Figure 367 Text Import Wizard dialog box – step two of three illustrating importing a print file.

Click Next to continue to the next and final step.

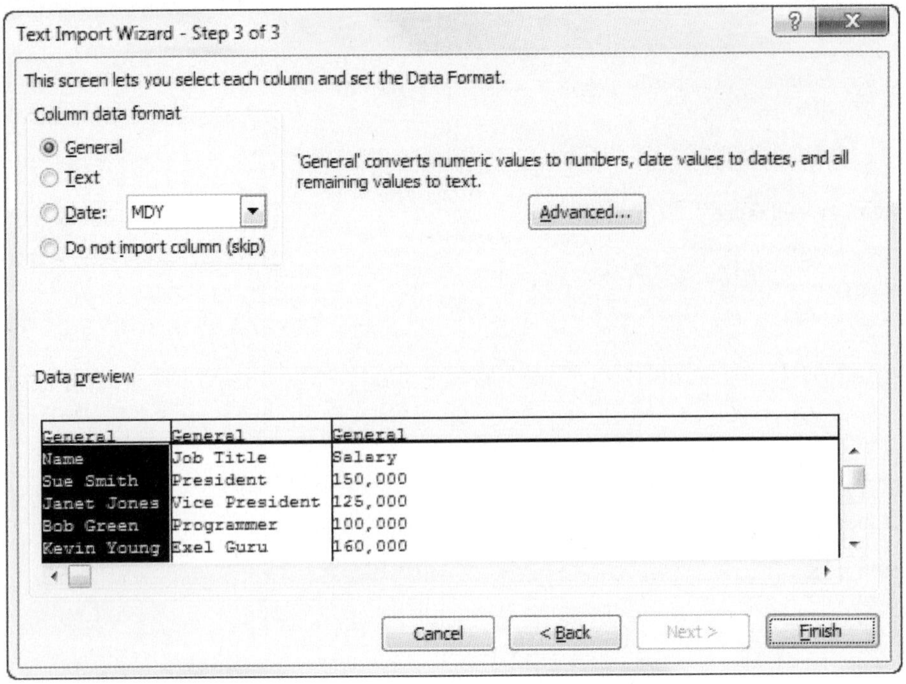

Text Import Wizard - Step 3 of 3

This screen lets you select each column and set the Data Format.

Column data format

◉ General
○ Text
○ Date: MDY ▾
○ Do not import column (skip)

'General' converts numeric values to numbers, date values to dates, and all remaining values to text.

Advanced...

Data preview

General	General	General
Name	Job Title	Salary
Sue Smith	President	150,000
Janet Jones	Vice President	125,000
Bob Green	Programmer	100,000
Kevin Young	Exel Guru	160,000

Cancel < Back Next > Finish

Figure 368 Text Import Wizard dialog box – step three of three.

In this step you can determine the format of each field. You can also select fields to be skipped (not imported.) Click Finish to complete the import process. Excel will ask you where to place the data before finishing.

How Can I Transfer Data from Excel to a Word Document?

I created a table or a chart in Excel and I want to embed this in the middle of some text in a Word document.

Open the Word document. Open the Excel workbook. Copy a range from Excel. Switch to Word. Ctrl+V to paste.

	A	B	C	D	E	F
1		Q1	Q2	Q3	Q4	Total
2	East	$144K	$180K	$226K	$282K	$832K
3	Central	$123K	$167K	$225K	$304K	$819K
4	West	$134K	$127K	$121K	$115K	$496K
5	Total	$401K	$474K	$571K	$700K	$2,147K

Figure 369 Copy a formatted range from Excel.

If you copied a range, the range will be pasted as a table. Here is the table in Word:

This is a table I created in Excel:

	Q1	Q2	Q3	Q4	Total
East	$144K	$180K	$226K	$282K	$832K
Central	$123K	$167K	$225K	$304K	$819K
West	$134K	$127K	$121K	$115K	$496K
Total	$401K	$474K	$571K	$700K	$2,147K

(Ctrl) ▾

Paste Options:

Set Default Paste...

Figure 370 Word adds ugly gridlines.

A small dropdown appears next to the pasted table. You can open this dropdown and choose if the range should have the Excel formatting or be reformatted to match the styles in Word. If you click the tiny Picture icon, Word will paste a picture of the table.

Provided you don't paste as a picture, you can use Word's table tools to further format the table.

This is a table I created in Excel after some formatting with Word's table tools:

	Q1	Q2	Q3	Q4	Total
East	$144K	$180K	$226K	$282K	$832K
Central	$123K	$167K	$225K	$304K	$819K
West	$134K	$127K	$121K	$115K	$496K
Total	$401K	$474K	$571K	$700K	$2,147K

Figure 371 You can apply additional formats in Word.

For a chart, select the chart in Excel and copy. Paste to Word. All three of Excel's Chart Tools Ribbon tabs will be available in Word.

After I Transfer an Excel Range to PowerPoint, Can I Edit the Data?

Say I need to change the data and have no access to the original file, can I do that? Will it still AutoSum if needed?

If this is going to happen to you in the future, you should get in the habit of embedding the Excel range or chart instead of linking. A standard copy from Excel pasted to PowerPoint will paste a linked copy of the workbook. This means that to get updates, you have to have access to the original file.

Instead of doing a normal copy and paste, you should copy from Excel. In Word or PowerPoint, right-click and choose to embed.

If you are pasting a chart, use either of these first two icons.

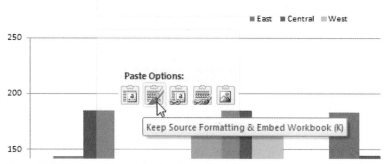

Figure 372 To be able to edit the chart data later, choose one of the first two icons.

When pasting an Excel range, use the third icon.

Figure 373 For a range, choose to Embed.

To edit the chart data later, select the chart. Go to Chart Tools Design, Edit in Excel. PowerPoint will open a special copy of your workbook in Excel that you can edit.

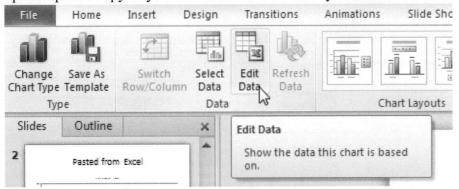

Figure 374 If the chart was embedded, you can edit the data later.

To edit a range later, double click inside the pasted range in PowerPoint. A border appears around the worksheet range. Although the application title bar says you are still in PowerPoint, all of the Ribbon tabs and icons are from Excel. In this tiny range, use the arrow keys to navigate around and change the data. Use the arrow keys to scroll back to the area that was originally shown and then click outside of the range.

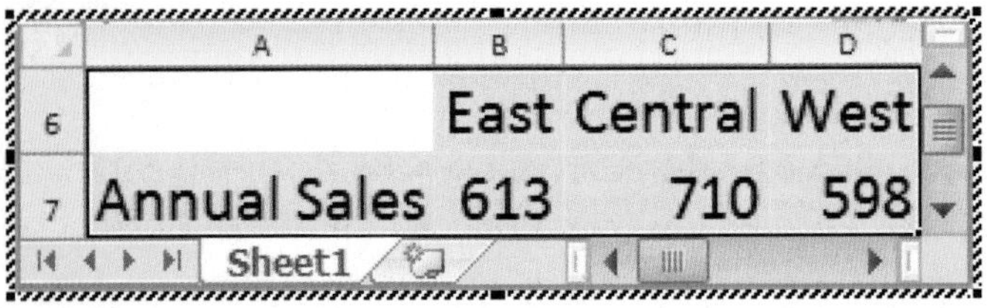

	A	B	C	D
6		East	Central	West
7	Annual Sales	613	710	598

Figure 375 This pasted range includes formulas pointing outside the range.

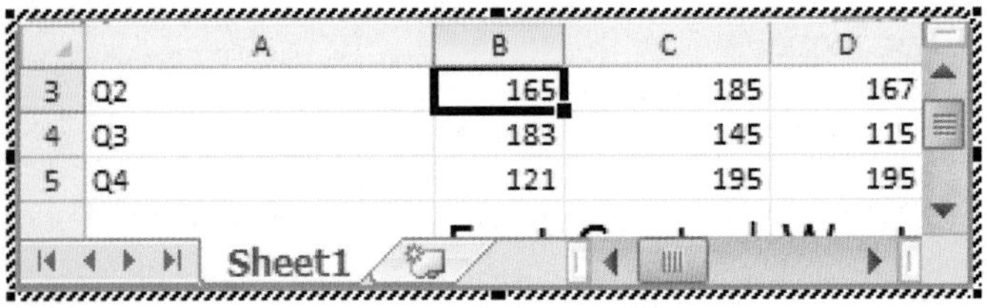

	A	B	C	D
3	Q2	165	185	167
4	Q3	183	145	115
5	Q4	121	195	195

Figure 376 Within PowerPoint, use the arrow keys to scroll up so you can change the source values.

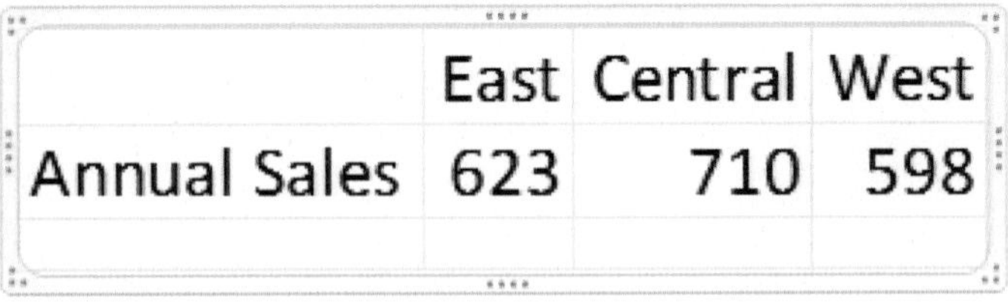

	East	Central	West
Annual Sales	623	710	598

Figure 377 After clicking outside the Excel range, you have the new results.

CHAPTER 8 - EVERY WAY TO

Tell Me Every Way to …

My manager is a control freak. He has been using Excel longer than I've been alive. He stands behind me and watches me work in Excel. If I don't do things exactly the way he does them, he throws a fit.

The topics in this next section will show you every conceivable way to perform some tasks. Some of these are just what your boss wants. Some of them are a lot slower than what your boss wants. Some of them may be faster than your boss wants.

My manager is a control freak

After becoming familiar with all the methods, you should consider using the method that is marked as the fastest. The speed difference between the slowest method and the fastest method will make the difference when you are faced with a several hour task.

Tell Me Every Way to Change Column Widths

Some columns are too wide, some are too narrow. I need to adjust so they fit my data.

Method 1: Click between two column headings and drag left or right to change the width of the column to the left. A tooltip will tell you the new width in both width and points.

Method 2: Double-click the same line as shown in Method 1. This will auto-fit the column to the longest value in the column. Note that this method will not work in column A of the figure. The title in A1 is longer than all of the other data in the column. Excel will resize column A to be too large.

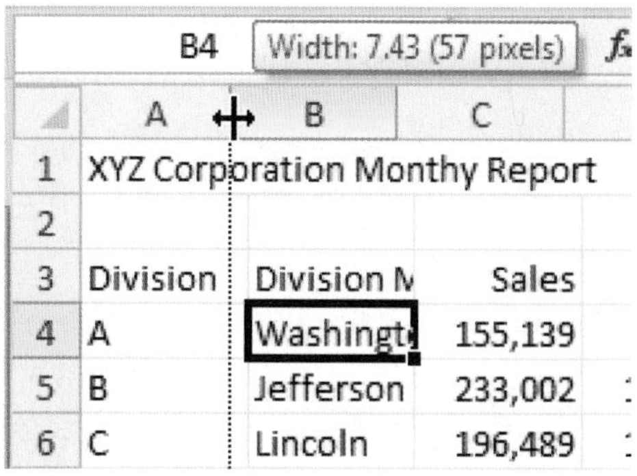

Figure 378 Click the line between two column letters and drag left or right.

Method 3: Select all of columns B:F. Double click the line between the "F" column label and the "G" column label. This will auto-fit all of the selected columns at once.

Method 4: Select one or more cells in a column or columns. Choose Home, Format, Column Width. Excel will display a dialog where you can type a column width. Click OK.

Method 5: Select A3:F9. Choose Home, Format, AutoFit Column Width. By excluding A1 from the selection, you can auto-fit all columns based on the longest value in each column of the selection. Instead of using the mouse to select from the Ribbon, you can use Alt+O+C+A (which stands for Format Column AutoFit). You can also use Alt+H+O+I (which stands for Home, Format, AutoFit).

Method 6: This method is particularly good if you have to copy a pattern of column widths to many other columns. For example, you have 24 columns. Each pair of columns represents sales and % of Sales for one month. After fixing the column widths for January, you can copy the two January columns. Then, select the 22 remaining columns. Do Home, Paste dropdown, Paste Special, Column Widths. This will paste the alternating wide and narrow column widths.

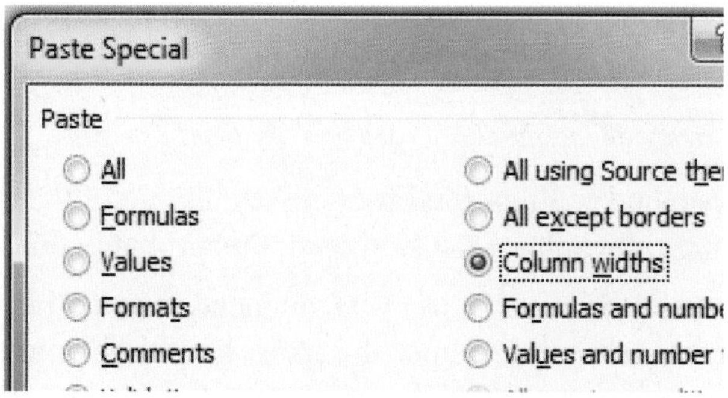

Figure 379 Adjust the column widths with Paste Special.

Tell Me Every Way to Copy Cells

Slowest Method: Use the Copy icon on the Home tab of the Ribbon.

Figure 380 Yes, the Copy icon works.

Method 2: Right-click the selection and choose Copy.

Figure 381 Right-click and choose Copy.

Fastest Method: Ctrl+C.

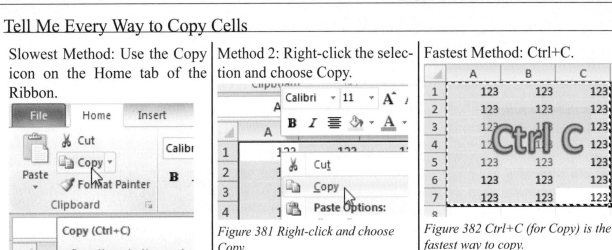

Figure 382 Ctrl+C (for Copy) is the fastest way to copy.

Tell Me Every Way to Paste Cells

I've copied some cells and selected a new location. What is the best way to do a true paste (not a paste special)?

Slowest Method: Press the Enter key. This is a fast way to paste, but pressing Enter will do the paste and then clear the clipboard. If you need to paste the selection to many different locations, using Enter will be horribly slow.

Method 2: Use the top half of the Paste icon on the Home tab of the Ribbon. The Paste icon is split into a top half and a dropdown menu bottom half. Simply clicking the top half of the icon will paste.

Method 3: Open the dropdown at the bottom of the Paste icon and choose Paste. This takes twice as many clicks as Method 2. Using the keyboard shortcut of Alt+H+V+P will navigate the same path and is even worse.

Figure 383 Click the top half of the Paste icon to paste.

Method 4: Right-click the cell where you are pasting and choose the first Paste icon. If your hand is already on the mouse, this might be an OK way to paste.

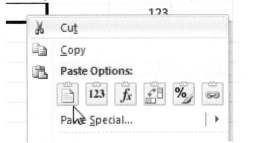

Figure 384 Right-click and choose the first Paste icon.

Method 5: Press the Program key. Let go of the Program key and press P. Since the program key is on the right side of the keyboard, this probably does not beat Ctrl+V.

Fastest Method: Ctrl+V. If you need to paste the same cell in many different locations, hit Ctrl+V with your left hand and use the arrow keys with your right hand to move to the next location.

Tell Me Every Way to Copy a Formula down a Column

I have hundreds of rows of data in A:E. I just entered a new formula in F2. How can I copy this down to all of the rows?

	F2		▼		f_x	=E2*2%	

◢	A	B	C	D	E	F	
1	Region	Date	Customer	Revenue	Profit	Bonus	
2	East	1/1/2014	Ford	22810	12590	251.8	
3	Central	1/2/2014	Verizon	2257	1273		
4	East	1/4/2014	Merck	18552	10680		

Figure 385 Copy this formula down to all rows.

Slowest Method: Select cell F2. The square dot in the lower right corner is called the Fill Handle. Using the mouse, grab the fill handle and start to drag down. Excel starts scrolling faster and faster, but will pause momentarily at the last row. If your reflexes are fast enough, release the mouse button, otherwise, you will quickly find yourself copying the formula hundreds of rows too far. If you currently use this method, jump ahead to Method 4.

Method 2: If your manager is a keyboard fanatic, he might use this method:
1. Ctrl+C to copy.
2. Left Arrow to move to the filled column E.
3. Ctrl+Down Arrow to move to the bottom of the data set.
4. Right Arrow to move back to the empty column F.
5. Ctrl+Shift+Up Arrow to select from the last row back to F2.
6. Ctrl+V to paste.
7. Ctrl+. (period) to move to the top of the column.

People who use this method are incredibly quick with the method. You can get as quick with the method if you do it once an hour for two weeks straight.

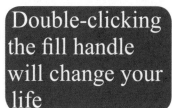

Method 3: The above method doesn't work well if there are many blanks in E. You can modify Method 2 as follows:
1. Ctrl+C to copy.
2. Ctrl+Down Arrow to move to last row in the grid.
3. Left Arrow to move back to column E.
4. Ctrl+Up Arrow to move to the last row with data. (look to make sure you are there. If the last few rows of column E are blank, you might have to press the Down Arrow to get to last row.)
5. Right Arrow to get back to column F.
6. Ctrl+Shift+Up Arrow to select back to F2.
7. Ctrl+V to paste.
8. Ctrl+. to move to the top of the column.

Fastest Method: Instead of dragging the fill handle as in Method 1, select cell F2 and double-click the fill handle. If you are in Excel 2010 or newer, the formula will always get copied to the bottom of the data set. If you are in Excel 2007 or earlier, you need to press Ctrl+Down Arrow to make sure that the formula was copied all the way.

Controversial Method That Your Boss Will Hate: Before entering anything in column F, select one cell in the data and press Ctrl+T. Click OK. This will define your data as a table. Once you enter a formula in F2, it will automatically get copied down to all rows of the table. While this sounds like a brilliant feature, having a Table causes the formula to use an unusual syntax. Also, features like the View Manager won't work any more once you use a table. Proceed only with your manager's approval.

Tell Me Every Way to Convert Formulas to Values

I created a new column C that points to column A and B. I only want to keep column C. I don't need column A and B anymore. However, when I delete columns A and B, the formula that I wrote changes to the #REF! error. I want to convert the formulas in C to their current values so I can safely delete A and B.

	A	B	C	D
	C2	▼	f_x =PROPER(A2&" "&B2)	
1	FIRST	LAST	Name	
2	THOMAS	STEWART	Thomas Stewart	
3	PAUL	MCCARTNEY	Paul Mccartney	
4	BILL	JELEN	Bill Jelen	
5	JON	TESSMER	Jon Tessmer	

Figure 386 This formula joins text from A and B with a space and converts to proper case.

	A	B	C	D	E	F
	A2	▼		f_x =PROPER(#REF!&" "&#REF!)		
1	Name					
2	#REF!					
3	#REF!					

Figure 387 If you delete A and B, the formula can no longer calculate.

The solution is to use Paste Special Values. There are many different ways to invoke this command.

Method 1: Select the range that contains your formula. Press Ctrl+C to copy. Open the Paste dropdown and choose Paste Special. In the Paste Special dialog, choose Values and then OK.

	A	B	C
1	FIRST	LAST	Name
2	THOMAS	STEWART	Thomas Stewart
3	PAUL	MCCARTNEY	Paul Mccartney
4	BILL	JELEN	Bill Jelen
5	JON	TESSMER	
6	SUSAN	HALLORAN	Paste Special
7	AMY	MCMASTER	
8	TAMMY	ROSSI	Paste
9	RANDOLF	COFFIN	○ All
10	FRANK	DOYLE	○ Formulas
11	TOYA	WHITE	◉ Values
12	STEPHANIE	LENNON	○ Formats

Figure 388 Choose Values in the Paste Special dialog.

Method 2: This is the same as Method 1, but it uses all keyboard shortcuts. Select the data. Press Ctrl+C. then Alt+E followed by S, then V, and then Enter.

Method 3 is for Excel 2007: Select the data. Press Ctrl+C to copy. Open the Paste dropdown and choose Values.

Method 4 is for Excel 2010: Select the data. Press Ctrl+C to copy. Press and release the Program key (it shows a mouse pointer on a menu and is usually to the right of the spacebar, between Alt and Ctrl). Press V.

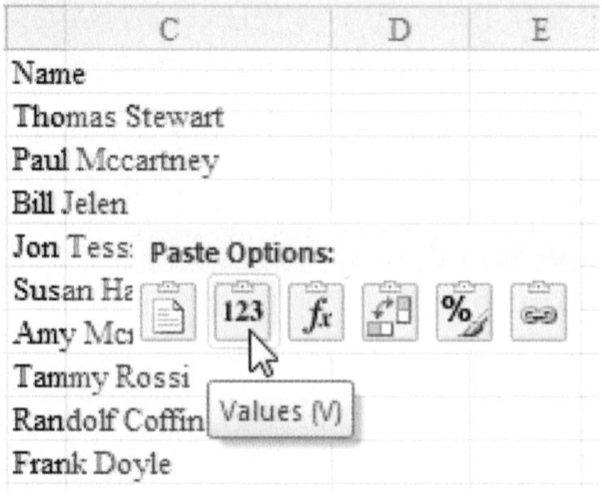

Figure 389 The 123 icon will paste as values.

Method 5 is for people who prefer the mouse: Select the data. Using the mouse, point to the right border of the selection. Hold down the right mouse button while you drag the selection to the right one column and then back to the original column. When you let go of the right mouse button, a super-secret menu appears with an option for Copy Here as Values Only.

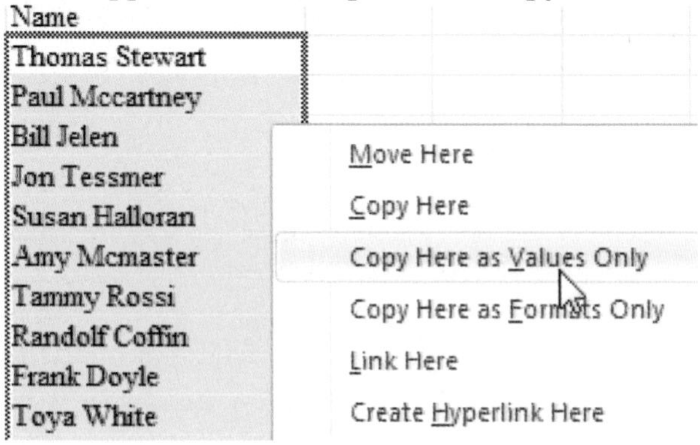

Figure 390 Right-drag the selection to get to this menu.

Tell Me Every Way to Total a Column

I need to put a total at the bottom of a column of numbers. How can I do that?

	A	B	C	D	E	F	G	H	I	J	K	L	M	N
1	Div.	Jan $	Feb $	Mar $	Apr $	May $	Jun $	Jul $	Aug $	Sep $	Oct $	Nov $	Dec $	Total
2	A	$218K	$150K	$462K	$130K	$376K	$335K	$285K	$317K	$314K	$353K	$162K	$333K	
3	B	$306K	$216K	$232K	$150K	$362K	$302K	$378K	$436K	$274K	$204K	$416K	$257K	
4	C	$132K	$138K	$195K	$297K	$450K	$120K	$382K	$149K	$118K	$339K	$126K	$369K	
5	D	$135K	$473K	$337K	$156K	$281K	$256K	$222K	$149K	$175K	$322K	$233K	$384K	
6	E	$374K	$350K	$383K	$439K	$139K	$189K	$344K	$402K	$166K	$411K	$191K	$107K	
7	Total													
8														

Figure 391 Add totals to this data.

If you know anyone who is using either of the first two methods, please photocopy this page and give it to them.

Really Bad Method 1: Grab a calculator. Type 217940+305556+131553+135497+374310=. Type the result shown in the calculator into cell B7. If you wonder why this is bad, please see Method 4.

Almost as Bad Method 2: Select cells B2:B6. Look in the lower right corner of Excel where the quick sum shows you the total of the selected cells. Repeat that number aloud three times so you don't forget it. Select cell B7. Type the number that you just repeated three times and hope you didn't transpose a couple of digits.

Light Years Ahead, but Still Not So Good Method 3: Select cell B7. Type =B2+B3+B4+B5+B6 and press Enter. Excel will calculate the total. Why this isn't so good – try using the same method when you have 100 cells to add instead of five.

Method 4: Select cell B7. Type the formula:

`=SUM(B2:B6)`

and press Enter. This is the best formula, but there are faster ways to enter it.

Method 5: Select cell B7. Type Alt+= (that is, hold down Alt and press Equals). Excel will propose a formula of `=SUM(B2:B6)`. Press Enter to accept the formula. This method won't work well if your heading in B1 is numeric or if there are blank cells for some divisions. Instead of Alt+=, you could also use the Sigma icon on the right side of the Home tab or on the left side of the Formulas tab.

◢	A	B	C	D	E	F
1	Div.	Jan $	Feb $	Mar $	Apr $	May
2	A	$218K	$150K	$462K	$130K	$376
3	B	$306K	$216K	$232K	$150K	$362
4	C	$132K	$138K	$195K	$297K	$450
5	D	$135K	$473K	$337K	$156K	$281
6	E	$374K	$350K	$383K	$439K	$139
7	Total	=SUM(B2:B6)				
8		SUM(**number1**, [number2], ...)				
9						

Figure 392 Alt+= will propose a SUM formula for you.

Method 6: Select B2:B7 (that is, all of your numbers plus one extra cell below. Type Alt+= or click the Sigma icon. Excel will put the following formula below your data: `=SUM(B2:B6)`

Method 7: Select B7:M7 and press Alt+= or click the AutoSum Sigma icon. Excel will put in all 12 formulas at once, without requiring you to review the selection.

Caution: Don't use this method if the headings in row 1 are numeric.

Method 8: Select B2:N7. This is all of your numbers plus one extra row and one extra column. Press Alt+= or click the AutoSum icon. Excel will add a total row and a total column.

◢	A	B	C	D	E	F	G	H	I	J	K	L	M	N
1	Div.	Jan $	Feb $	Mar $	Apr $	May $	Jun $	Jul $	Aug $	Sep $	Oct $	Nov $	Dec $	Total
2	A	$218K	$150K	$462K	$130K	$376K	$335K	$285K	$317K	$314K	$353K	$162K	$333K	
3	B	$306K	$216K	$232K	$150K	$362K	$302K	$378K	$436K	$274K	$204K	$416K	$257K	
4	C	$132K	$138K	$195K	$297K	$450K	$120K	$382K	$149K	$118K	$339K	$126K	$369K	
5	D	$135K	$473K	$337K	$156K	$281K	$256K	$222K	$149K	$175K	$322K	$233K	$384K	
6	E	$374K	$350K	$383K	$439K	$139K	$189K	$344K	$402K	$166K	$411K	$191K	$107K	
7	Total													
8														

Figure 393 Select all numbers, one extra row + column, then press Alt+=.

The advantage of Methods 3 through 8 is that if you change any numbers in B2:M7, the total cells will automatically recalculate!

Tell Me Every Way to Format Every Other Row

I have hundreds of rows of data in A:M. It is difficult to follow the data across the row in order to match up the label in column A with the value in column M. I want to shade every other row in a different color.

First, you have to ask yourself if you will be inserting, deleting or sorting the data after this point in time. If you are sure that the rows are complete and you won't be adding or deleting rows, then you can use one of the static methods shown below.

If you use a static method and then delete a row, the effect will be ruined, as shown here:

	A	B	C	D
1	Region	Date	Customer	Revenue
2	East	1/1/2014	Ford	22810
3	Central	1/2/2014	Verizon	2257
4	East	1/4/2014	Merck	18552
5	East	1/7/2014	State Farm	21730
6	East	1/7/2014	General Motors	8456
7	Central	1/9/2014	General Motors	16416

Figure 394 After deleting the old row 5, the alternating colors are wrong in this static solution.

There are dynamic solutions that can adapt as the rows are inserted, deleted, or sorted. But they are more difficult to set up.

Static Method 1: This method only works in Excel 2007 or newer.
1. Select one cell in your data.
2. Press Ctrl+T to declare the range as a table.
3. Excel will temporarily show a Ribbon tab called Table Tools Design. There is a large gallery on the right side called Table Styles. At the right edge of the gallery are three arrow icons. Click the bottom icon to open the gallery. Choose one of the 48 styles shown.
4. Some people dislike tables. Formulas that point to tables have a strange and unfamiliar nomenclature. Some Excel features don't work with tables. There is an icon called Convert to Range on the Table Tools Design tab. Choose this to remove the table features but keep the formatting.

This is a really quick method to apply the every-other row formatting. You are somewhat limited in the color choices, but this is a quick way to solve the problem.

Static Method 2: This method works in any version of Excel.
1. Select row 2 of your data and use the Fill Color (aka Paint Bucket) dropdown to apply a color to row 2.
2. Select row 3 of your data and apply a contrasting color.
3. Select the data in rows 2:3.
4. Ctrl+C to copy.
5. Select all of the data. After step 4, you can usually do Ctrl+Shift+Down Arrow.
6. Paste Special Formats. If you are in Excel 2010, right-click and choose the Paste Formats icon shown in the next figure. If you are in earlier versions, choose Paste Special from the right-click menu. In the Paste Special dialog, choose Formats and click OK.

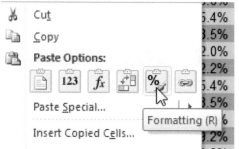

Figure 395 In Excel 2010, right-click and choose this icon.

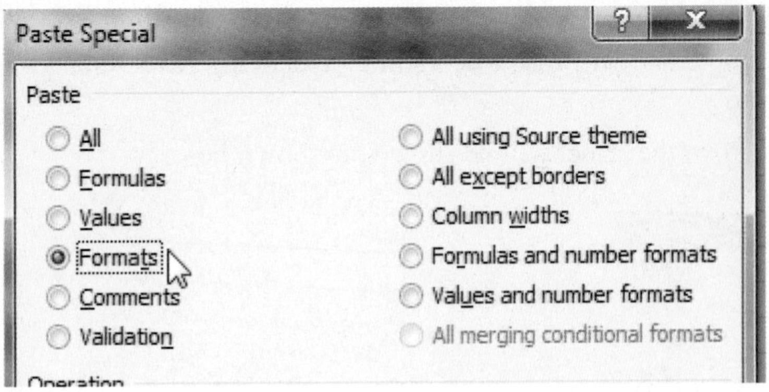

Figure 396 In earlier versions, choose Paste Special... and then Formats.

Dynamic Method for Excel 2007 or Newer: If your manager agrees that it is OK to use the new table functionality, follow steps 1-3 in Method 1, but do not convert the table back to a range. As you insert rows, Excel will automatically adjust the formatting.

Dynamic Method for any version of Excel: This method uses conditional formatting to shade all of the even numbered rows. It takes the longest to set up but then causes the least hassle in the future.

1. Choose two colors that you will use for the formatting. Apply color one to all rows in the data.
2. Select all data from A2 down and to the right of your data.
3. Type Alt+O followed by D to bring up conditional formatting.

If you are in Excel 2003, you will see a dropdown that says Cell Value Is. Open this dropdown and choose Formula Is. If you are in Excel 2007 or newer, choose New Rule and then choose Use a Formula to Determine Which Rows to Format. In either case, you will now have a large area where you can type a formula.

Look in the name box to the left of the Formula Bar to see the name of the active cell. In this case, the active cell is A2. You will use whichever cell is your active cell in place of A2 in the following formula.

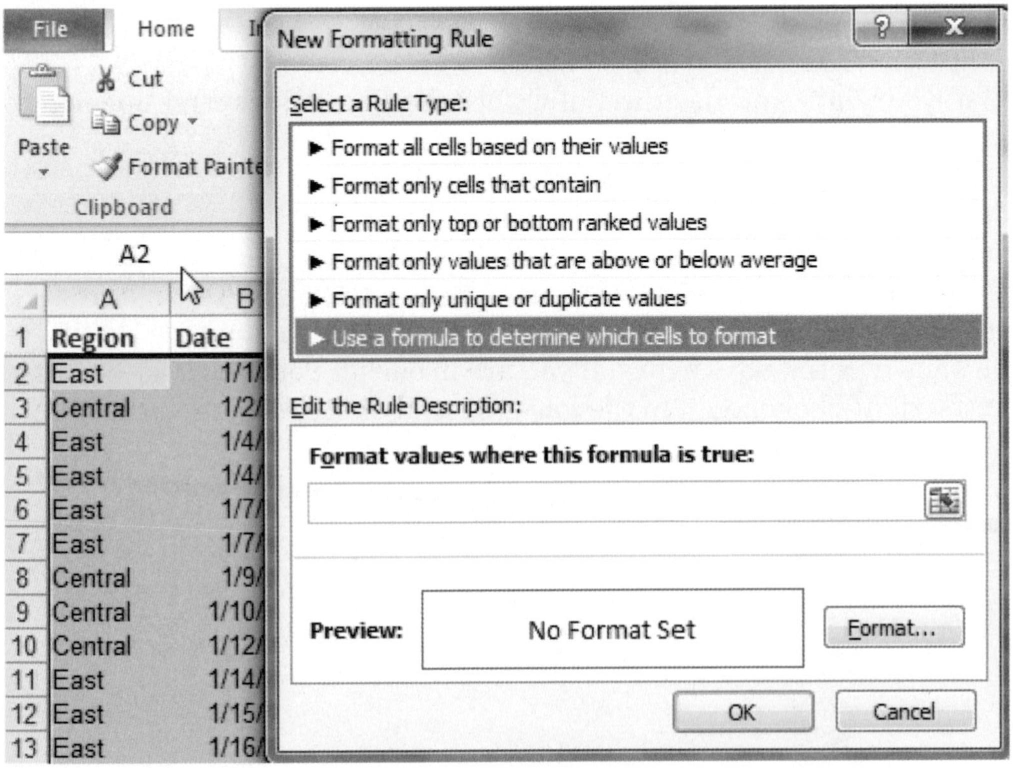

Figure 397 Note the active cell in the name box. In this case, it is A2.

4. Type the formula: =MOD(ROW(A2),2)=0
5. Click the Format button.
6. Choose a fill color that contrasts the color you used in step 1.

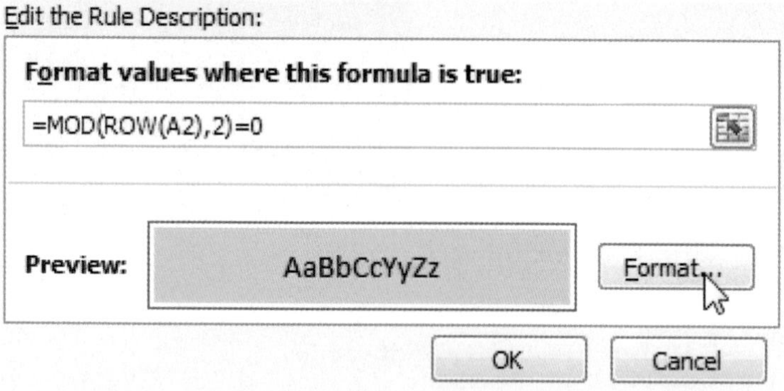

Edit the Rule Description:

Format values where this formula is true:

=MOD(ROW(A2),2)=0

Preview: AaBbCcYyZz   Format...

OK   Cancel

Figure 398 This cryptic formula will be true for every other row.

7. Click OK until you return to the worksheet. Magically, every other row will be formatted.

	A	B	C	
1	Region	Date	Customer	Re
2	East	1/1/2014	Ford	
3	Central	1/2/2014	Verizon	
4	East	1/4/2014	Merck	
5	East	1/4/2014	Texaco	
6	East	1/7/2014	State Farm	
7	East	1/7/2014	General Motors	

Figure 399 Every other row is formatted using conditional formatting.

The advantage of this method is that if you sort the data, the formatting continues to appear on every other row.

Region	Date	Customer
West	9/1/2014	AIG
East	4/14/2015	AIG
Central	6/25/2015	AIG
West	11/5/2015	AIG
East	1/14/2014	AT&T
West	3/22/2014	AT&T

Figure 400 Even after sorting, the formatting continues to work.

In case you are wondering about the formula, it uses the ROW function to return the row number for each cell. In A2, the row number is 2. In M55, the row number is 55. The formula then sends that row number into the MOD function. While MOD stands for Modulo, think of it this way: when you were first learning to divide, you would come up with an answer and a remainder. For example, 55/2 would have been 27 R 1 or 27 with a remainder of 1. The MOD function returns only the remainder. When you divide by 2, the only possible remainders are 1 (for the odd rows) and 0 (for the even rows). By checking to see if the remainder is 0, the conditional formatting applies the second color to the even numbered rows. For the odd rows, nothing is applied, so the base color remains.

Tell Me Every Way to Turn Data Sideways

I figured out a wild SUMIF formula to summarize data by month. I built the table with months going across. My manager wants me to re-do the analysis so that the months go down. Is there an easy way to turn this sideways?

The feature that you are looking for is called Transpose. There are several ways to transpose the data, but you have to understand one limitation.

You can turn a range sideways and copy it to a new location such as

> The paste area can not overlap the copied range when transposing

shown in Figure 401.

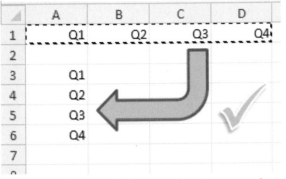

Figure 401 Transposing from one location to another.

However, you cannot have the twisted copy overlap the original data in any way. This seems to be a common need when you want to pivot headings. If you want to do the transpose shown below, you will first have to transpose to another location, then cut and paste the transposed data.

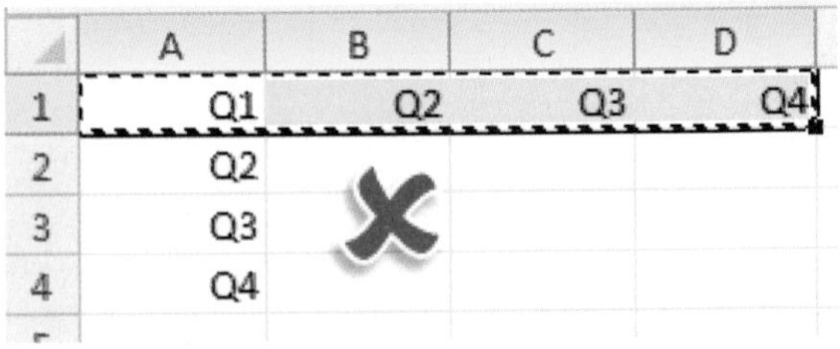

Figure 402 The pasted location cannot overlap the original location.

Method 1: To turn data, follow these steps:
1. Select the data to be turned.
2. Ctrl+C or click the copy icon to copy the data.
3. Select a new cell location for the transposed data.
4. Open the dropdown at the bottom of the Paste icon and choose Transpose.
5. If you want to delete the original data, re-select the data. Open the Eraser icon in the Editing group of the Home tab and choose Clear All.

Caution: These steps create a one-time copy of the original data. If the original data later changes, the twisted copy will not change.

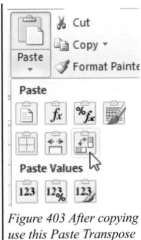

Figure 403 After copying use this Paste Transpose option.

Method 2: If you are using Excel 2003 or earlier, the classic solution is to use the Transpose option in the Paste Special dialog. You will copy the horizontal range; select a completely new cell, then Paste Special. In the Paste Special dialog, choose the Transpose checkbox near the bottom right of the dialog as shown in Figure 404.

It is important to check the formulas in the new section to make sure that they are still working. Because the original formulas used some absolute ranges and one relative range that pointed to the copy range, the formulas worked in Figure 405.

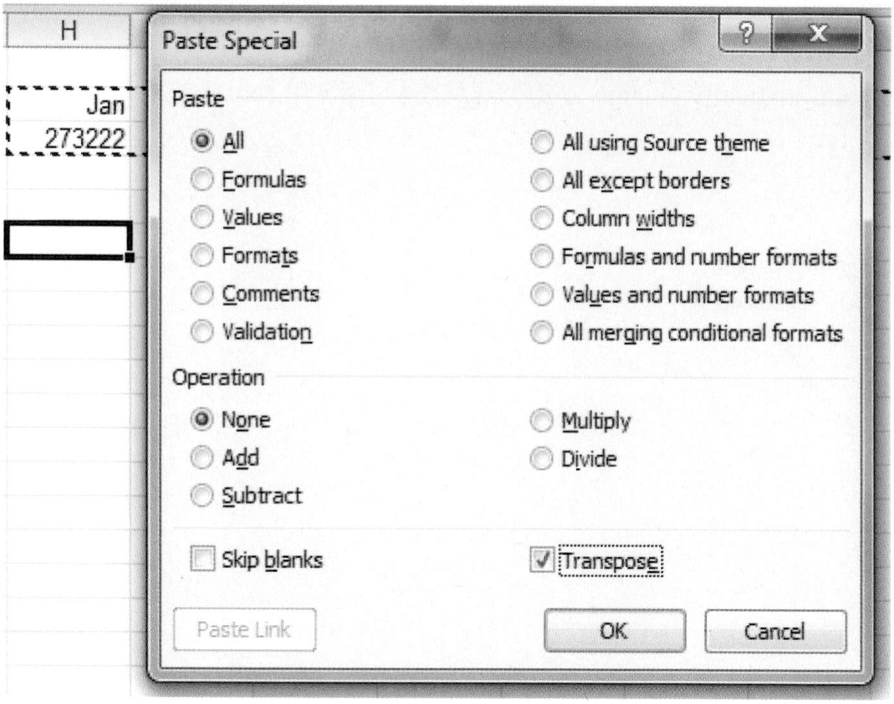

Figure 404 Select Transpose in the Paste Special dialog.

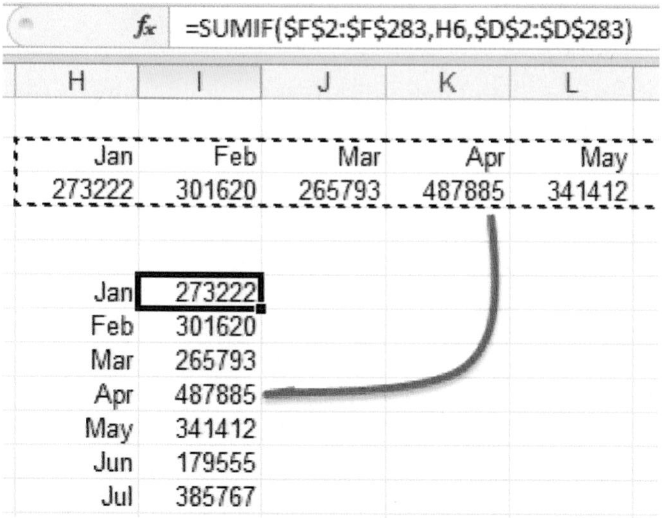

Figure 405 Check the formulas after the transpose.

The Paste Special Transpose method will also work for turning vertical data back to horizontal.

Method 3: If you plan to leave the original range where it is, you can transpose with a formula.

The goal is to take the results in H3:S3 and turn them sideways.

In the first row of the new range, you want the first value from H3:S3.

In row 12 of the new range, you want the twelfth value from H3:S3.

The function to return a specific value from a range is called INDEX.

The formula for the first cell would be:

```
=INDEX($H$3:$S$3,1)
```

However, if you used this formula, you would have to edit the formula to change the 1 to a 2 in the second row, then a 3 in the third row, and so on.

When you need an argument to automatically change from 1 to 2, 3, 4, as it gets copied, replace the 1 with ROW(A1). The ROW function will return a 1 since cell A1 is in the first row. As you copy the formula down, the formula will automatically change to ROW(A2) which will return a 2.

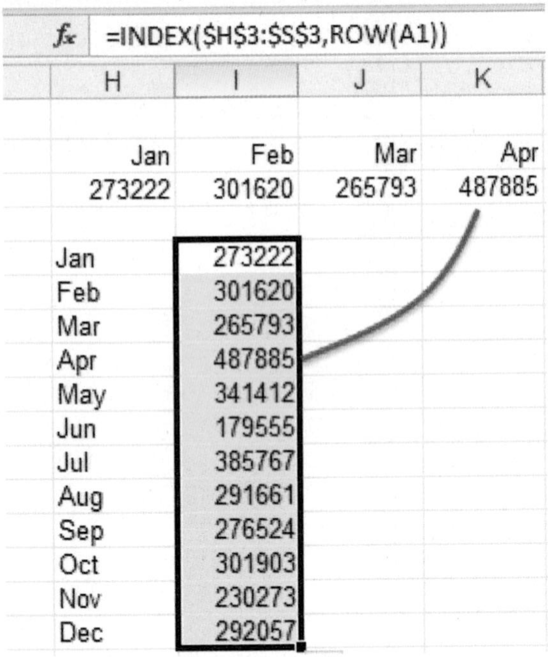

f_x	=INDEX($H$3:$S$3,ROW(A1))		
H	**I**	**J**	**K**
Jan	Feb	Mar	Apr
273222	301620	265793	487885
Jan	273222		
Feb	301620		
Mar	265793		
Apr	487885		
May	341412		
Jun	179555		
Jul	385767		
Aug	291661		
Sep	276524		
Oct	301903		
Nov	230273		
Dec	292057		

Figure 406 This formula will turn horizontal data to vertical.

The formula method needs to be adjusted to turn vertical data back to horizontal. Rather than using ROW(A1), you will use COLUMN(A1) to generate the 1. As this gets copied across, it will point to COLUMN(B1) which is 2, and so on.

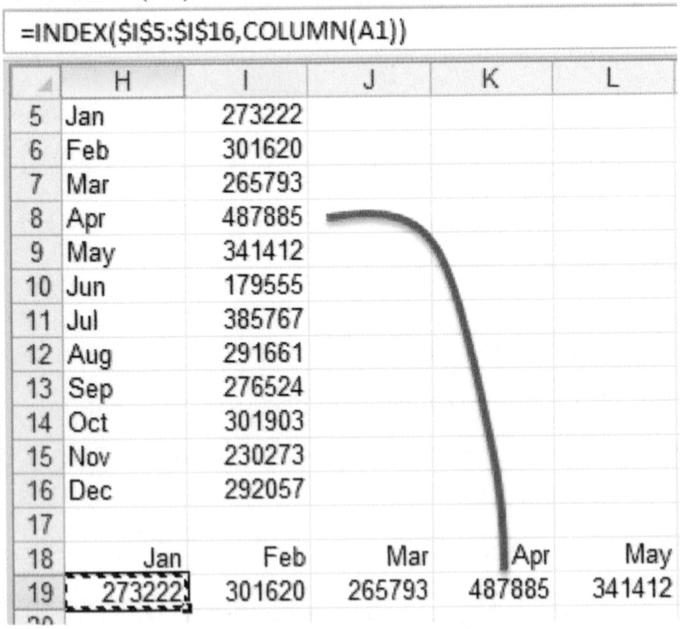

=INDEX($I$5:$I$16,COLUMN(A1))				
H	**I**	**J**	**K**	**L**
5 Jan	273222			
6 Feb	301620			
7 Mar	265793			
8 Apr	487885			
9 May	341412			
10 Jun	179555			
11 Jul	385767			
12 Aug	291661			
13 Sep	276524			
14 Oct	301903			
15 Nov	230273			
16 Dec	292057			
17				
18 Jan	Feb	Mar	Apr	May
19 273222	301620	265793	487885	341412

Figure 407 This formula will turn vertical data to horizontal.

CHAPTER 9 - DATA ANALYSIS INTRO

Introduction to the Data Analysis Chapter

I have an interview this afternoon and I have to know about some of those Level 4 and Level 5 topics. Can you help me out?

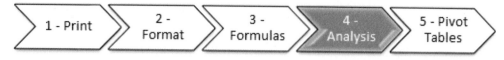

Figure 408 If the job description asks for Excel, you will have to know the items in this chapter.

Before you try anything in this chapter, you have to understand the rules for setting up data. I call this List Format.

In list format, you have:

- A single row of headings at the top of the data set.
- If the headings are not in row 1, you have a blank row above the headings to separate it from any titles.
- There are no blank columns in the data. If your manager wants tiny blank columns between the columns to make the lines under the headings look good, do not do it. Search the Internet for Learn Excel Podcast 1259 for an alternative method.
- There should be no blank rows.
- If there is a total row, keep one blank row above the total row to separate it from the rest of the data. It is fine to make that row have a height of one or to hide it, but there has to be a blank row.
- If you need to jot a grocery list to the right of your data, leave one completely blank column to the right of the data.

	A	B	C	D	E	F	G
1	Region	Date	Customer	Revenue	Profit	Bonus	GP%
2	West	9/1/2014	AIG	18072	9896	197.9	54.8%
3	East	4/14/2015	AIG	14004	8100	162	57.8%
4	Central	6/25/2015	AIG	4060	2092	41.84	51.5%
5	West	11/5/2015	AIG	15104	8328	166.6	55.1%
6	East	1/14/2014	AT&T	2401	1379	27.58	57.4%
7	West	3/22/2014	AT&T	6765	3699	73.98	54.7%
8	Central	3/28/2014	AT&T	21357	12501	250	58.5%
9	Central	4/1/2014	AT&T	14448	8316	166.3	57.6%

Figure 409 This is data in list format.

Tip: If you follow these rules, the techniques in this chapter will work wonderfully and you will be the hero at your office. If you skip any one of these rules, you run the risk of really screwing something up and presenting bad analyses that get sent to the boardroom resulting in a lot of screaming and yelling. Listen to what I say, I've had it happen to me. I've had it happen to people who work for me. It isn't fun. Follow the rules. They are there for a reason.

How Do I Sort Data?

My data is sorted by customer. I want it sorted by date.

If your data is in list format, it is very simple to sort the data.

Select one cell in the date column. It can be the heading cell. It can be the first date. It can be the 52nd date. But you have to select exactly one cell in the data column.

	A	B	C	D	E	F	G
1	Region	Date	Customer	Revenue	Profit	Bonus	GP%
2	West	9/1/2014	AIG	18072	9896	197.9	54.8%
3	East	4/14/2015	AIG	14004	8100	162	57.8%
4	Central	6/25/2015	AIG	4060	2092	41.84	51.5%
5	West	11/5/2015	AIG	15104	8328	166.6	55.1%
6	East	1/14/2014	AT&T	2401	1379	27.58	57.4%

Figure 410 Select a single cell in the column that you want to sort by.

On the Data tab, click AZ to sort ascending or ZA to sort descending.

Figure 411 Sort the current region around the active cell. Select a single cell in the column that you want to sort by.

Select exactly one cell when sorting using the AZ or ZA icon

The result: data is sorted by date.

	A	B	C	D	E	F	G
1	Region	Date	Customer	Revenue	Profit	Bonus	GP%
2	East	1/1/2014	Ford	22810	12590	251.8	55.2%
3	Central	1/2/2014	Verizon	2257	1273	25.46	56.4%
4	East	1/4/2014	Merck	18552	10680	213.6	57.6%
5	East	1/4/2014	Texaco	9152	5064	101.3	55.3%
6	East	1/7/2014	General Motors	8456	5068	101.4	59.9%

Figure 412 Two clicks to sort.

Caution: Be sure there are no blank columns in your data.

Caution: Do not select two cells or the whole column. Do not. Disaster awaits. Don't do it.

If you are sorting money columns, you will often sort descending. This data has the largest profit at the top.

	A	B	C	D	E	F	G
1	Region	Date	Customer	Revenue	Profit	Bonus	GP%
2	East	7/17/2014	Bank of America	25350	15130	302.6	59.7%
3	West	5/2/2015	AT&T	25310	15090	301.8	59.6%
4	Central	2/26/2014	Wal-Mart	25140	14920	298.4	59.3%

Figure 413 Sort descending.

What if you need to sort by two columns, such as Descending Profit with Region? Sort by the inner sort field first (Profit). Then sort by Region. You could continue this pattern to do a ten-level sort if you needed to.

What Is the Filter on the Data Tab?

It says AutoFilter in Excel 2003, but in Excel 2010, it just says Filter.

Figure 414 AutoFilter is now Filter.

Say that you have a large worksheet with a few hundred records with data for different customers all mixed in. Your manager wants you to quickly find all of the March 2015 sales to General Motors.

Choose one cell in the data set and click the Filter icon. Excel will add filter dropdowns to each heading cell.

	A	B	C	D	E	F
1	Region ▾	Date ▾	Customer ▾	Reven ▾	Pro ▾	GF ▾
2	East	1/1/2014	Ford	22810	12590	55%
3	Central	1/2/2014	Verizon	2257	1273	56%
4	East	1/4/2014	Merck	18552	10680	58%
5	East	1/4/2014	Texaco	9152	5064	55%

Figure 415 You have 560 rows of data in this worksheet. Excel adds Filter dropdowns to each heading in row 1.

Open the Customer dropdown in column C. Initially, all customers are selected. Uncheck the box called (Select All) to unselect all customers.

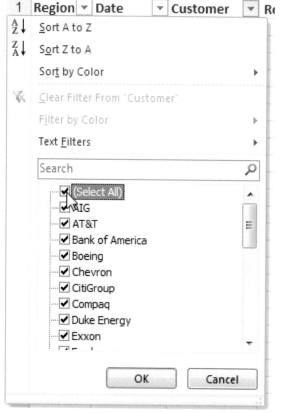

Figure 416 First, click Select All to turn off all customers.

Once you've cleared all the customers, choose General Motors. (In another situation, you might want to choose both Ford and General Motors – that would be fine.)

Figure 417 Choose the customers you want to see.

Starting in Excel 2010, the filters handle dates in a new way. Open the dropdown in B2 for date. Rather than show 500 date values, Excel collapses them in an outline. First, uncheck (Select All). Click the + next to 2015 so you can see the months. Choose March and click OK.

Figure 418 It is easier to filter dates in Excel 2010.

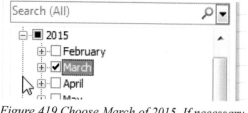

Figure 419 Choose March of 2015. If necessary, you could expand March to choose certain days.

Excel hides all the rows that are not General Motors records from March 2015. Notice the row numbers in the figure below. The other data is still there, but those rows are hidden.

At this point, you could copy the range and you would only get the five visible rows when you paste.

To clear the filter, click the Clear button next to the Filter icon. To hide the filter dropdowns, click the Filter icon again.

Figure 420 To go back to seeing all records, use Clear.

Note: If you have to add the rows that are visible from a filter, use the AutoSum button after you've applied a filter. Excel will put in =SUBTOTAL functions that show only the rows selected in the filter.

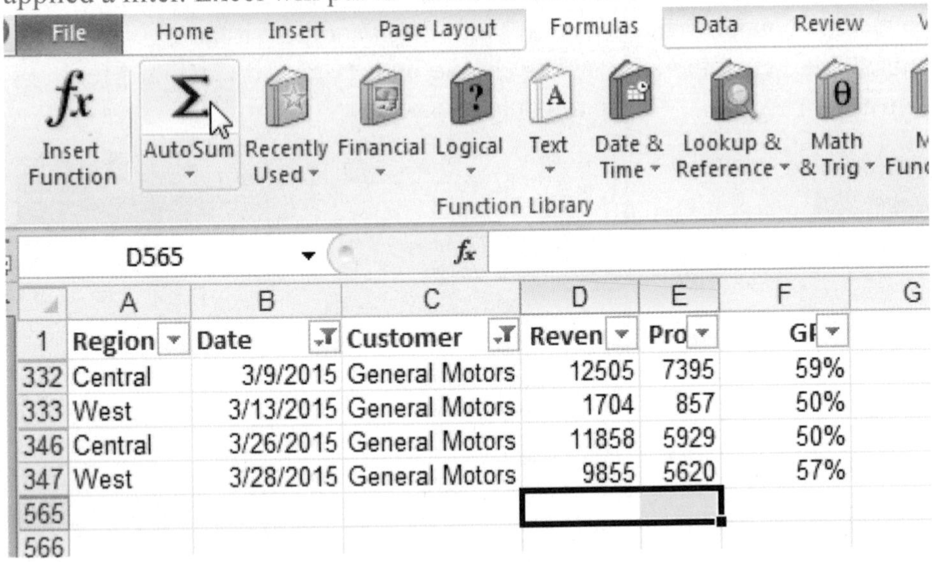

	Region ▾	Date	Customer	Reven ▾	Pro ▾	GF ▾	G
332	Central	3/9/2015	General Motors	12505	7395	59%	
333	West	3/13/2015	General Motors	1704	857	50%	
346	Central	3/26/2015	General Motors	11858	5929	50%	
347	West	3/28/2015	General Motors	9855	5620	57%	
565							
566							

Figure 421 Apply a filter first, and then use the AutoSum.

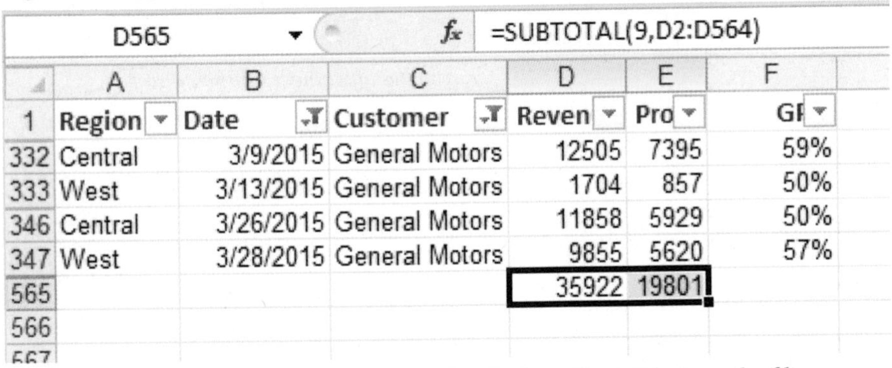

D565 f_x =SUBTOTAL(9,D2:D564)

	Region ▾	Date	Customer	Reven ▾	Pro ▾	GF ▾	F
332	Central	3/9/2015	General Motors	12505	7395	59%	
333	West	3/13/2015	General Motors	1704	857	50%	
346	Central	3/26/2015	General Motors	11858	5929	50%	
347	West	3/28/2015	General Motors	9855	5620	57%	
565				35922	19801		
566							
567							

Figure 422 Excel will use a formula to total only the cells visible from the filter.

👀 You Did What?

Why Can't I Filter to All of the Arizona Records?

Patricia received a call from a co-worker. This co-worker was fairly advanced in Excel, in that she had added the AutoFilter icon to her Quick Access Toolbar in order to have one-click access to Filter by Selection. The co-worker selected a cell containing the state code of "AZ". She clicked the AutoFilter icon in the Quick Access Toolbar. She went to the blank row below the data and clicked the AutoSum icon to generate a sub-total formula that sums the visible cells.

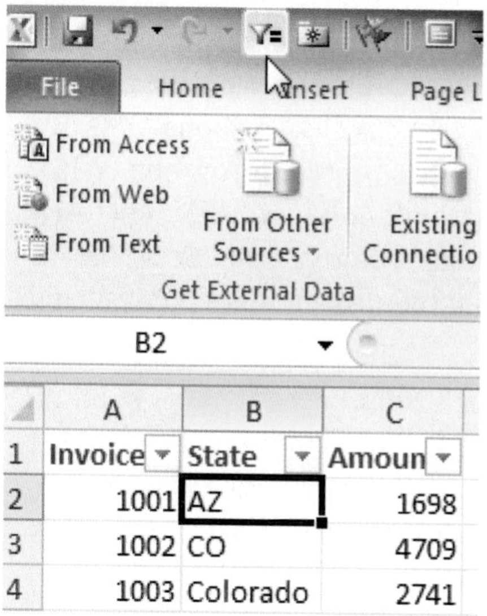

Figure 423 Select an AZ cell and click the AutoFilter icon.

The icon labeled AutoFilter can be added to your Quick Access Toolbar, it really does Filter by Selection

=SUBTOTAL(9,C2:C15)

	A	B	C	D	E
1	Invoice ▼	State ▼	Amoun ▼		
2	1001	AZ	1698		
7	1006	AZ	2839		
11	1010	AZ	3168		
15	1014	AZ	4510		
16	Total Visible		12215		
17					
18		Arizona	12215	<--Manual Note	

Figure 424 After filtering to AZ, use the AutoSum to add a subtotal formula.

The co-worker manually noted the total for Arizona, then repeated the process for "CO" to get the Colorado records. The database only contained records for Arizona and Colorado. However, the co-worker noticed that the total for AZ + CO did not match the grand total. Why wouldn't the AutoFilter work?

	A	B	C	D	E
13	1012	Colorado	2476		
14	1013	Colo.	4989		
15	1014	AZ	4510		
16	Total Visible		45726		
17					
18		Arizona	12215	<--Manual Note	
19		Colorado	6715	<--Manual Note	
20		Total	18930		
21					

Figure 425 The filtered total for each state doesn't add up to the total for the database.

Patricia headed over to the co-worker's computer. The database is shown in this figure.

=SUBTOTAL(9,C2:C15)

⊿	A	B	C	D
1	Invoice ▼	State ▼	Amoun ▼	
2	1001	AZ	1698	
3	1002	CO	4709	
4	1003	Colorado	2741	
5	1004	Ariz.	2584	
6	1005	Arizona	4140	
7	1006	AZ	2839	
8	1007	CO	2006	
9	1008	Colo.	2347	
10	1009	Arizona	3139	
11	1010	AZ	3168	
12	1011	Ariz	4380	
13	1012	Colorado	2476	
14	1013	Colo.	4989	
15	1014	AZ	4510	
16	Total Visible		45726	
17				

Figure 426 There are only two states in the data; Arizona and Colorado.

While the human brain can easily scan through column B and see that there are only two states, Excel does not understand that "AZ", "Arizona", "Ariz" and "Ariz." are all ways to represent Arizona. When you filter to "AZ", you will only get "AZ", not "Arizona", not "Ariz". Excel will give you "az", "Az" or even "aZ". But it cannot figure out that you want any spelling of Arizona.

If you are using Excel 2003 or earlier, the solution is to be consistent. Make sure that you always enter each state the same way. Repeating the exercise with data where all the states are entered the same way produces totals that match.

1009	AZ	3139
1010	AZ	3168
1011	AZ	4380
1012	CO	2476
1013	CO	4989
1014	AZ	4510
Total Visible		45726
	AZ	26458
	CO	19268
	Total	45726

Figure 427 When all the states are entered in a consistent manner, the AutoFilter technique works again.

Note: If the goal is to total each state, you could skip the Filter trick and use the SUMIF function shown in Figure 428.

=SUMIF($B$2:$B$15,B18,$C$2:$C$15)

⊿	A	B	C	D
13	1012	CO	2476	
14	1013	CO	4989	
15	1014	AZ	4510	
16	Total Visible		45726	
17				
18		AZ	26458	<--SUMIF
19		CO	19268	<--SUMIF
20		Total	45726	
21				

Figure 428 Patricia could have shown her co-worker to use COUNTIF instead.

If you are in Excel 2007 or newer, you can use the big Filter icon on the Data tab. Open the State drop-down. You can now choose multiple items, including all possible spellings of Arizona.

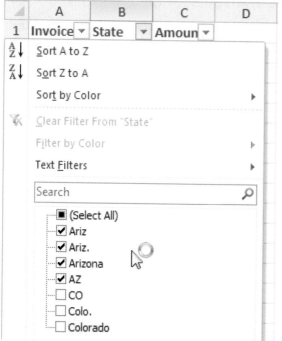

Figure 429 Starting in Excel 2007, you can select multiple items from the filter dropdown.

If you are in Excel 2010 or newer, you can use the new Text Filters choice.

Figure 430 Choose everything starting with A.

How Can I Get Just the Unique Items from a List?

From a column showing many repeated items, you want a list of unique items.

In the following figure, you see a list of names, many of which are repeated two, three, or more times. Here is how you can create a shorter list to show each unique name only once.

A1 ▼	*fx* Names		
	A	B	C	D
1	**Names**			
2	Nancy			
3	Nancy			
4	Madison			
5	Nancy			
6	Steve			
7	Steve			
8	Nancy			
9	Tucker			
10	Nancy			
11	Steve			
12	Madison			
13	Tucker			
14	Tucker			
15	Miley			
16	Steve			
17				

|◄ ◄ ► ►| Sheet1

Figure 431 Original list with many repeated names.

To create a list of unique names in column C based on the list of many repeated names from column A, follow these three steps:
1. Select any single cell in the list. In the figure, cell A1 is selected.
2. From your keyboard, press the Alt key, and while doing so, press the D and F keys. Then, press the A key as shown in the next figure.

Figure 432 From your keyboard, simultaneously press the keys for Alt, D, and F, and then press the A key.

3. You will see the Advanced Filter dialog box as shown below. Click to select the options for "Copy to another location" and "Unique records only". In the Copy to field, you see that $C$1 is entered, which is where the new list of unique items will start. After that, click OK.

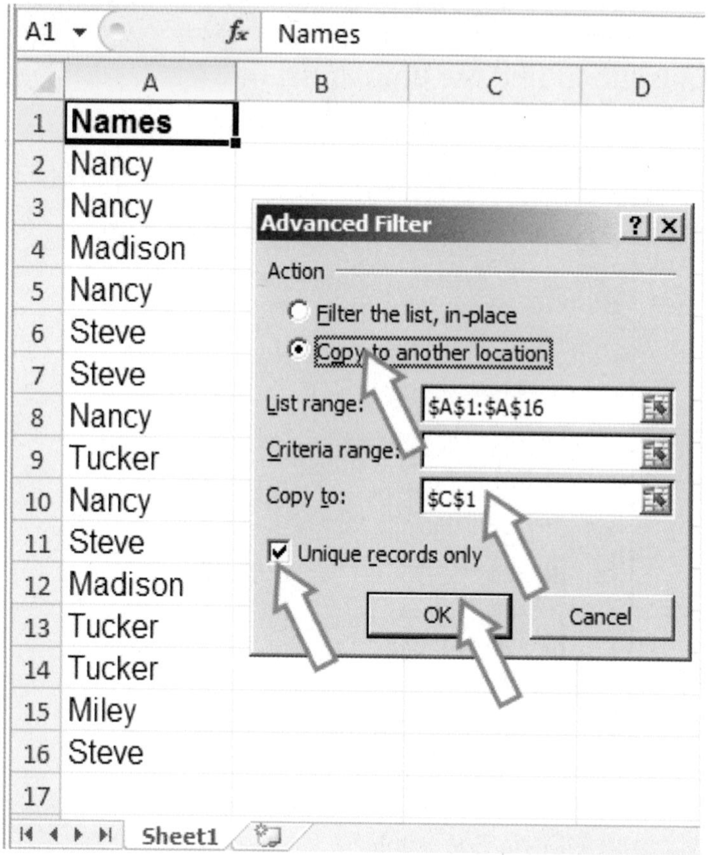

Figure 433 The Advanced Filter dialog with selections to create a unique list.

And that's it! Your list of unique names will be shown in column C, as seen by example in the following figure.

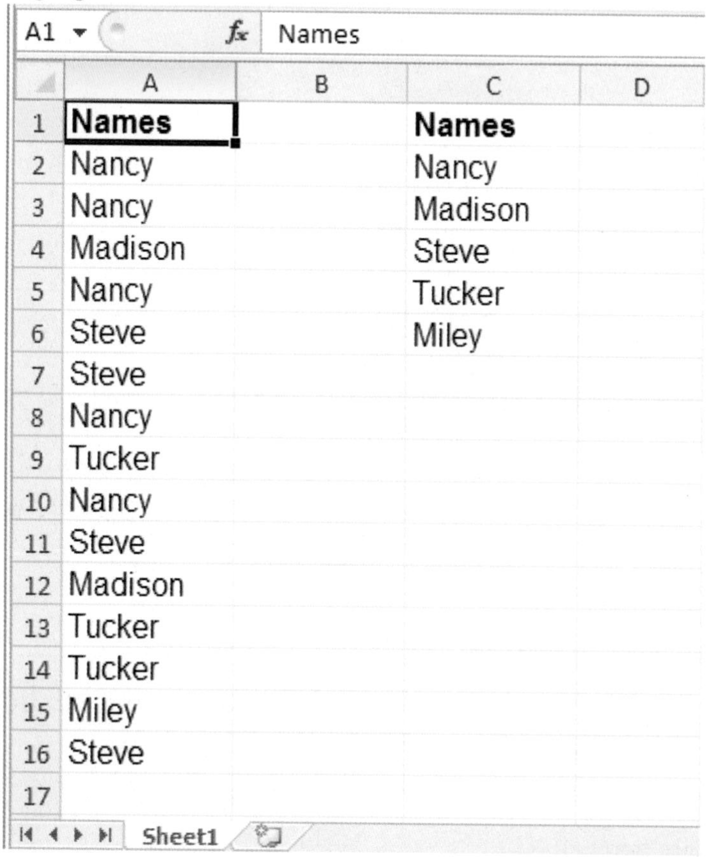

Figure 434 A list of unique names was extracted from column A and placed in column C.

How Do I Remove Duplicates?

I have a big list of data and my boss wants me to find the unique list of customers.

This became dramatically easier starting in Excel 2007.

The new command is destructive, so make sure to do the command on a copy of the data. You can copy the Customer column and paste it a few columns to the right of your data.

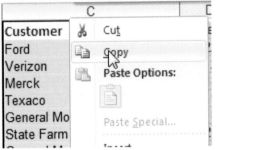

Figure 435 Copy the column and paste somewhere away from your data.

On the Data tab, click the Remove Duplicates button.

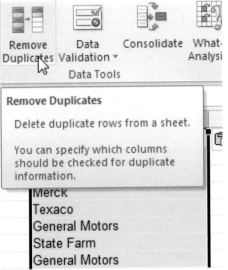

Figure 436 This is new in Excel 2007.

If you have more than one column, uncheck everything but the Customer column.

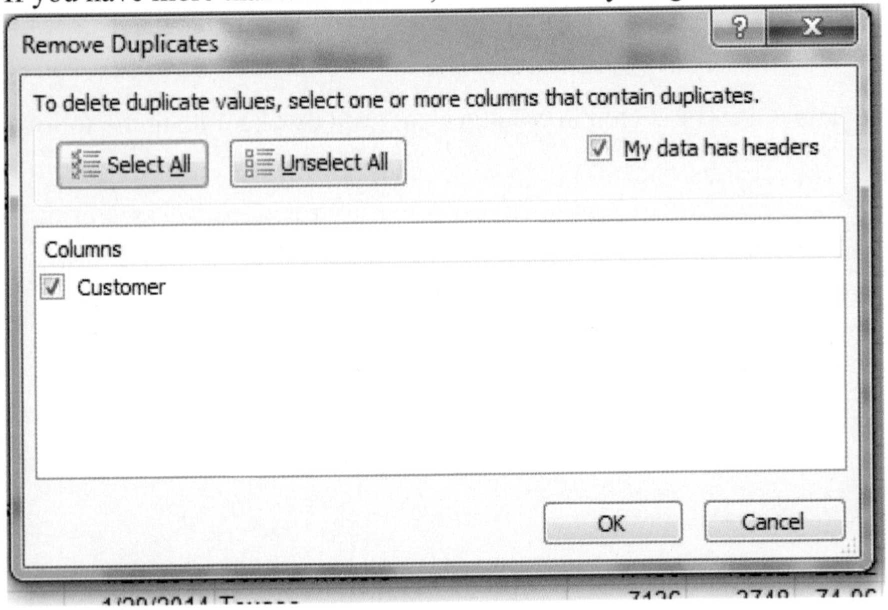

Figure 437 Select the customer column.

The result will be a list of the unique customers. In this case, there are 30 unique customers from the 564 row data set.

Note: The unique list of customers is not sorted. Select one cell and use the AZ icon to sort.

My Boss Wants Me to Sort by Customer and Add Totals after Each Customer.

It takes me two minutes per customer to add the totals and we have 30 customers, but he wants it done in five minutes. Is he insane? How can I do this in five minutes?

Sort the data by customer using the steps on page 171.

Select one cell in the data set. Any cell, but only one cell.

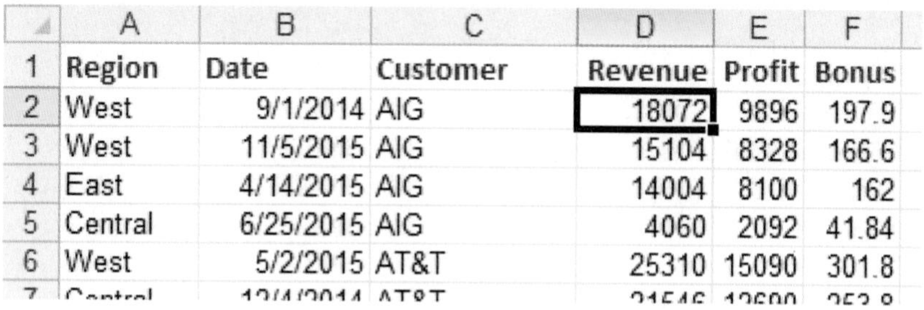

	A	B	C	D	E	F
1	Region	Date	Customer	Revenue	Profit	Bonus
2	West	9/1/2014	AIG	18072	9896	197.9
3	West	11/5/2015	AIG	15104	8328	166.6
4	East	4/14/2015	AIG	14004	8100	162
5	Central	6/25/2015	AIG	4060	2092	41.84
6	West	5/2/2015	AT&T	25310	15090	301.8
7	Central	12/4/2014	AT&T	21546	12600	252.9

Figure 438 Select a single cell in the data set.

On the Data tab, find the Subtotal icon. It is in the Group & Outline group, near the right. It is a big icon in the figure below, but on most monitors, it ends up as a tiny icon. You might have to hover over a few icons to find it, but it is worth the hunt.

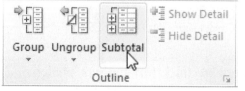

Figure 439 The big version of the Subtotal icon.

Click the Subtotal icon and you get the Subtotal dialog. Every assumption in this dialog is wrong. Spend two minutes here checking everything.

Open the At Each Change in dropdown, and choose Customer.

Open the Use Function dropdown and choose Sum. There are eleven functions in the dropdown, but sum is the one used 99% of the time.

In the Add Subtotal To area, choose all of your numeric fields. You might have to scroll to see them all.

If you want every customer on their own page, choose Page Break Between Groups.

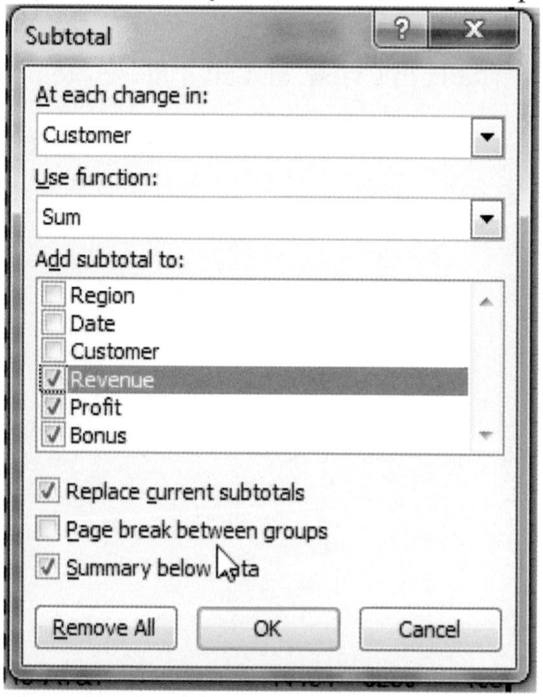

Figure 440 Carefully fill out this dialog box.

Click OK. In a few seconds, Excel has completed the task! After every customer, there is a new row and a total for that customer. At the bottom, there is a grand total. It is simply amazing.

1 2 3		A	B	C	D	E	F
·	133	Central	9/14/2015	CitiGroup	2058	1036	20.72
·	134	Central	2/8/2014	CitiGroup	1817	970	19.4
−	135			**CitiGroup Total**	613514	338409	6768
·	136	West	11/16/2014	Compaq	17250	8780	175.6
·	137	Central	6/7/2015	Compaq	9064	4976	99.52
·	138	West	11/25/2015	Compaq	8556	4468	89.36
·	139	East	8/7/2015	Compaq	4380	2412	48.24
−	140			**Compaq Total**	39250	20636	412.7
·	141	East	4/29/2014	Duke Energy	18264	10088	201.8
·	142	Central	9/19/2014	Duke Energy	16784	8912	178.2
·	143	West	10/6/2014	Duke Energy	16936	8760	175.2
·	144	East	8/29/2015	Duke Energy	5532	2991	59.82
−	145			**Duke Energy Total**	57516	30751	615
·	146	Central	8/19/2014	Exxon	21120	12650	253

Figure 441 Excel added the 30 subtotals in seconds instead of 2 hours.

But wait, there is more! To the left of column A, at the top, there are three tiny buttons labeled 1, 2, 3. Right now, in #3 view, you are seeing everything. Click the #2 icon and you only see the customer totals and the grand total!

1 2 3		A	B	C	D	E	F
	1	**Region**	**Date**	**Customer**	**Revenue**	**Profit**	**Bonus**
+	6			AIG Total	51240	28416	568.3
+	47			AT&T Total	498937	278959	5579
+	76			Bank of America Total	406326	227741	4555
+	81			Boeing Total	71651	39180	783.6
+	86			Chevron Total	54048	30268	605.4
+	135			CitiGroup Total	613514	338409	6768

Figure 442 See the tiny #2 in the top left of this figure?

Data in this collapsed #2 view is amazing. You can sort the data in this view, and all of the customer detail records get sorted with the customer total.

fx   =SUBTOTAL(9,D2:D5)

C	D	E	F
Customer	**Revenue**	**Profit**	**Bonus**
AIG Total	51240	28416	568.3
AT&T Total	498937	278959	5579
Bank of America Total	406326	227741	4555
Boeing Total	71651	39180	783.6
Chevron Total	54048	30268	605.4
CitiGroup Total	613514	338409	6768

Figure 443 Even your manager doesn't know you can sort in collapsed mode. It is one of the great secrets of Excel.

Caution: Seriously, if you try to sort with the data in collapsed mode in front of your manager he will gasp and tell you it cannot be done. Show him this page. It can be done. I've done seminars for thousands of people and one guy, Derek, from Springfield Missouri knew this trick and taught it to me. I am still amazed that it works. Show you manager this page and tell him to try it on a fake data set or a second copy of the file. It works.

The one huge gotcha with subtotals is when you try to copy the collapsed subtotal rows and paste to a new book. Excel brings the hidden rows along. To successfully copy, follow these steps in this order:

1. Select the data.
2. Press Alt+Semicolon.
3. Ctrl+C to copy. You will see the marching ants around each row.
4. Go to the new sheet and paste.

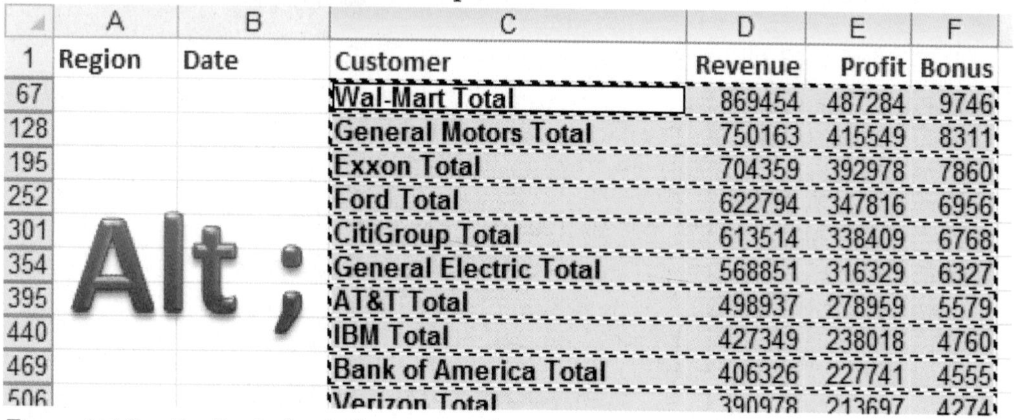

	A	B	C	D	E	F
1	Region	Date	Customer	Revenue	Profit	Bonus
67			Wal-Mart Total	869454	487284	9746
128			General Motors Total	750163	415549	8311
195			Exxon Total	704359	392978	7860
252			Ford Total	622794	347816	6956
301			CitiGroup Total	613514	338409	6768
354			General Electric Total	568851	316329	6327
395			AT&T Total	498937	278959	5579
440			IBM Total	427349	238018	4760
469			Bank of America Total	406326	227741	4555
506			Verizon Total	390978	213697	4274

Figure 444 Do Alt+Semicolon before copying from collapsed mode.

To go back to seeing all rows, click the #3 group and outline button in the top left of the worksheet.

To get rid of subtotals, select one cell in the data, go back to the Subtotals command, and choose Remove All.

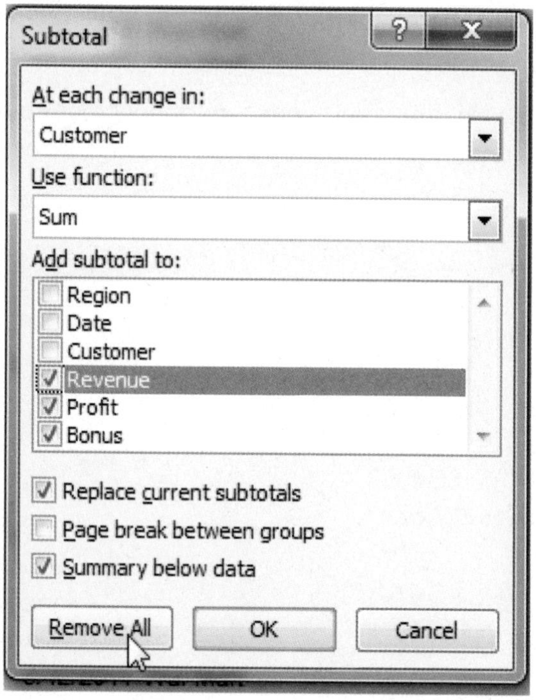

Figure 445 To get rid of subtotals, use the Remove All button in the Subtotal dialog.

How Can I Bold the Numbers in My Subtotaled Data?

Why is it that my Subtotal numbers wont bold?

With the Subtotal feature, the Subtotal labels are bold but not the numbers themselves. Here's a way to bold your Subtotaled numbers too.

When you have your data Subtotaled, Excel automatically bolds the Subtotal labels in their cells. However, the actual Subtotaled numbers along that same row are not bolded by default. The figure below shows a comparison of what you first get with Subtotaled data, and what you want to achieve:

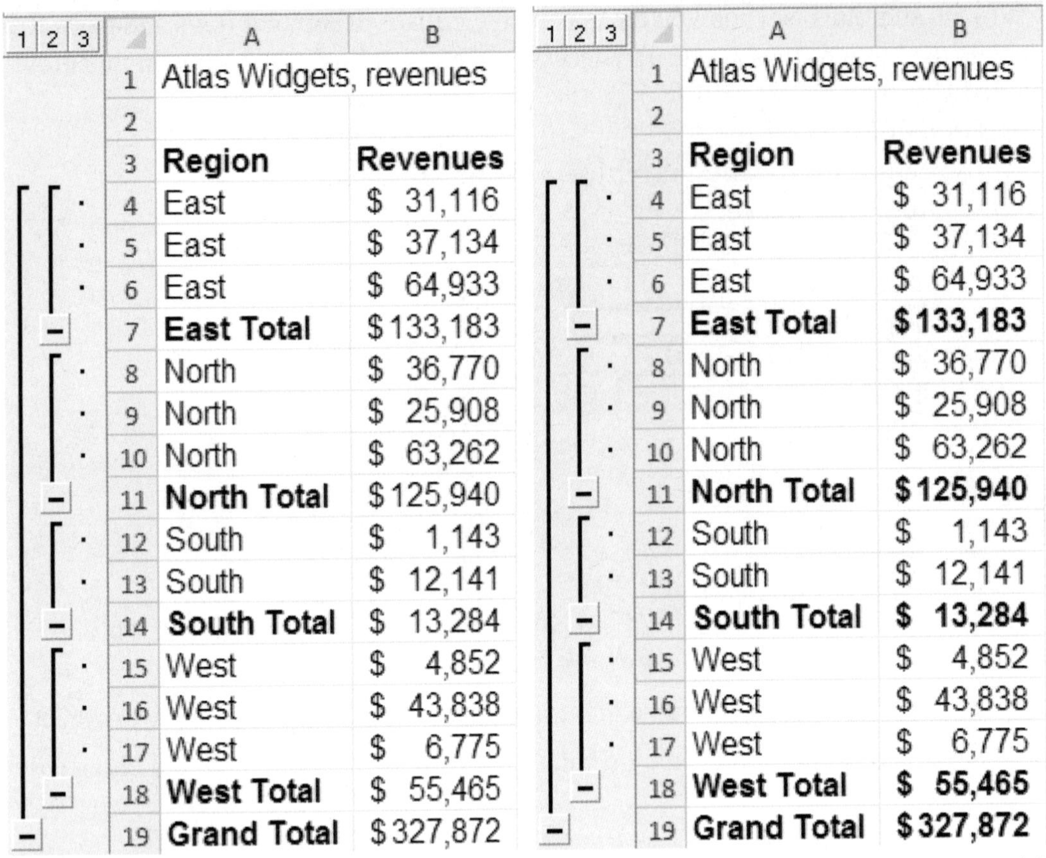

	A	B
1	Atlas Widgets, revenues	
2		
3	Region	Revenues
4	East	$ 31,116
5	East	$ 37,134
6	East	$ 64,933
7	East Total	$133,183
8	North	$ 36,770
9	North	$ 25,908
10	North	$ 63,262
11	North Total	$125,940
12	South	$ 1,143
13	South	$ 12,141
14	South Total	$ 13,284
15	West	$ 4,852
16	West	$ 43,838
17	West	$ 6,775
18	West Total	$ 55,465
19	Grand Total	$327,872

	A	B
1	Atlas Widgets, revenues	
2		
3	Region	Revenues
4	East	$ 31,116
5	East	$ 37,134
6	East	$ 64,933
7	East Total	**$133,183**
8	North	$ 36,770
9	North	$ 25,908
10	North	$ 63,262
11	North Total	**$125,940**
12	South	$ 1,143
13	South	$ 12,141
14	South Total	**$ 13,284**
15	West	$ 4,852
16	West	$ 43,838
17	West	$ 6,775
18	West Total	**$ 55,465**
19	Grand Total	**$327,872**

Figure 446 A before and after look at what an original Subtotaled result is, and what you want with bolded numbers.

You can accomplish this in two easy steps. As seen in the next figure, click your Subtotal's hierarchy number that will expose just the subtotaled rows. In the figure, button 2 is being clicked. Then, select that collapsed range.

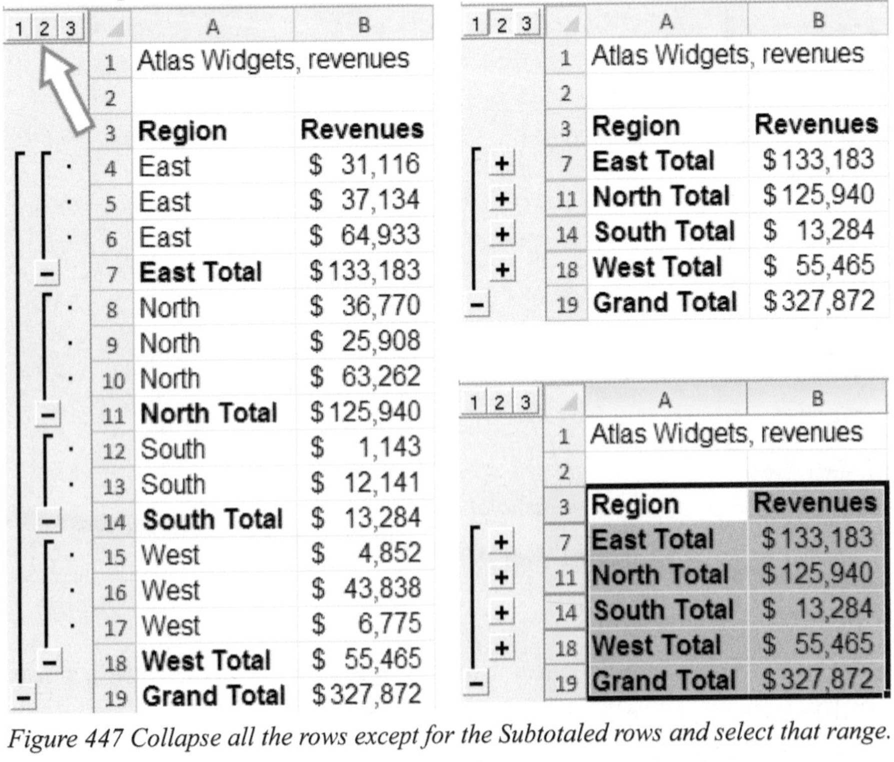

	A	B
1	Atlas Widgets, revenues	
2		
3	Region	Revenues
4	East	$ 31,116
5	East	$ 37,134
6	East	$ 64,933
7	East Total	$133,183
8	North	$ 36,770
9	North	$ 25,908
10	North	$ 63,262
11	North Total	$125,940
12	South	$ 1,143
13	South	$ 12,141
14	South Total	$ 13,284
15	West	$ 4,852
16	West	$ 43,838
17	West	$ 6,775
18	West Total	$ 55,465
19	Grand Total	$327,872

	A	B
1	Atlas Widgets, revenues	
2		
3	Region	Revenues
7	East Total	$133,183
11	North Total	$125,940
14	South Total	$ 13,284
18	West Total	$ 55,465
19	Grand Total	$327,872

	A	B
1	Atlas Widgets, revenues	
2		
3	Region	Revenues
7	East Total	$133,183
11	North Total	$125,940
14	South Total	$ 13,284
18	West Total	$ 55,465
19	Grand Total	$327,872

Figure 447 Collapse all the rows except for the Subtotaled rows and select that range.

Finally, from your keyboard, press the Ctrl and semicolon keys, which will select only the visible cells. From there, click the Home tab on the Ribbon and click the Bold icon as shown by where the arrows are pointing. Finally, to see all the worksheet data, you can click the button (number 3 in the figure) to expand the Subtotal range.

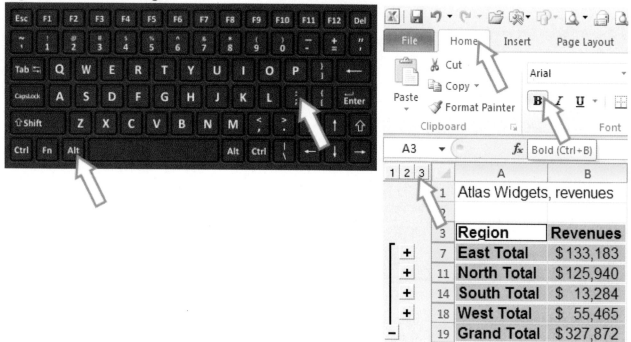

Figure 448 Press Ctrl+; to select the visible cells, bold the selected visible range, and optionally expand the Subtotal range.

What Is a Pivot Table?

I think my boss would marry Pivot Tables if he could.

Pivot Tables are the most powerful data analysis feature in Excel. I've written a whole book on Pivot Tables. This introduction will get you started.

Select one cell in your data.

On the Insert tab, choose PivotTable.

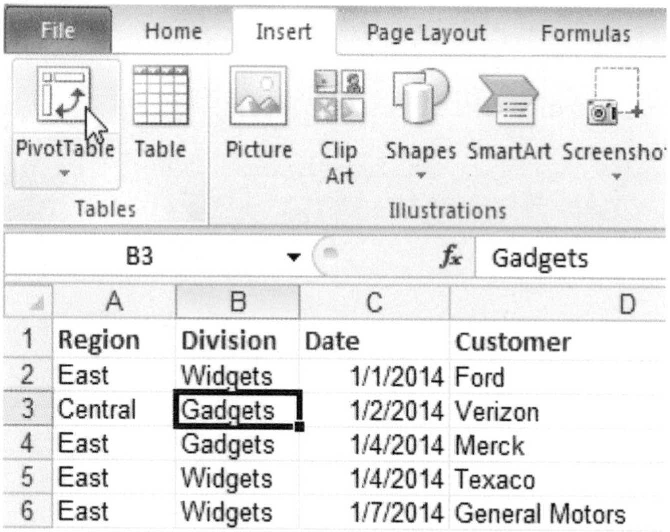

Figure 449 Select one cell and choose Pivot Table.

Excel will guess the reference for your data and offer to put the Pivot Table on a new sheet.

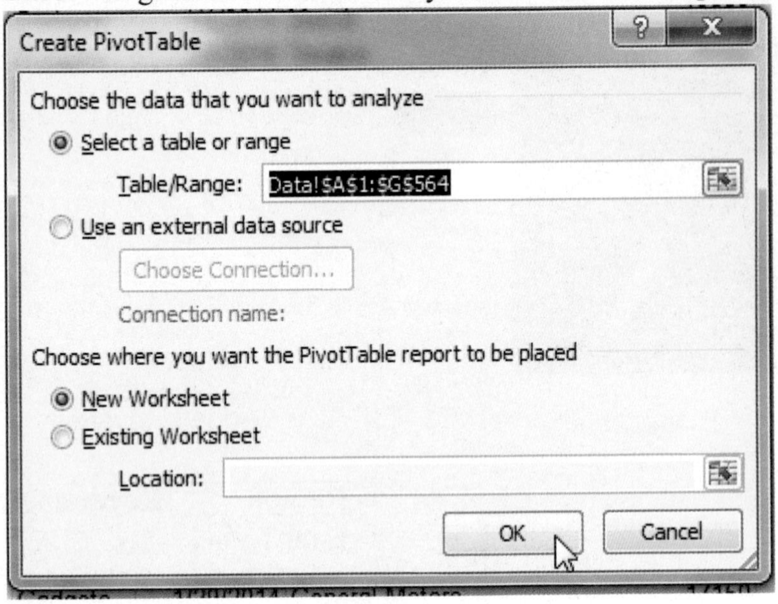

Figure 450 *The defaults are usually correct.*

Click OK. You are now on a new blank sheet. On the right side of the sheet is a tall Pivot Table Field List. At the top of the list is a list of fields in your data set.

Figure 451 *A list of all the fields in your original data set.*

At the bottom are four drop zones. These correspond to different areas of the report.

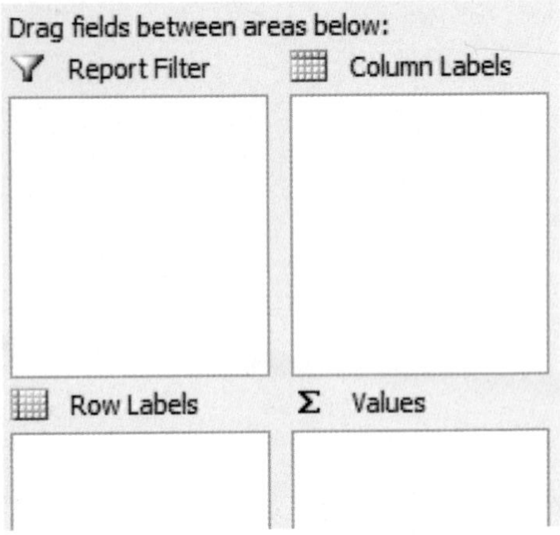

Figure 452 *Four drop zones where you can arrange fields to build a report.*

To build your summary report, drag fields from the top of the list to one of the drop zones. To see total revenue by Region and Division, drag the fields as shown below.

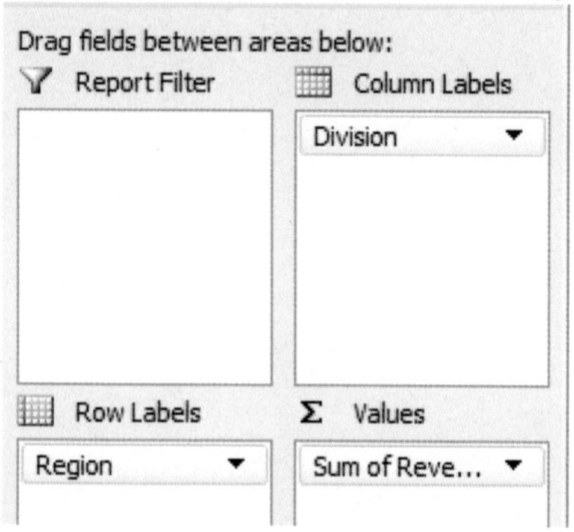

Figure 453 Region going down the side, Division going across the top.

You now have the report shown below. This is an amazing feature! You didn't have to write any formulas. The entire process from start to finish takes six clicks of the mouse.

▲	A	B	C	D
1				
2				
3	**Sum of Revenue**	**Column Labels** ▼		
4	**Row Labels** ▼	**Gadgets**	**Widgets**	**Grand Total**
5	Central	1070892	1304987	2375879
6	East	799703	1693300	2493003
7	West	542234	1296696	1838930
8	**Grand Total**	**2412829**	**4294983**	**6707812**
9				

Figure 454 Pivot Tables are fast to create.

When you are inside the Pivot Table, there are two Ribbon tabs for dealing with the Pivot Table. Go to the second tab – the Design tab. Open the Report Layout dropdown and change to Tabular form. This changes the bizarre headings to real words.

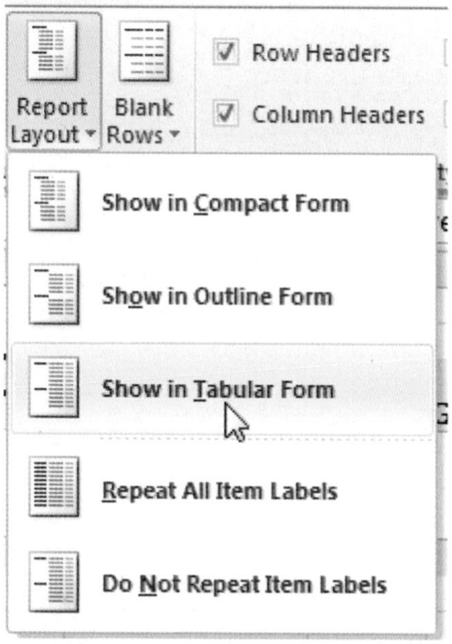

Figure 455 You have better headings in B3 and A4 now.

You can move fields in the drop zones to change the report. Here is a report after adding the Customer field below the Region field in the Row Labels drop zone:

▲	A	B	C	D	
1					
2					
3	Sum of Revenue	Division ▼			
4	Region ▼	Gadgets	Widgets	Grand Total	
5	Central	1070892	1304987	2375879	
6	East	799703	1693300	2493003	
7	West	542234	1296696	1838930	
8	Grand Total	2412829	4294983	6707812	
9					

Figure 456 Add a field to the drop zone and the report changes.

You can rearrange fields. Maybe you want Region going across the report and Division going down. Drag each field to the right place. It is easy.

CHAPTER 10 - FORMULAS III

How Can I Make a Decision in a Formula?

I have to calculate a rate. If the Job Code is "Copyedit", the rate is $20. Otherwise the rate is $15.

The IF function can be used to make a decision. If something is true (JobCode="Copyedit") then you use one value, otherwise you use another value. The IF function starts out with a logical test. Some examples of logical tests are: D2="Copyedit", E2>100, C2<=5, C2>=D2, C2<>"No".

The second argument in the IF function is the calculation to use when the logical test is true. The third argument is the value to use if the logical test is false.

In the figure below, a formula of =IF(D2="Copyedit",20,15) assigns a rate of 15 to everything except the Copyedit rows.

=IF(D2="Copyedit",20,15)

	D	E	F	G
1	Job Code	Description	Hours	Rate
2	Copyedit	Faces/Anxiety	0.733	$20.00
3	Layout	DFSS	1.083	$15.00
4	Copyedit	XL Small Biz	1.333	$20.00
5	Layout	Red Headed Geek	2.083	$15.00

·Figure 457 Use one of two different rates using the IF Function.

The IF Function is powerful, but sometimes you need to test for multiple conditions. For example, say that you wanted to calculate a bonus for all records where the product was a jacket and the sale price is greater than 200. One way is to nest one IF statement inside of another: =IF(A4="Jacket",IF(B4>200,10,0),0). This formula only pays the $10 bonus once A4 is Jacket and B4>200. You can simplify this formula by using the AND function as your logical test. Every logical test inside of the AND function must be true for the AND function to be true. =IF(AND(B4>200,A4="Jacket"),10,0).

=IF(AND(B4>200,A4="Jacket"),10,0)

	A	B	C	D
1	Pay a $10 Bonus on Jacket sales over $200			
2				
3	Product	Sale $	Bonus	
4	Jacket	300	10	
5	Jacket	150	0	
6	Shirt	225	0	
7	Jacket	450	10	
8	Shirt	75	0	
9	Shirt	50	0	

Figure 458 With the AND function, all conditions must be true.

You can put up to 255 conditions inside the AND function. Excel also offers OR and NOT functions. With the OR function, any one condition has to be true for the OR to return true. For anyone stuck in a logic chapter in a math class, using NOT(AND()) will simulate the NAND operation in Boolean logic.

What Is VLOOKUP and How Can I Use It?

I've heard about the VLOOKUP function's ability to look up values in tables and return related values but I'm not sure how to use it. How can I use it to do something useful like look up a product price so I can calculate the extended price?

The VLOOKUP function is one of the most used functions in Excel workbooks. The basic operation is to look up a value in one column and return the value on that same row in a column to the right of the found value. Let's start with the following example:

	A	B	C	D	E	F
1	Product Code	Product Description	Quantity Sold	Unit Price	Extended Price	
2	A100		12			
3	A101		15			
4	A100		6			
5	A102		24			
6	A100		30			
7	A102		4			
8						

Figure 459 Our project.

We are starting with the product sales for the day. We have entered the product code and the quantity sold. But we need to add the description and unit price and calculate the extended price (quantity times unit price.)

The extended price is a simple formula: column C times column D. But how will we get the description and the unit price without entering it over and over for each sale? This is where VLOOKUP comes into play along with a second table containing the information we need.

F	G	H	I	J
	Product Code	Product Description	Unit Price	
	A100	Bat	35.00	
	A101	Glove	45.00	
	A102	Ball	12.00	
	A103	Cap	18.00	

Figure 460 The second table containing the information we need to complete the task.

The second table contains, for each product code, the product description and the unit price. To pull the description into our main table we use this formula in cell B2:

```
=VLOOKUP(A2,$G$2:$I$5,2,FALSE)
```

Copy that formula down to the end of the table. The parameters to the VLOOKUP function are:

VLOOKUP(lookup_value, table_array, col_index_num, [range_lookup])

lookup_value – The value to search in the first column of the table.

table_array – The range of cells that contains the data being searched. The first column is used to find a match using Lookup Value.

column_index_number – The column number in the table from which the matching value is returned.

range_lookup – Specify False to have Excel look for an exact match. Using False is the most common use of VLOOKUP and does not require that the table be sorted. When you need to find a value that is in a range then specify True or omit this argument. See below for a detailed explanation of how this works.

Tip: Since the second parameter (table_array) has absolute row references (using the dollar sign), the range reference won't be changed by Excel as you copy the formula down the column. Since the reference to column A (A2) is not an absolute reference it will be changed by Excel as the formula is copied down the column so that it always references the cell in column A in the same row.

To pull the unit price into the main table we'll use this formula:

```
=VLOOKUP(A2,$G$2:$I$5,3,FALSE)
```

Notice that the only difference between this and the formula that pulls the description is the column_index_number which is 3 instead of 2.

Finally we add the formula for the extended price. It's a simple multiplication:

```
=C2*D2
```

The formula is entered into cell E2 and copied to the end of the table.

And here is the final result:

	A	B	C	D	E	F
1	Product Code	Product Description	Quantity Sold	Unit Price	Extended Price	
2	A100	Bat	12	35.00	420.00	
3	A101	Glove	15	45.00	675.00	
4	A100	Bat	6	35.00	210.00	
5	A102	Ball	24	12.00	288.00	
6	A100	Bat	30	35.00	1,050.00	
7	A102	Ball	4	12.00	48.00	
8						

Figure 461 Product description and unit price came from the lookup table.

Above we used the exact match version of VLOOKUP which will return #N/A if the product code is not found in the table. This is an appropriate use of VLOOKUP because we would like to know if the product code is valid. We certainly don't want Excel giving us the information for the next lower product code!

But suppose we want to find a value in a range such as determining the fine for an overdue library book. For this we can use the range match version of VLOOKUP. In the figure below, the yellow lookup table contains fine amounts. If a book is less than three days late, there is no fine. If it is three or more days late but less than 10 days late, there is a $15 fine. In this system, what would the penalty be for something 7 days late? A human can tell this is a $15 fine, but VLOOKUP will not find 7 in the first column of the lookup table. When you tell Excel to use the range version of VLOOKUP, it will look for 7 but if it can't find 7, it will use the row with the closest value that is smaller than 7.

```
=VLOOKUP(A2,$E$2:$F$5,2,TRUE)
```

=VLOOKUP(A2,$E$2:$F$5,2,TRUE)

	A	B	C	D	E	F
1	Days Late	Penalty			Days	Fine
2	7	15			0	$0
3	0	0			3	$15
4	35	100			10	$50
5	14	50			30	$100
6	2	0				
7						

Figure 462 Rarely used, the True version of VLOOKUP does an approximate match.

Tip: When you are doing the range version of VLOOKUP to find an approximate match, the lookup table must be sorted in ascending sequence.

How Can I Look up a Value across a Row Instead of down a Column?

Is there a way that I can look up a value horizontally?

Most lookup activities seem to take place vertically, in columns. The HLOOKUP function is a tool for horizontal lookups along rows.

HLOOKUP is a function not as easily grasped nor as widely used as its VLOOKUP counterpart. This is probably because most lists are vertical in nature. The figure below shows an example using the HLOOKUP function to find a lookup the value ("Mar" in this case) along row 1, hence the "H" in "HLOOKUP" referring to a horizontal lookup action.

	B8	▾		*fx*	=HLOOKUP(A8,A1:M5,3,0)							
	A	B	C	D	E	F	G	H	I	J	K	L	M
1	Income	Jan	Feb	Mar	Apr	May	Jun	Jul	Aug	Sep	Oct	Nov	Dec
2	Sales	639	654	163	997	930	222	299	343	416	793	942	178
3	Videos	277	594	108	899	679	309	133	169	665	309	522	533
4	CD's	920	353	932	111	79	531	165	230	465	856	335	55
5	Training	65	53	688	108	238	915	425	114	933	154	684	190
6													
7	Criteria	Result											
8	Mar	108		The formula in cell B8 is =HLOOKUP(A8,A1:M5,3,0)									
9													
10													
11				The lookup value is in cell A8.									
12													
13				The range of your table is A1:M5.									
14													
15				You are interested in the third row of the table.									
16													
17	A zero, or "False" means you want an exact match of the lookup value.												
18													

Figure 463 Example of the HLOOKUP function.

The arguments in the HLOOKUP function can be translated as questions:
1. What value do you want to look up?
2. What is the range of the table?
3. Which row of the table do you want to return a value for?
4. Do you want to find an exact match, or an approximate match of the lookup value?

Questions one and two are easy to answer. All you need to know is what you are looking for, and the range address of the data you are working with.

Question three requires a tiny bit of thought, in that you need to enter the row *index* of the table, not necessarily the row of the worksheet. In the figure shown, the row index and the row of the worksheet happen to be the same, because the table starts on row 1. If the table occupied, say, range A8:M15 and you were interested in the third row of that table, you would still enter a 3 to fulfill the row_index argument, even though the actual worksheet row number of that table would be 10. Just remember that HLOOKUP does not care about the worksheet row number, it only cares about the row in reference to the table itself…in this example the third row of the table.

As for the final argument called range_lookup to find an exact match, you know in this example that "Mar" exists as a column header because you have the table arranged by months. Therefore, you set the fourth argument to FALSE (or to 0 as done here, meaning the same as FALSE).

Tip: When I use HLOOKUP I always set the range_lookup argument to FALSE. This is because I build my tables with simple headers, and I would have (in this case) cell B8 data-validated for a drop down list of months Jan, Feb, Mar, and so on. That way, an exact match is assured and the proper number (9111 in the example) would be returned.

How Can I Avoid Those Ugly Formula Errors like #DIV/0! and #N/A?

#DIV/0! and #N/A really make me crazy! How can I make them go away?

Errors in formulas can help you identify mistakes, but sometimes you'd rather show nothing than an ugly error message.

When you create formulas, Excel is always on the lookout for errors. Some errors are good because they alert you of a mistake you made with your formula.

However, some errors are a legitimate part of spreadsheet work and cannot be avoided. For times like this, you'd rather have the cell display a pleasant-looking value than an error message.

In the first figure, a ratio of widgets made to widgets sold is being calculated. The numbers in range B3:E3 are being divided by the numbers in range B4:E4. Cell D5 displays a #DIV/0! error because its formula D3/D4 is trying to divide the number in cell D3 by zero, which is mathematically impossible.

	f_x =D3/D4			
	A	B	C	D	E
1	Atlas Widgets, Inc.				
2		Q1	Q2	Q3	Q4
3	Widgets made	15	12	13	19
4	Widgets sold	13	9	0	17
5	Ratio of made to sold	115%	133%	#DIV/0!	112%
6					

Figure 464 A #DIV/0! error occurs when a formula attempts to divide a number by zero.

For this company, there are times when no widgets will be sold. Therefore, zeros will exist on the worksheet, but the company wants the related cells to show a zero other than an ugly error message.

Normally, you might use a formula of =IF(D4=0,0,D3/D4). However, testing if D4 is zero is the same as testing if it is false, so this cool shortcut works: =IF(D4,D3/D4,0).

	f_x =IF(D4,D3/D4,0)			
	A	B	C	D	E
1	Atlas Widgets, Inc.				
2		Q1	Q2	Q3	Q4
3	Widgets made	15	12	13	19
4	Widgets sold	13	9	0	17
5	Ratio of made to sold	115%	133%	0%	112%
6					

Figure 465 If a number exists in cell D4, divide the number in cell D3 by the number in cell D4. Otherwise, show a zero.

Note that the first argument of the IF function generally is looking for a logical test such as D4=0, D4>0, or D4<>0. However, the IF function will treat any zero as False and and non-zero number as True, so the above formula works.

There are many other error types than attempting to divide by zero. Such an example is the #N/A error that can occur when Excel is told to look for a value that does not exist. In the following figure, the name Joe does not exist in range A2:A6, so Excel shows a #N/A error in cell E1 with the formula:

```
=VLOOKUP(D1,A2:B6,2,0)
```

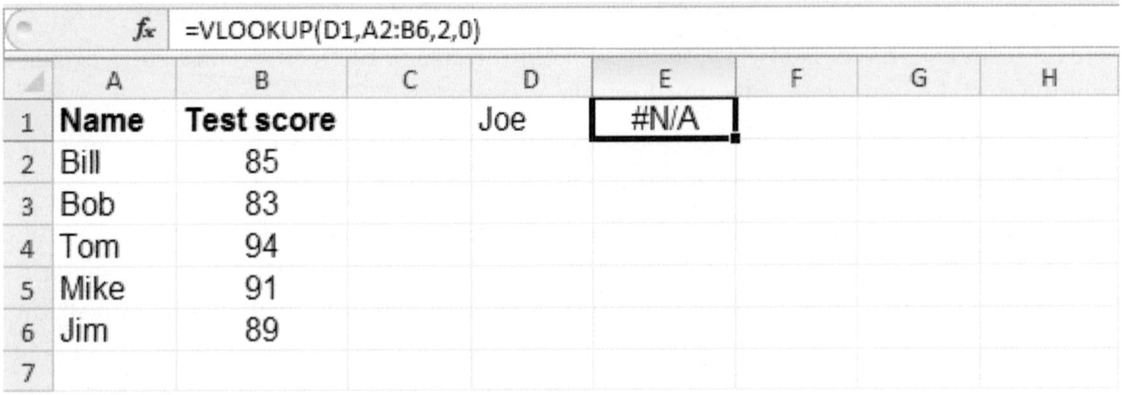

	fx	=VLOOKUP(D1,A2:B6,2,0)						
	A	B	C	D	E	F	G	H
1	**Name**	**Test score**		Joe	#N/A			
2	Bill	85						
3	Bob	83						
4	Tom	94						
5	Mike	91						
6	Jim	89						
7								

Figure 466 Example of how a #N/A error can be caused.

Instead of showing an error, you might understandably prefer a friendlier notation in the cell. This next figure shows how cell E1 displays "Not found" when (in this case) the criteria value of Joe does not exist in range A2:A6.

The formula in cell E1 is a *conditional* formula, meaning the possibility of a #N/A error is evaluated first. If that test evaluates to True, "Not found" is returned; otherwise the formula carries out the VLOOKUP action:

```
=IF(ISNA(VLOOKUP(D1,A2:B6,2,0)=TRUE),"Not found",VLOOKUP(D1,A2:B6,2,0))
```

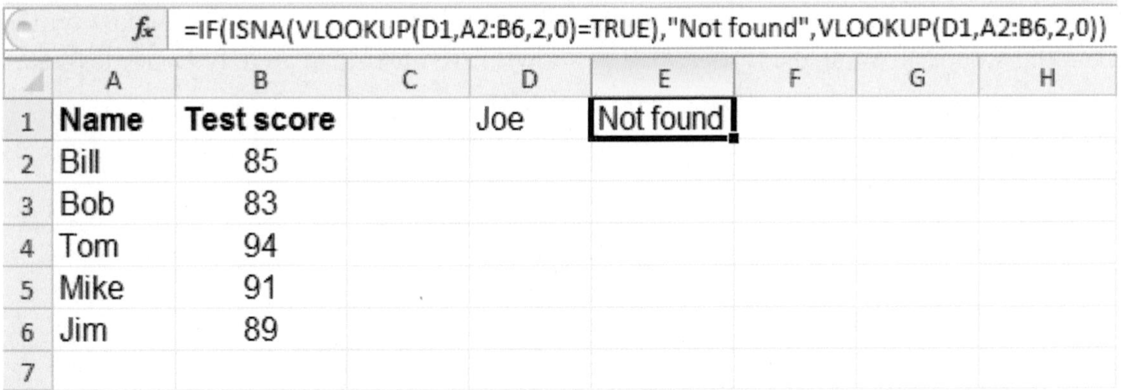

	fx	=IF(ISNA(VLOOKUP(D1,A2:B6,2,0)=TRUE),"Not found",VLOOKUP(D1,A2:B6,2,0))						
	A	B	C	D	E	F	G	H
1	**Name**	**Test score**		Joe	Not found			
2	Bill	85						
3	Bob	83						
4	Tom	94						
5	Mike	91						
6	Jim	89						
7								

Figure 467 Bypassing the #N/A error.

Note: You may also employ a catch-all technique for almost any error without specifying its error type. Using the two previous examples, these formulas would have worked in any version of Excel.

- =IF(ISERROR(D3/D4),0,D3/D4)
- =IF(ISERROR(VLOOKUP(D1,A2:B6,2,0)),"Not found",VLOOKUP(D1,A2:B6,2,0))

If you are using Excel 2007 or newer and everyone who might open the workbook also has Excel 2007 or newer, you can use the new =IFERROR(any formula,value if error) function. This function is easier to use and often calculates faster.

- =IFERROR(D3/D4,0)
- =IFERROR(VLOOKUP(D1,A2:B6,2,0),"Not Found")

How Do I Convert Numbers to Words?

I have an amount and need to spell it out, like a checkwriter would do.

Amazingly, Excel does not natively support this feature.

If you need to do this, Microsoft provides a macro that you can add to your workbook. To see a short video about how to add the macro, visit: http://youtu.be/HJ-2OZSsFhk. To find the macro, go to http://support.microsoft.com/kb/213360.

Once you've installed the macro in your workbook, you can use the =SPELLNUMBER function.

	A	B	C	D	E	F
1						
2		1,234,567.89		One Million Two Hundred		
3				Thirty Four Thousand Five		
4				Hundred Sixty Seven Dollars		
5				and Eighty Nine Cents		
6						
7						

D2   fx =spellnumber(B2)

Figure 468 This function won't work unless you copy the macro into a module behind your workbook.

Why Does Excel Ask to Update Links When There Aren't Any Links in My Workbook?

How do I find and delete phantom links?

If you've ever wondered why this message pops up after you are sure you've deleted all your workbook's links, well, join the club. It's a common problem because some links can be difficult to find.

Microsoft Excel

This workbook contains links to other data sources.

• If you update the links, Excel will attempt to retrieve the latest data.
• If you don't update the links, Excel will use the previous information.

Note that data links can be used to access and share confidential information without your permission and possibly perform other harmful actions. Do not update the links if you do not trust the source of this workbook.

[Update]   [Don't Update]   [Help]

Figure 469 Excel shows this message when you open a workbook that contains links to outside sources.

In my twenty years working with Excel, I have not yet seen a case when this message appeared and there was not a link; Excel is very good at recognizing an existing link. So, how do you find a link when you have looked throughout your workbook, yet you still cannot locate a link Excel says is there?

Here are some tactics for searching and destroying phantom links:

Tactic 1

Right-click on any sheet tab, left-click Select All Sheets, press Ctrl+F and in the Find what field enter:

= [

or

!

The idea is to look through all sheets for formulas referencing external workbooks, so be sure to unhide any hidden sheets with this tactic.

Tactic 2

Look closely at your list of defined names, not just in the name box but also in the Define Name dialog, and make sure you do not have any named ranges that refer to an outside workbook. In Excel version 2003 or before, from the worksheet menu click Insert , Name , Define. In version 2007 or after, from the Ribbon click the Formulas tab and in the Defined Names section click Name Manager.

Tactic 3

Open a new workbook, create a link to it and save that workbook. Now go to Edit , Links (version 2003) or the Name Manager (version 2007 or after), click the Edit button, and use the "Change Source" option to refer the link to the new workbook. Save again and then delete the link you created.

Tactic 4

If you have Pivot Tables or charts, they may contain source data that is derived from outside workbooks and hence being the links culprit. Take a look at the chart series and the Pivot Table source ranges.

Good luck! The above tactics are by no means a comprehensive list. With persistence you will find the link(s), maybe with the above suggestions, or from your own ideas or suggestions by others.

How Can I Track Billable Hours in a Weekly Time Sheet?

I do work on a variety of projects. I get paid two different rates depending on the type of work that I am doing. Thus, I need to track hours in two different categories. While I have to submit this once a week to get paid, I also want to use the worksheet so I know how much I am making each week, so I know if I can buy those new shoes or not. I actually tried downloading the calendar template, but it did not seem good at holding hours and didn't provide a way to total hours.

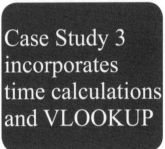

You can build a worksheet that will help you to log and calculate the hours.
The worksheet will be reusable each week. It is designed to let you enter the data in a minimal amount of time.

If you have worked through Case Study 1 on page 29, you can easily build the starting point shown in the following figure. Cell A3 is using Italics and a cell style of 20% Accent 6 from the Cell Styles dropdown. Cells B3 & C3 are using 20% Accent 4. The column widths are 24, 10, 11, 11, 19, 9, 9, and 10.

	A	B	C	D	E	F	G	H
1	**Weekly Billable Hours**							
2	Week Ending: June 10, 2015							
3	*Use Ctrl ; for date!*	*Use Ctrl : for time*						
4								
5	Date	Start Time	End Time	Job Code	Description	Hours	Rate	Amount
6								

Figure 470 Start with these headings.

Think about your work week. How many projects could you have a day? Say that you do one-hour projects. You might have eight projects a day, seven days a week, for a total of 56 projects. If that is an estimate of the likely maximum, then go even larger. Also, say that there might be a week with 90 projects or so. For each of the steps below, you will be initially formatting from row 6 to row 100.

1. Select A6:A100. From the Number Format dropdown on the Home tab, choose Long Date.
2. Select B6:C100 (two columns). Choose a Format of Time.
3. Select F6:F100. Choose a Format of Number. Click Decrease Decimal once to go to one decimal place. (You can't see the decimals yet, just trust me).
4. Select G6:H100. Choose Currency from the Format dropdown.

To make data entry easier, the Job Code in column D will contain a dropdown with the valid job codes. Go out to a blank section of the worksheet and enter the values shown in the figure below:

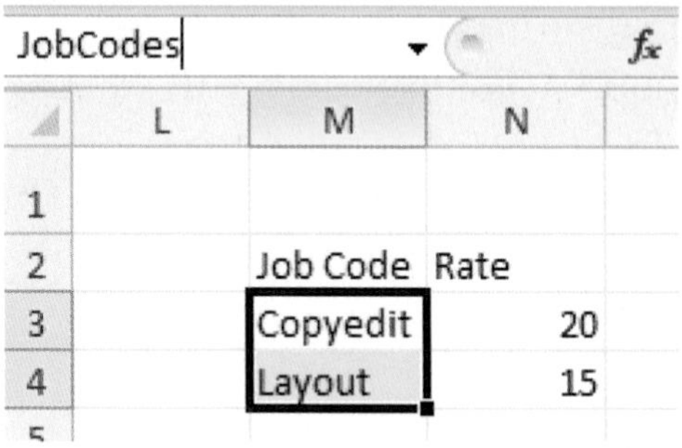

Figure 471 This table will be used for VLOOKUP and for the dropdown list.

Select the list of job codes in M3:M4. Click in the name box to the left of the Formula Bar and type a one-word name such as JobCodes. Press Enter. When you press Enter, nothing really happens except the word JobCodes is centered. Behind the scenes, you've created a name for that range which you can use in formulas and elsewhere.

Select M3:N4. Assign this two-column range as name of Rates. This will help when using the VLOOK-UP later.

Select D6:D100. On the Data tab, choose Data Validation. It is right of center, in the Data Tools group. The Data Validation dialog has a dropdown called Allow that says Any Value. Change that dropdown to List. New fields will appear in the dialog so it looks like the following figure. In the Source box, type =JobCodes. This is the name you defined above.

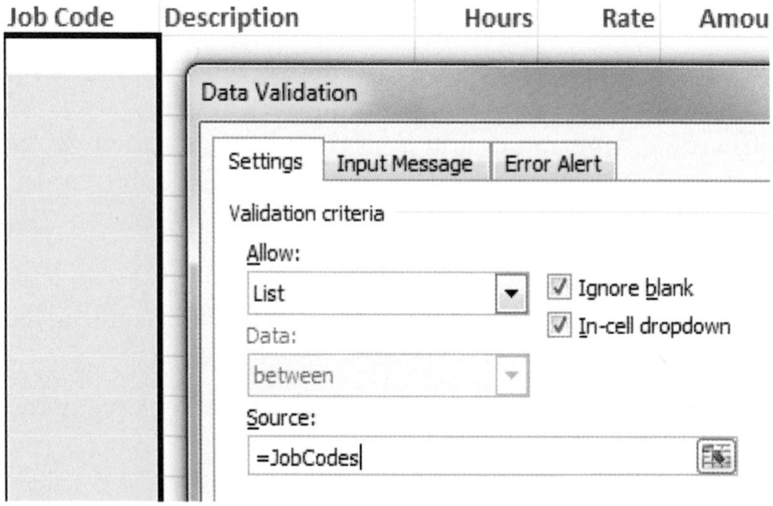

Figure 472 Validation is how you create a dropdown list in a cell.

You can now test what you've built so far. Go to A6 and press Ctrl+;. A date appears. Go to B6 and press Ctrl+:. A time appears. Type a later time in C6. Go to D6 and a dropdown box appears. Choose from the dropdown box.

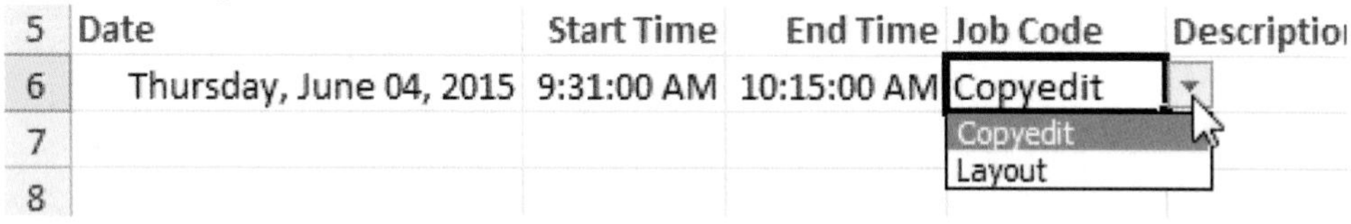

Figure 473 The dropdown is working!

Type a description in E.

To calculate billable hours in F, you have to multiply 24 times the (End time – Start time). This formula is =(C6-B6)*24. However, since this is the last case study in the book, I want to teach you the incredibly fast way to enter formulas. If you can master this arrow key method, you will be faster at Excel than your manager.

1. Go to cell F6. Type an equals sign and the opening parenthesis.
2. Press the Left Arrow key three times in succession. A flashing box will appear around C6 and the Formula Bar will show =(C6.
3. Type the minus sign. When you type a mathematical operator, the "focus" leaves C6 and you are back in F6.
4. To point to B6, you will press the Left Arrow key four times.
5. Type)*24 and press Enter.

F6			*fx* =(C6-B6)*24		
	B	C	D	E	F
5	Start Time	End Time	Job Code	Description	Hours
6	9:31:00 AM	10:15:00 AM	Copyedit	Faces/Anxiety	0.733
7					

Figure 474 To convert time to hours, multiply by 24.

Tip: I am absolutely serious. Using the Left Arrow key seven times in the above steps is much faster than reaching for the mouse twice. Try it for a day. Once you get the hang of the arrow key method, it is very efficient.

To get the Rate in G, you can use a VLOOKUP. Here are the steps for entering VLOOKUP:

1. Select cell G7
2. Type =VL and press Tab. This will insert the VLOOKUP function and the opening parenthesis.
3. Press the Left Arrow key three times to select D6.
4. Type a comma.
5. Type rat. The tooltip is now offering a function called RATE and your named range of Rates. Press the Down Arrow to choose the named range, then press tab to enter that name in the formula. Type ,2,False) and press Enter.

The formula in H6 is =F6*G6.

Copy the three formulas in F6:H6 down to row 100. You can select F6:H6, click the Fill Handle in the lower right corner of the selection and drag down to row 100.

In real life, nothing ever goes as planned in Excel. The formulas that are copied down look really bad for all the blank rows.

Hours	Rate	Amount
0.733	$20.00	$14.67
0.000	#N/A	#N/A
0.000	#N/A	#N/A
0.000	#N/A	#N/A
0.000	#N/A	#N/A

Figure 475 Argh. I say Argh a lot when using Excel, and I am MrExcel.

Edit the formula in G6 to wrap an IFERROR around it.

=IFERROR(VLOOKUP(D6,Rates,2,FALSE),0)							
F	G	H	I	J	K	L	
0.733	$20.00	$14.67					
0.000	$0.00	$0.00					

Figure 476 Starting in Excel 2007, the new IFERROR function makes preventing #N/A errors easy.

For each cell in G6:H6, select the cell and press Ctrl+1 (the number one). On the Number tab, choose Custom. A code will appear in the Type box. Click after the code and type two semicolons. This is a good way to show positive numbers, but to hide negative and zero numbers.

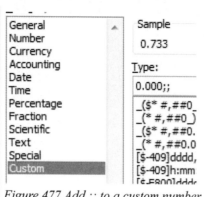

Figure 477 Add ;; to a custom number format to hide zeroes and negative.

Once G6:H6 is fixed copy it down.

You now have a great way of tracking hours, but no way to report the totals by job code. Enter Copyedit and Layout in E2 and E3. The formula in F2 is =SUMIF($D$6:$D$100,$E2,F$6:F$100). If you are careful to enter the seven dollar signs exactly where I've shown them, you can copy that formula to F3 *and* to H2:H3. Normally, totals go at the bottom, but since this is money that you've earned this week, you definitely want to keep it in view all the time. Once you Freeze Panes, those totals will always be visible.

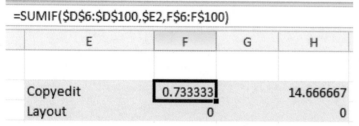

Figure 478 You might remember SUMIF from page x

Add a formula in F1 and H1 to sum the two rows below it.

Do some final formatting. Select cell A6 and choose Freeze Panes.

Before you start using the worksheet, rename this sheet to "Blank." Hold down the Ctrl key and drag the tab for this worksheet to the right. Rename that worksheet to be the date for this week. Then… each week, you can simply drag a new copy of Blank into the workbook and start over. The following figure shows the workbook in use:

	A	B	C	D	E	F	G	H
1	**Weekly Billable Hours**				Total for Week	38.73		$758.83
2	Week Ending: June 10, 2015				Copyedit	35.57		$711.33
3	Use Ctrl ; for date!		Use Ctrl : for time		Layout	3.17		$47.50
4								
5	Date	Start Time	End Time	Job Code	Description	Hours	Rate	Amount
6	Thursday, June 04, 2015	9:31:00 AM	10:15:00 AM	Copyedit	Faces/Anxiety	0.733	$20.00	$14.67
7	Thursday, June 04, 2015	10:25:00 AM	11:30:00 AM	Layout	DFSS	1.083	$15.00	$16.25
8	Thursday, June 04, 2015	11:40:00 AM	1:00:00 PM	Copyedit	XL Small Biz	1.333	$20.00	$26.67
9	Thursday, June 04, 2015	2:05:00 PM	4:10:00 PM	Layout	DFSS	2.083	$15.00	$31.25
10	Friday, June 05, 2015	9:00:00 AM	5:00:00 PM	Copyedit	XL for CFO	8.000	$20.00	$160.00
11	Saturday, June 06, 2015	8:00:00 PM	9:30:00 PM	Copyedit	Indexing	1.500	$20.00	$30.00
12	Monday, June 08, 2015	9:00:00 AM	5:00:00 PM	Copyedit	XL for CFO	8.000	$20.00	$160.00
13	Tuesday, June 09, 2015	9:00:00 AM	5:00:00 PM	Copyedit	XL for CFO	8.000	$20.00	$160.00
14	Wednesday, June 10, 2015	9:00:00 AM	5:00:00 PM	Copyedit	Red Headed Geek	8.000	$20.00	$160.00

Blank | June 10

Figure 479 The final worksheet.

CHAPTER 11 - OTHER RESOURCES

I Have a Question That Is Not Answered in This Book.

What do I do if I have questions that were not answered in this book?

A. There is a large community of Excel gurus who love to spend their coffee break at work helping people who are trying to learn Excel. It is completely free. You can usually get your answer within ten or fifteen minutes.

Go to the Internet. Browse to http://www.mrexcel.com/forum

In the top right corner, choose the link to Register. It is free to register and I will never spam you for registering. You can register with your name (MarySmith) or with a secret name, such as "Rather-BeTanning". When you register, our website will send a confirmation e-mail to your e-mail address. Click the link in that e-mail to confirm that you are not a bot.

Figure 480 Register once – there is no charge to register.

Go back to the forum. Choose the category called Excel Questions.

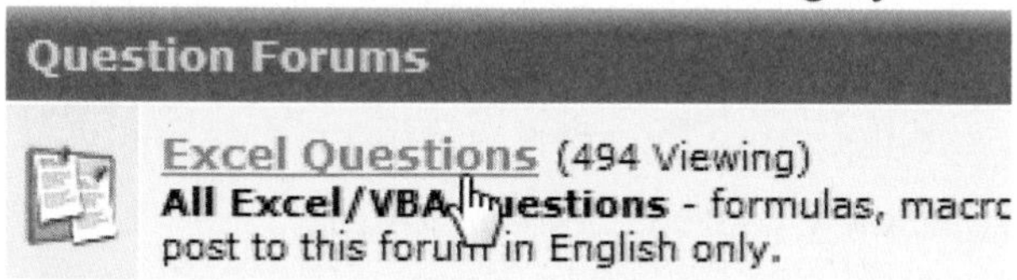

Question Forums

Excel Questions (494 Viewing)
All Excel/VBA questions - formulas, macrc
post to this forum in English only.

Figure 481 Post all Excel questions here.

Click New Topic.

THIS IS THE MOST IMPORTANT PART: Type a really descriptive title for your post. Bad titles are "Help me please", or "Urgent!" or "Excel Help!" We know that you are looking for Excel help. We know this is urgent. You wouldn't be here if you weren't urgently looking for Excel help.

Let me give you a peek inside the mind of the people who are helping you out. They are currently at work, doing some mind-numbing huge number-crunching project for their manager. They come to their coffee break and they decide to pop in to the MrExcel message board to see if they can help one or two people in the next ten minutes.

This person is looking for a recent question. A question that has zero replies. One that they think they have the expertise to help. To convince this person to look at your question instead of the other questions, you need to be able to describe, in eight to ten words, what you are trying to do.

Are you trying to build a chart and it won't cooperate? Use the word Chart in your title: "Chart keeps plotting years as an unwanted line."

Are you trying to do a VLOOKUP and you are getting #N/A! errors? Use a title of "VLOOKUP returns #N/A! in every cell."

Are you getting 300 extra printed pages every time you print your worksheet? "300 blank pages print after my report."

<u>Searching for a Match - returning a cell's content</u>
Asrampd

<u>Date Picker to default to named range</u>
inarbeth

<u>Drop Down List with multiple columns</u>
Alexjj

<u>If and/or formula</u>
ChrissieCox

Figure 482 Example of four good titles.

After you post your question, give it about five to ten minutes. Come back and refresh the page. You will see how many people have viewed your post. Be prepared that the first answer is often NOT your answer. The first answer is usually a clarifying question. The person has several solutions in mind, but wants to know if you are trying to do X or Y. Expect the clarifying question. Clarifying questions are great, because now this person is notified whenever anyone (including you) posts to your topic.

Don't be snotty or rude when you answer the clarifying question. This person has not been dealing with your problem all morning. What might be completely obvious to you may not be obvious to the person trying to answer your question. Thank the person for their clarifying question. Try to address their questions. It is very possible that you are neither trying to do X nor Y. You might be trying to do something completely different. Let the community know if they are barking up the wrong tree.

What Should I Do after I Have Mastered Every Technique in This Book?

Are there any other resources that you have that will expand my knowledge and proficiency in using Excel?

Once you finish this book, you might want to consider moving up to Bill Jelen's Learn Excel 2007-2010 From MrExcel. This book covers 512 questions and goes into far more details on data analysis.

For a daily video tip about Excel, watch Bill's podcast at www.youtube.com/bjele123

Kevin regularly answers questions at www.Experts-Exchange.com. This forum is great for Excel and all Office products.

Bill runs the forum at http://www.mrexcel.com/forum/index.php. The forum is free after you register. Post your question and hundreds of Excel gurus will have a look to see if they can help.

Tom Urtis, co-author of this book and a Microsoft Excel MVP, created the XAT, an acronym for Excel Aptitude Test. The XAT is an innovative test that measures knowledge and develops aptitude for Microsoft Excel. Tom's goal for the global Excel community is to increase employee work efficiency, operational productivity, and financial profitability through XAT's unique testing system. Most users of Excel only touch upon its basic features. Businesses, employees, and job-seekers prosper when they understand what features are available in Excel and how to use them. The XAT can help businesses of any size, and Excel users of every skill level, to become more productive and more profitable. If you'd like to know more, you can email Tom at tom@atlaspm.com, or you can go ahead and take the XAT test, at xat.atlaspm.com.

INDEX

QUICK REFERENCE

Popular shortcut keys:

- F2 Edit cell
- Ctrl+; Enter date
- Ctrl+: Enter time
- F4 while entering formula: toggle relative/absolute with $
- F4 repeats last command
- F5 Go To
- F7 Spell check
- Ctrl+Shift+- Remove borders
- Alt+F1 Create default chart from selection
- Ctrl+Enter Fill selection with entry
- Alt+Enter Start new line in cell
- Ctrl+Arrow Go to edge of range

Useful custom number formats

- #,##0,K displays numbers in thousands
- #,##0,,"M" displays numbers in millions
- [h]:mm displays hours and minutes, even if the value is over 24 hours
- dddd, mmmm d, yyyy Tuesday, June 9, 2015
- "Please pay "$#,##0.00 will display the text in quotes followed by the value
- 0;-0; Hides zero values
- ;;; Hides all values
- 00000 shows leading zeroes to ensure 5 digits

Useful functions

- =COUNT() to count numeric cells
- =COUNTA() to count non-blank cells
- =INT() to remove decimals
- =ROUND(,0) to round to nearest whole number
- =TODAY() to return current date
- =PMT(5%/12,60,-10000) to calculate loan payments
- =UPPER() to convert text to upper case
- =LOWER() to convert text to lower case
- =PROPER() to convert text to proper case
- =MONTH() to return the month number from a date
- =TEXT(,"MMMM") to return the month name from a date
- =TEXT(,"DDDD") to return the weekday name from a date

EXCEL APTITUDE TEST

TO LEARN MORE

Ready to improve your Excel skills even further? Learn Excel 2007-2010 from MrExcel offers 512 questions and answers, including charts, data analysis, pivot tables, subtotals, VLOOKUP and much more!

ISBN 978-1-932802-44-3 $39.95 also available for iPad, Kindle, or Nook.

Watch Bill Jelen's informative Power Excel seminar - 75 lessons that you can watch on your computer. Learn a cool trick in 2 to 5 minutes. Watch at your own pace. Topics on Formulas, VLOOKUP, Pivot Tables, Subtotals and more.

ISBN 978-0789743930 $39.99

Available wherever books are sold or at MrExcel.com